# teach yourself...
# Lotus Notes 4

Bill Kreisle

MIS:
PRESS

**A Subsidiary of
Henry Holt and Co., Inc.**

First Edition—1996

Printed in the United States of America.

**Library of Congress Cataloging-in-Publication Data**

Kreisle, William.
   Teach yourself : Lotus Notes 4 / by William Kreisle
     p.   cm.
  ISBN 1-55828-417-6
  1. Lotus Notes. 2. Business--Computer programs. 3. Database
management--Computer programs.  I. Title.
HF5548.4.L692K74  1996
650' .0285'46--dc20                               96-233
                                                  CIP

10 9 8 7 6 5 4 3 2 1

MIS:Press books are available at special discounts for bulk purchases for sales promotions, premiums, fund-raising, or educational use. Special editions or book excerpts can also be created to specification.

For details contact:      Special Sales Director
                            MIS:Press
                            a subsidiary of Henry Holt and Company, Inc.
                            115 West 18th Street
                            New York, New York 10011

**Associate Publisher:** *Paul Farrell*         **Production Editor:** *Stephanie Doyle*
**Managing Editor:** *Cary Sullivan*         **Technical Editor:** *Mike Falkner*
**Development Editor:** *Debra Williams Cauley*     **Copy Editor:** *Karen Tongish*

*To my mother (who made me take typing in high school), my wife (who convinced me not to use "alas" on a resume), and my daughter whom I love as "big as Clifford".*

# Contents

# Chapter 2:
# How are Businesses Using Notes? ....................23

# Chapter 3:
# Using Notes to Locate Databases ....................37

## Chapter 4:
## Using the Database Window to Locate
## and Track Documents in a Notes Database .....59

# Chapter 5:
# Adding Information to Notes Databases .......103

# Chapter 6:
# More Ways to Add Information to
# Notes Databases ............................................133

# Chapter 7:
# Using Plain- and Full-Text Searching
# to Locate Information .......................................179

# Chapter 8:
# Replication .................................................207

# Chapter 9:
# Lotus Notes Mail .........................................251

# Chapter 10:
# Mobile Notes .................................................291

# Chapter 11:
# Working Faster and Smarter ........................323

# Appendix A:
# The Appearance of the Notes Client on Different Operating Systems .................395

# Appendix B:
# Installing the Sample
# Applications that Ship with this Book ..........417

# Appendix C:
# Glossary .......................................................419

# Acknowledgments

If you think that because my name's on the outside of this book I'm the person responsible for writing it, I'd like to share a secret with you...

In large part, my name is there to make the book easier to find in the library.

The people who are actually responsible for taking this book from an idea to reality are listed here on this page, and, if you would indulge me, I'd like to take a moment to thank them for their support, encouragement, advice, kindness, editing, and even deadlines.

Undoubtedly, the award for Best Supporting Family Member goes to my wife, Susan, without whose encouragement and willingness to entertain a four-year-old girl who wanted to see her daddy more often, this book would never be here trying to separate you from your money.

The award for Most Encouragement from a Friend goes to Mike Falkner, a successful author who wanted to see me become a writer so badly that he negotiated a contract for this book himself, only to turn it down and suggest that I take his place.

In the Kindness from Strangers category, I'd like to thank the contributing regulars of the Lotus Partner Forum for their help throughout the years with Notes, and single out Janet Moyer, Don Bechtold, and Jon E. Johnston in particular for offering several helpful suggestions to increase the usefulness of this book.

The award for Best Editing goes to a group of men and women whose excellence in their craft has allowed them to take the tens of thousands of words that I wanted to share with you and arrange them so that they communicated my intentions more accurately and effectively. Skilled in the use of English, Notes, and psychiatry, these people are commonly called editors, but I know that there is nothing common about them. Thank you Chris Maio, the Falkner brothers (Eric and Jon), Karen Tongish, Stephanie Doyle, and Susan Kreisle for your willingness to read, reread, and read again every word in this book.

Lastly, in the category for publisher deadlines, I'd like to thank Jono Hardiworogo for creating one, and Debra Williams Cauley for making it flexible.

In addition to the people who've supported this—my perspiration (that's an unusual way to put it, don't you think?)—there is someone whom I would like to acknowledge for giving me inspiration. In that category, I salute Doug Burgum, the CEO of Great Plains Software. Doug's relentless pursuit of dreams and tireless encouragement to others to pursue their own fills the air at Great Plains so much and so often that I must have accidentally swallowed some of it.

Of course, many more people who deserve recognition for their help in making this book, even if they don't realize that it's being published. The list includes Gregg Wemes, Don Bulens, Katherine Spanbauer, Scott Vrusho, Ray August, and many others whom I'm sure I should mention but whose names, in the excitement of having this book finished escape me.

My heartfelt thanks to each person named here and to the others whom I will be apologizing to for forgetting in very short order.

# Introduction

# LNA (Lotus Notes, Anonymous)

The scene opens in a high-school classroom on loan for the evening to a local self-help group. Twenty or so people are in the room, talking among themselves. Their conversations quiet as a short, round, hairy (yet handsome) man rises from his seat and approaches the lectern.

"Hi, I'm Bill," the speaker begins. "I'm new to the group, and...." He pauses, clearly struggling with the words he wants to say next.

The audience looks at him with understanding.

Finally, he blurts out, "I'm a Notes evangelist!"

"Hi Bill!" the audience responds, "Welcome to our workgroup!"

Encouraged by the response, Bill continues, "When I first started using Notes, I never thought it would become such a huge part of my daily life." He looks out at some of the members of the group and makes eye contact. "Heck, I've never been addicted to anything before, except maybe Twinkies."

The audience laughs politely. Bill draws a deep breath and goes on. "I'll just use it for e-mail, is what I first thought. 'Maybe I'd look through some of the other databases when I get time.'"

Members of the audience nod their heads as Bill speaks.

"But then, slowly, the power of Notes began to take hold. I discovered that Notes was more than just electronic mail, more than just forms—it was a place where you could store knowledge. I found myself learning about different departments and procedures as I looked through the company's Notes databases. I began following, and eventually participating in, discussions about products. I even learned more about our customers!"

"Not long after that, someone showed me how to make my own Notes databases from templates that were already designed by Lotus and our internal development staff. Almost overnight, I began creating Notes databases, solving problems my company faced in terms of tracking and routing knowledge! I became more productive personally, and I started helping others by sharing databases I'd created."

Several members of the group begin to fidget or wince at this point, remembering their own experiences. This was clearly a familiar story to them.

"Then, one day," Bill continued, "I discovered replication."

A collective groan of recognition emanates from the audience.

"Suddenly, I realized that all of the solutions I was building and all of the knowledge my company was accumulating in Notes didn't have to be kept in our building. Our employees in the field, our branch offices, even offices we haven't opened yet could share and add to the knowledge we were collecting!

I knew I was hooked, but I didn't want to stop!" Bill pauses, and then looks down at the floor as he continues.

"So, I didn't stop. And it wasn't long after replication that I started turning to workflow and dealing with Agents."

The audience nods appreciatively while Bill speaks.

"Now, not only was knowledge flowing freely throughout the company, empowering teams and raising overall productivity-it was moving through the company automatically. Then, recently, I found out about InterNotes."

One overly enthusiastic member of the audience jumps up and shouts "Amen!" Others in the room turn toward her and smile knowingly. Sheepishly, she sits down. Bill begins speaking again, clearly working himself into a frenzy.

"Using Lotus Notes and InterNotes together allowed subsets of the information I was sharing company-wide to be shared world-wide using the Internet and the World Wide Web. Plus, the tremendous resources of the Internet, like News Discussions and other World Wide Web pages, could be brought into the company in a controlled environment!"

"Seeing the tremendous difference Notes can make to a company changed me. People didn't think I was the same person. But I didn't care." A single tear rolls down his cheek. Several people in the audience fumble for tissues as the sound of first one, then several noses blowing fills the room. Bill looks out over the audience. After regarding them for a moment, he stands up straight and says, "And I still don't."

The group gasps and begins trying to interrupt Bill's speech. Bill climbs on top of the lectern and shouts, "Notes is a powerful tool, and I'm going to make the whole world understand it! Even if I have to spend five hours a night and every weekend for the next six months in a hotel room writing a book about Notes, I will be heard!"

The group surrounds Bill at the podium. As the scene fades, some members of the group are applauding wildly, while others are reaching to pull him from the lectern.

## About this Book

While I think of myself as (surprise) Bill in the opening story, the scene I've laid out is obviously fictitious. Well, except for the short, round, hairy (yet handsome) part. And the laptop in the hotel room thing. And, well, the emotion from the scene is real, too.

I honestly believe that Notes is a powerful tool, unlike anything else on this planet. I also believe that learning about it can change not only the way you work, but the way your company works.

And I'm not alone. According to figures from Lotus, there are over 3 million Notes users out there as of this writing, and with the introduction of Notes Release 4, that number is projected to increase to over twenty million by 1997. That translates into quite a few people like me—Notes administrators, developers, and evangelists—dedicated to preaching the gospel of Notes.

Gospel of Notes? Where did that come from? Why do I compare Notes to a religion and write about it like something you can become addicted to? Well, because for some people out there, it is and you can. But it's not such a bad religion. And unlike an addiction to say, Twinkies, the only thing being addicted to Notes increases is your earning power.

Perhaps you've already dealt with someone like me. Someone who almost seems to explode into your department, bringing you the good news that you're about to have Notes installed department-wide, promising you the rewards of client/server architecture, replication, mail-enabling, workflow, and enterprise-wide data distribution. Of course, these terms are guaranteed to make your eyes glaze over if you're new to Notes, so you tell yourself, "After they install Notes, I'll start it up and figure it out."

Notes was installed. There was a training session. You'd heard so many buzz-words about Notes before the training started, however, that you decided it was too complicated for you and you didn't pay as much attention as you should.

And there you sat. Looking at the workspace, saying to yourself, "Now what?" That's pretty much how it happened the first time I did a major Notes installation. I was so concerned with making Notes available to everyone, I didn't work at making Notes *usable* to everyone. Oh, the installation didn't fail, by any stretch of the imagination—those initially perplexed masses that believed Notes was being inflicted upon them are now some of the most creative Notes users around. Their company was actually given an award by Lotus in 1995 for innovation using Notes. It just didn't go as well as it could have.

So I began concentrating on creating a document that would explain Notes in easy to understand terms and provide a user with step-by-step examples. It was my hope that the next time I did an installation, users could take my document and learn the basics of Notes and use those basics to begin to explore more advanced topics.

That document eventually turned into this book, a work modeled after some of the most successful "Introduction to Notes" classes I've taught. Designed to provide a working knowledge of Notes after completion, the book builds, chapter by chapter, toward answering three questions:

❖ What is Notes?

❖ How are businesses using Notes today?

❖ How can I use Notes?

Chapters 1 and 2 answer the first two questions, providing you with a definition of Notes and its concepts followed by a discussion of how businesses are using

Notes. The remaining chapters are dedicated to the third question. Chapters 3–7 introduce the basics of finding and adding information to Notes, and the remaining chapters build on the more advanced features, including Notes Mail, replication, using Notes with the Internet, and building your own Notes Databases from templates.

Here's a quick chapter-by-chapter breakdown.

Chapter 1 defines Notes, and introduces terms and concepts we'll use throughout the book including Documents, Views, Navigators, workflow, mail enabling, replication, Responses, and Notes Clients and Servers.

Chapter 2 reinforces the concepts we discussed in Chapter 1 by discussing what types of applications Notes is generally used for, as well as providing a real-life example of how Notes is being used at a software company in North Dakota.

Chapter 3 discusses the Notes Client and its Workspace, explains how to locate Notes databases and add them to the Workspace, and shows you how to preview information about each database before opening it.

Chapter 4 covers how to use Views, Navigators, and Folders to locate documents in a Notes database.

Chapter 5 explains how to add information to a Notes database, expands on the use of the Access Control List, and introduces the different types of fields available in Notes.

Chapter 6 explores the possibilities of the Rich Text Field, a special field in Notes designed to hold just about anything!

Chapter 7 introduces plain-text searching and full-text searching, two powerful ways to locate information in a Notes database.

Chapter 8 is dedicated to the concept of replication and putting it into practice using the Replication Page on the Workspace.

Chapter 9 covers Notes Mail, and explains how your understanding of all of the previous chapters will make it an extremely powerful tool in your daily life.

Chapter 10 covers Mobile Notes, Lotus collection of tools for using Notes remotely.

Chapter 11 collects the features of Notes designed to help you work faster and smarter, including the InterNotes Web Browser, SmartIcons, word processing features in Notes, and Notes Client commands designed to help you maintain your databases.

Appendix A covers the appearance of the Notes Client on different operating systems.

Appendix B explains how to install the sample applications that are included with this book.

You'll notice as you read the chapter outline, this book differs from similar titles in that I spend a great deal of time early on presenting the concepts behind Notes. I do this because I know that once you have an understanding of replication, workflow, mail-enabling, and client/server, you'll look at Notes from a whole new perspective. You'll also be better-equipped to make Notes become what it's capable of—a tool that makes you more knowledgeable, more productive, and better equipped to use Notes to solve problems your business faces tracking information and knowledge.

Because of my emphasis on concepts and building on the basics, this book can be used for Notes, Notes Desktop, and Lotus Mail users. The sample database that I use in all of the step-by-step exercises can be opened by any of these applications.

If during your reading your eyes glazed over because I wrote *replication, client/server,* and *solve problems* in the same sentence, please don't put the book down yet. I promise you, you won't need a masters degree in computer science to read what I've written. I've worked very hard to make the concepts easy to understand. I draw out analogies between these technologies and things you use every day (like Post-It notes and three-ring binders). I make this extra effort because, as I said earlier, I believe that once you have the concepts that Notes is built around down pat, learning it will become easier (and much, much more rewarding).

There are three other things I'd like to mention about this book:

1.  I work to keep my writing casual (translated: I try not to sound like a computer geek).

2.  Occasionally, I try to interject a bit of humor (although humor is a relative concept when a computer-geek is trying hard not to sound like one).

3.  Lastly, while I try to be casual and humorous, I think that learning is still the main thing (meaning I try not to be so cute that I'm annoying, and I provide plenty of hands on exercises for you to follow).

That said, all that's left is to find some subtle way to blurt out "Buy this book, please!" to keep my publisher happy and to start answering the three questions I've built the book around.

# Chapter 1

# What Is Lotus Notes?

## In this Chapter...

In this chapter, I'll provide you with a working definition for Lotus Notes and introduce several important terms and ideas Notes relies upon along the way. The material we'll cover will include:

- ❖ What is Lotus Notes?
- ❖ Comparing knowledge to information
- ❖ Databases, documents, rich text, and responses
- ❖ Folders, navigators, and views
- ❖ Notes Clients and Notes Servers
- ❖ The Access Control List (ACL)
- ❖ Replication
- ❖ Mail enabling
- ❖ Agents
- ❖ Workflow

# What is Lotus Notes?

Imagine, as you read these words, someone is being introduced to Notes for the first time.

This person may be a corporate decision maker evaluating using Notes in her company or a new employee being given a class on Notes as part of his orientation. Regardless of the circumstances, imagine this person asking, "What is Lotus Notes?"

Now, imagine a second person, responsible for explaining what Notes is, talking to the first. Maybe he's a member of the IS department or a trainer. Quite possibly, she's a consultant, specifically hired to introduce Notes. Regardless, picture the second person drawing in a deep breath and saying, "Notes is...darned hard to explain."

As someone who has attended (and given) dozens of discussions and classes on Notes, I can tell you from experience that that's a common answer. It's also a true answer. Notes *is* hard to explain. Not because the concept of Notes is complicated. Its main purpose is simply to share knowledge and information. The problem is that in being a tool used to share knowledge and information, there's not much that Notes isn't:

❖ Notes is a database technology.

❖ It's a workflow engine.

❖ It's a compound document store.

❖ It's client/server computing.

❖ It's word processing.

❖ It's electronic mail.

❖ It's enterprise data distribution.

❖ It's even a multiplatform integrated development environment.

Frankly, almost all the buzzwords we're accustomed to reading in the computer press every day apply to Lotus Notes in some fashion.

Consequently, distilling the essence of Notes into a couple of short sentences is a challenge even Lotus faces. As recently as 1993 (several years into the life of Notes), Lotus was criticized by the computer press for not being able to define Notes "in 25 words or less."

Fortunately, I have the rest of this chapter to help you understand what Lotus Notes is. My approach to defining Notes is to introduce and then build onto this simple sentence:

> *Lotus Notes is a tool to collect, organize, and share knowledge and information.*

I'll use the rest of this chapter to expand on what that definition means, word by word.

# Comparing Knowledge to Information

> *Lotus Notes is a tool to collect, organize, and share KNOWLEDGE and INFORMATION.*

Knowledge, in the context of our definition of Notes, is loosely structured information that is difficult to break down into small fields. Take a discussion among several people at a meeting as an example. While listening to the conversation, one attendee learns something about the personality of another and perhaps picks up an insight into that second person's profession. However, another attendee may learn something completely different from it. You see, she already knew the part the first person picked up on and was paying attention to something someone else said. What was learned by each person participating in the meeting, taken in total, is their knowledge. It can't be collected; it must be shared. (Meaning that if one person in the room was responsible for writing down the meeting's minutes, their interpretation of the meeting would be different from the person sitting next to them. Everyone must participate in summarizing the meeting to share their knowledge.)

This is very different from data, or information. Information is something that breaks easily into discrete components. Some examples of information include:

❖ A spreadsheet of sales figures where everything fits into a row or column

❖ A database of hardware vendors which contains a collection of short text and numeric fields for names, addresses, and telephone numbers

Of course, information is still important—you couldn't organize your knowledge without it. (Imagine a library with no card catalog or a list of customer likes and dislikes but no customer list!) Like the card catalog in a library, information in Notes is peripheral to the goal of collecting knowledge.

# Databases, Documents, and Responses

*Lotus Notes is a tool to COLLECT, organize, and share knowledge and information.*

## Databases

Notes collects knowledge by storing it in Databases of Documents. If you aren't familiar with the term database, imagine a three-ring binder filled with pages (see Figure 1.1). The binder is the database, and the pages are the Documents contained within it. A three-ring binder lets you remove or add pages to it, or turn to a specific page and add or erase information. In similar fashion, a Notes Database allows you to add, remove, navigate, and edit the Documents contained within it.

**Figure 1.1** *A Document in a Notes database can be compared to a page in a three-ring binder.*

## Documents and Rich Text

Each Notes Document is intended to be a combination of information and knowledge. Fields contain information (text, numbers, and dates) that allow Documents to be sorted and retrieved later based on common values. Examples include the Document's creation date and the name of the Document's author. A specially designed Notes field called a *rich text* field holds knowledge. Rich text fields can contain text with formatting, sounds, pictures, or even other programs, making them well suited for containing loosely structured information (see Figure 1.2).

This brings us to a few questions you're probably asking:

❖ How does a Document in Notes translate into a container for a discussion?

❖ What's the difference between a Notes Document and a word processing document?

❖ Doesn't it boil down to one person typing in the meeting's minutes?

The answer to these questions is this:

What turns Notes into a container for knowledge is the combination of rich text, the Notes document we've just discussed, and another special type of Notes Document, called a *Response Document.*

**Figure 1.2** *In a Notes Document, rich text fields allow you to store formatted text and pictures.*

## Responses

Response Documents (generally referred to in Notes as *Responses*) are similar to standard Notes Documents in that they can combine information and knowledge using different types of fields. However, Response Documents are special in that they are designed to be associated with other Notes Documents or Responses in a parent-child relationship. Borrowing from the binder analogy, you can think of Responses as yellow Post-it Notes you might attach to a specific page in the binder (Figure 1.3).

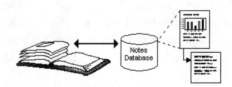

**Figure 1.3** *Response Documents in Notes are similar to Post-it Notes on the pages of our binder.*

Just as you can have more than one Post-it Note on a page, a Document can have more than one Response associated with it. Keeping that analogy, a Response to a Response Document would be similar to a Post-it Note placed on top of a Post-it Note.

Responses and rich text are the keys that allow Notes to store discussions. A conversation in a meeting may start with a main subject and follow different threads based on one or more person's response. In the same fashion, Notes databases can store a main topic as a Document with one or more Responses associated with it and each other.

Responses also allow the creation of Documents that aren't discussion related but should be associated with a main topic. For example, imagine a database of magazine articles. Each article is a Document. After creating a magazine article, Documents containing reference information used in writing the article are associated with it through Response Documents. Articles based on a single source will have only one Response associated with them. Articles based on many sources will have many Responses.

## Folders, Navigators, and Views

> *Lotus Notes is a tool to collect, ORGANIZE, and share knowledge and information.*

This brings us to the next key word in my definition of Notes—the word *organize*. Once collected, Notes organizes knowledge by presenting it to the user in one or more Folders, Views, and/or Navigators. All three items are similar in Notes, but each is designed to present and group information differently.

Navigators and Views are usually developer-defined windows that help you organize the Documents stored in the database. Views use lines of text grouped in categories to help you find information, while Navigators often combine text and images. Going back to our three-ring binder analogy, a View would be similar to a table of contents or an index that allowed you to organize the information on each of the binder's pages concisely. A Navigator might be a map or a collection of pictures that symbolize the type of data you will see if you select them.

Figure 1.4 shows a screen shot of one of the sample databases included on the diskette that accompanies this book. In this illustration, the Navigator is shown in the leftmost pane of the window, and the View is in the rightmost pane.

Folders are containers that allow you to collect Documents from multiple Views or Navigators into a logical group. In our binder analogy, a Folder might be thought of as a separate pad where you make a list of page numbers you'll want to refer to in the future.

Navigator Pane ⟶ 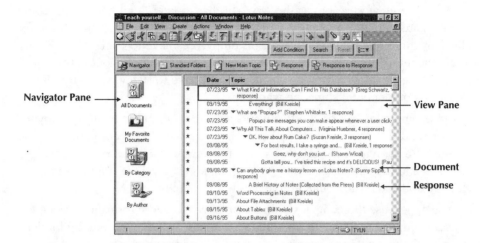 ⟵ View Pane

Document

Response

*Figure 1.4* *An illustration of a Notes Navigator and a Notes View.*

# The Notes Client and the Notes Server

*Lotus Notes is a tool to collect, organize, and SHARE knowledge and information.*

The next key word of our definition, *sharing*, requires a bit of storytelling before we expand on it. With that in mind, let's go back to the binder analogy we introduced when talking about database and take it in two directions—backward and forward.

Going backward, let's assume that a company maintains a library of three-ring binders available for check-out by its employees. Each binder contains something that is knowledge or information oriented within the company (accounting policies and procedures, leads, or executive memos, for example). Let's also assume that I am the keeper of this library. The idea behind my library is not only to create an environment where new employees can learn by reading, but one where more experienced employees learn and teach by adding to or changing the pages of the binders they check out. Essentially, the library is a repository of company knowledge.

This is a great idea, but as the guy who has to keep it all going, I'm telling you it's hard to put into practice. The first requirement is a physical location for all of my three-ring binders. That means employees have to come to my library to get the information they need, which isn't convenient for anyone. (They have to make a special trip to get information, and I have to stay close to the library to check a binder out if someone wants one.)

If an employee in a field office wants to borrow a binder, I make a copy for him or send him the original binder. If the employee has a copy and not the original, I must remember to send a set of changes or make a new copy every time something in the original binder is updated. If I send the original binder, it can't be updated by any other employees until it is returned.

Next, because the company wants employees to add information freely, I'm constantly updating the tables of contents and indexes to my three-ring binders. If an employee who is an expert on networking adds comments to three or four pages, that change must be reflected in the binder's index. I also have to repaginate the books each time to keep the tables of contents up-to-date!

Then, of course, there's the issue of security. While it would be ideal to keep one binder of memos, some memos are for company officers' eyes only and others are sensitive to some employees but not all. Because of this, I cannot have one binder of memos. I must have several, organized according to content. Now whenever an employee adds a memo to a binder, I decide if the new document is copied to the other memo binders as well.

Lastly, I'm part of a growing company. What happens when we open a branch office in another location? How am I going to keep the two libraries synchronized?

Obviously, I have problems. Can taking the analogy forward and including Notes help? (We're only in the first chapter, but I bet you know the answer to that question.)

Instead of using three-ring binders to store knowledge, let's look at using Notes databases. Since Notes databases are stored on computer disks, I must replace the library in our analogy with something better suited to providing information that is stored on a computer to multiple users. This replacement is a Notes Server.

The first thing this changes is how employees access the information (check out the binders) I have stored in my library. Because I'm using a Notes Server instead of a physical room, each employee now has direct access to the databases through a Notes Client. The Notes Client is a program installed on each computer that can use an existing network to connect Notes Servers.

Employees in the field can also access the library (now the Notes Server) using their computers and a modem.

Figure 1.5 illustrates our new on-line library.

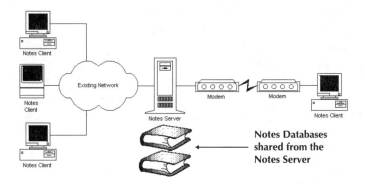

**Figure 1.5** *Notes Clients connect to a Notes Server by a network or modem and use it to share databases.*

Besides providing desktop access to our information, the Notes Server allows our employees to check out the same binder (open the same database) at the same time. That means I don't have to keep multiple copies of each binder (which means I only have one table of contents and one index to update). Speaking of tables of contents and indexes, since my binder is a Notes database, I get to replace them with Notes' Navigators and Views.

As I mentioned earlier, Navigators and Views are windows into the contents of a Notes database created by the database's designer. They serve the same purpose as our index and table of contents, but they go much farther in terms of functionality. Now my table of contents and index are updated automatically every time someone adds information to our databases. In addition, I can create multiple tables of contents, sorted not by page number but by the information stored in our database's Documents. For example, along with the traditional table of contents View, consider a second View called "table of contents, by author." This new View could sort every Document in the database by the name of the person who wrote it, providing a different method of locating specific information.

## The Access Control List (ACL)

You might expect that I'll still have to maintain multiple copies of databases for information that requires some level of security (such as our executive memo binder). However, thanks to another feature of Notes called Access Control, that isn't the case. Every Notes database I create contains an Access Control List. The ACL of a Notes database is basically a list of names that the Notes server uses to determine (you guessed it) access.

Because every name in the list is associated with an access level, I can create a database that is very specific about who does what with it. For example, I may allow some employees to open a database and read information already published but not to add new information or change what's already in the database. Other employees may have the right to open the database, read or edit any existing information, and create new Documents. A smaller group of employees yet again may have the right to do everything we just talked about, plus create new Views or otherwise change the design of the database.

As the librarian, I'm almost out of a job! Notes is handling everything. They'll still need someone to keep the databases synchronized when they open the branch office in Fargo, won't they?

No, they won't. And the reason is one of the most powerful features of Notes.

# Replication

Stepping back for a moment, remember how one of the biggest challenges of my three-ring binder library was allowing remote employees to have a copy of each binder and keeping the copy and the original up-to-date? I solved this by converting the library of binders into a Notes server with databases and letting the remote employees call the server from their computers at home.

This is a big step forward for the remote employee and my library. But won't the remote employee need to keep an open phone line between his computer and the server to see the database or make changes to it? What will that mean if we have 20 or 30 remote employees? That's a lot of modems to handle all the incoming calls and a hefty phone bill.

If only there were a way for the remote employees to synchronize their copies of a database with the copy on the server, some process where only the information that has changed in one of the copies is transferred to the other.

Of course, you know from those leading sentences, that there is, indeed, a way. The synchronizing process is what Notes calls *replication*, and, as I said earlier, it is one of the most powerful features of Notes. (I'll also add that, for my money, it's one of the most amazing.)

Here's how it works.

Instead of using copies of the databases from the Notes Server, remote employees maintain replicas. The field employees can work with each replica on their local hard drives without being connected to the Notes Server. They add changes, or create new pages just as all the other employees do on the network at the office.

Periodically, each remote employee calls the Notes Server and initiates a replication between his version of the database and the server's. During this process, any Documents that the employee has changed are sent to the Notes Server, and any changes made by the other employees on the network are sent to the remote employee. Once the replication process is complete, the databases are mirror images of each other.

Since replication is a process of synchronization, only information that has changed moves across the network or modem connection. This means an employee working remotely can use his replica of a database off-line all day and call in to replicate at day's end in a matter of minutes! It also means that two or three modems can take care of 30 employees because each employee needs to connect only to move the changes in the two databases back and forth.

Figure 1.6 illustrates our library with the concept of replication for our remote employees.

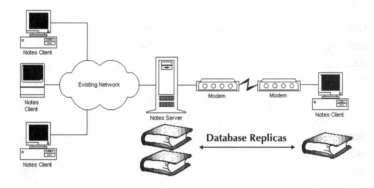

**Figure 1.6** *Remote Notes Clients can maintain a replica of a Notes Server database and share information by initiating a replication between them.*

Getting back to the branch office in Fargo, replication gives me two options:

1. I can allow the employees in the Fargo office to dial in to the Notes Server in the main office and replicate information to their local hard drives. This solution will work, but it's inconvenient for the employees in the branch office. Whenever one employee makes a change, the other employees at the remote location have to call and replicate with the main server to move the change to their local hard drives.

2. I can set up another Notes server in Fargo, and have the Fargo server call our main server and replicate. Essentially, this is the same as having two libraries that automatically keep the three-ring binders in both locations

up-to-date. Now, all the employees at the Fargo office can share changes in real-time on their Notes Server, while periodic replication with the main office keeps both branches working with up-to-date information.

If I'm going to have a number of employees in the branch office, the second option makes more sense.

So, thanks to Notes databases, Notes servers, and replication, I'm now out one librarian's job. (As the company's new Notes administrator, however, I'm just getting started.)

# Mail Enabling

Up to this point, we've looked at network and/or modem connections and replication as ways to share information in Notes. Before we move on to the next chapter, let's look at the third way Notes uses to share knowledge—mail enabling.

Mail enabling allows Notes Servers to route Documents as messages. (We typically think of e-mail as a means for people to send messages to other people, but Notes' mail enabling allows people to send information to databases or people.)

To put this in context, imagine sending a Document you are working on directly from your desk to a three-ring binder in the library. When the Document arrives, the table of contents and the index of the binder are automatically updated. Or imagine telling a three-ring binder in one library to automatically move or copy some of its pages into a binder at another library whenever a value on one page changes. As you can imagine, this is a powerful part of Notes.

# Agents

Another powerful feature of Notes is the ability to create and run Agents. Agents are user-created programs that automate or streamline common user processes. Agents can be simple or complex. A simple Agent might be a single instruction telling Notes to save a Document whenever a button is pressed. A more complex Agent could be many instructions executing in sequence. These instructions might create a new Document and automatically fill in some of the Document's fields based on who the user is and what she was doing when the Agent was started. With Notes Release 4, Agents can also include external programs written in languages such as Visual Basic or C++.

Agents can be scheduled to run at specific times on a Notes Client or a Notes Server, or they can be launched by the user on demand.

# Workflow

Agents and mail enabling are both powerful tools in their own right. When they are combined, however, they create an even more powerful tool in Notes called a *Workflow*. Workflow is difficult to define for the same reason Notes is difficult to define—there are so many components that go into a workflow that there's not much that workflow isn't. To keep things simple, I'm going to go by Lotus' definition of a workflow for this book:

A workflow is a combination of Notes' features that automate or streamline common user processes or tasks.

In other words, a workflow is anything that makes knowledge or information move more efficiently throughout your organization.

Like Agents, Notes workflows can be extremely simple or very complex.

An example of a simple workflow would be a Notes database that periodically sends a mail message to a user telling her how many Documents have been added in the last day that mention her name or the name of a product that she is researching. In this workflow, an Agent runs automatically on the server, checking any new Documents for her name or the name of her product. If it finds new Documents that match the search conditions, it sends the user a message using mail enabling. This saves the user from having to open the database every day to search for new Documents that may interest her.

For a more complex workflow example, imagine that a company using Notes wants to track its employees' time cards more effectively. Using Notes, the company creates a series of time card databases. The first database is shared by all employees from a public Notes Server. In this database, employees can enter their time cards and save them. Once the time card is saved, the employee is no longer allowed access to it, nor can he see any other employees' time cards because the database's Access Control Lists allows users only depositor access.

Weekly, a supervisor reviews the time-card database. If the supervisor agrees with the information an employee has entered on his time card, she marks the time card as approved. If she disagrees with the information, she runs an Agent that sends the employee an electronic memo asking for more information.

Every night, an Agent that scans the time-card database for Documents marked approved runs on the Notes Server. If it finds any, it forwards them using mail-enabling to another time-card database on the accounting department's Notes Server. By moving the time cards to another server where only members of the accounting department have access, the time cards are less likely to be altered by a supervisor or employee later. Figure 1.7 illustrates this process.

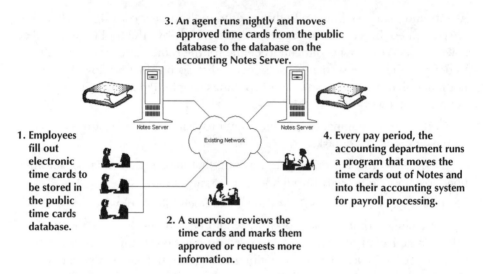

**3.** An agent runs nightly and moves approved time cards from the public database to the database on the accounting Notes Server.

**1.** Employees fill out electronic time cards to be stored in the public time cards database.

**4.** Every pay period, the accounting department runs a program that moves the time cards out of Notes and into their accounting system for payroll processing.

**2.** A supervisor reviews the time cards and marks them approved or requests more information.

***Figure 1.7*** *Notes uses mail-enabling as the basis for creating a workflow.*

The accounting department uses many different Notes Views in their time-card database to analyze the information:

❖ One View displays how many employees worked more than 40 hours per week.

❖ Another View sorts the total hours worked from the most to the least.

❖ A third View displays employees who haven't submitted time cards for the last pay period.

❖ On payday, the accounting department runs another Agent that exports the information in the time-card database into a format that can be read by the company's accounting software, and payroll checks are generated.

As you can see, the concept of Agents, Mail Enabling, and Workflow are extremely powerful extensions to Lotus Notes. As you can also see, my saying that there's not much that Notes isn't may be an understatement!

## Summary

Let's summarize what we've discussed so far:

❖ Lotus Notes is a tool to collect, organize, and share knowledge.

❖ Knowledge is not the same as information or data in that knowledge is loosely structured and difficult to break into consistent components for storage and retrieval. Because knowledge is loosely structured, it depends on information to organize it (similar to a card catalog at a library).

❖ Notes collects knowledge into Databases of Documents.

❖ Documents are containers designed to combine information and knowledge through the use of text, number, and date fields combined with a special Notes field called a *rich text* field.

❖ A rich text field can contain formatted text, graphics, sound, video, or even other programs.

❖ Response Documents are a special type of Notes Document designed to be related to other Documents or Responses just as a Post it Note is related to the sheet of paper it is attached to.

We'll discuss rich text, Documents, and Responses and how they're used by Notes in greater detail in Chapters 2, 3, and 4.

N O T E

❖ Notes organizes information using Navigators, Folders, and Views.

We'll discuss Folders, Navigators, and Views in greater detail in Chapter 3.

N O T E

❖ Notes shares information by allowing Notes Clients to share the same database on a Notes Server. The Notes Clients use Navigators and Views to locate and work with Documents.

❖ Notes also shares information through replication, mail enabling, and workflow.

1. Replication allows multiple replicas, or mirrored copies, of a database existing in a number of physical locations to synchronize their contents on command.

**N O T E**     We'll discuss Replication in exhaustive detail in Chapter 8.

2. Mail enabling allows Notes users to exchange electronic mail and Documents with each other or with Notes databases. It also allows Notes databases to exchange mail and Documents with users or other databases.

3. Mail enabling, combined with Agents, creates the basis for Workflow in Notes.

❖ Workflow is defined for this book as any system that helps to move information and knowledge throughout an organization through automating or streamlining user processes or tasks.

**N O T E**     We'll discuss e-mail in greater detail in Chapter 9.

# Chapter 2

# How are Businesses Using Notes?

## In this Chapter...

In this chapter, we'll discuss how businesses are using Lotus Notes to store knowledge and information, and we'll cover the five categories that most "out-of-the-box" solutions built in Notes fall into. Next, we'll look at how Notes can be used to collect information for other applications. At the end of the chapter, we'll examine how a software company uses Notes combined with the five standard application types we discussed to create a powerful business solution.

The material we'll cover will include:

❖ How businesses are using Lotus Notes

❖ Discussion, reference, broadcast, tracking, and workflow applications

❖ Using notes to collect information for other applications

❖ A real-life example of how Notes is being used

# How Businesses Are Using Lotus Notes

We spent a good part of Chapter 1 discussing how Notes is optimized for storing knowledge because of replication, Documents, Responses, and rich text. Near the end of the chapter, we also discussed how Notes can use workflow to collect what is essentially data (the time-card example). These types of applications are the out-of-the-box tools Notes provides an organization to solve business problems, which generally fall into five categories:

❖ Discussion applications

❖ Tracking applications

❖ Broadcasting applications

❖ Reference applications

❖ Workflow/approval applications

In the following section, we'll examine each of these application types in greater detail.

## *Discussion Applications*

Discussion applications are one of the flagship applications of Notes as they showcase Notes' strengths. To understand the power of a discussion application, consider the following information. Every business is the sum of the experience and knowledge contained in its people. Because of this, it is extremely important to an organization to ensure that it creates an environment in which individual knowledge is collected and shared across a company or a team. In a traditional setting, this occurs through discussions in person, meetings, by way of telephone, or through electronic mail (e-mail).

Except for e-mail, most of the knowledge transferred in this fashion is rarely recorded on a computer. It's recorded on whiteboards, tablets, or Post-it Notes. While having a notepad or collection of papers satisfies individual or small-group needs, it makes the knowledge obtained difficult to share on a large scale. As a result, a person with specialized knowledge often answers the same question repeatedly as different people arrive at the conclusion that they need a given piece of information. Additionally, most of the traditional methods of discussion (telephone calls, person-to-person conversations, or meetings) require that people be available at the same time. Discussion applications in Notes eliminate many of these issues.

Discussion applications are databases that use Documents to enter main topics and Response Documents to collect individual information or opinions that should be associated with them.

Discussion applications are the most commonly imitated feature of Notes by competitors in the workgroup software market. However, no competitor to date has combined all the following features in their imitation.

Because discussion applications are stored on a Notes Server, topics in a database are collected and shared by people throughout an organization. New members to a group can review long-standing discussions before asking questions to reduce the number of times shared knowledge must be repeated by the discussion participants.

Security on the server (the Access Control List) can limit the number of people allowed to participate in a discussion. The ACL can control the discussions a user can participate in, as well as establish the level at which a user can participate in a discussion. What this means is that some users can be allowed to create new topics and edit topics posted by others, while another group of users might be allowed only to read what is being discussed but not add to it or change it.

Rich text allows discussion participants to be more appropriately communicate their information than plain text. As an example, a user wanting to know about a particular feature of a computer program might include a screen shot of the actual button or menu command along with his question. Or a discussion participant who responds to a question might include illustrations explaining the steps needed to solve a problem.

Finally, replication allows the database to be distributed to many physical locations and still remain current.

All of these strengths combine to make an application that is effective because it is unconstrained by time, distance, or software incompatibilities. If a person wants to respond to a question at 3:00 AM using his Macintosh at home and then replicate his response with an OS/2 server in the morning so that a coworker using a PC can read it, he can! If someone else takes a two-week vacation, she can easily catch up on the discussion when she returns because everything has been stored in a Notes database.

Some examples of discussion applications include:

❖ **New Ideas Discussion**. Marketing or product-development departments can post new ideas or brainstorming topics, and each member of the group has the opportunity to respond to the idea or provide supporting information.

❖ **Project Discussion**. Project descriptions are the main Documents, and informal discussions regarding the project's scope or status are entered as Responses.

❖ **Executive Discussion**. By using Notes' security to restrict access to executive-level employees, the database can serve as a collection of topics and Responses relating to company officers. This type of application is especially useful to companies in which the senior officers spend a great deal of time traveling.

❖ **Sales Discussion**. A database of sales-related questions or topics and Responses can be extremely powerful in companies where the sales force includes remote employees.

❖ **Expert Discussion**. Company employees post questions as Documents to a discussion database that is "owned" by an employee or group of employees with specialized skills. Answers to each question and supporting information are added as Responses.

## *Broadcast Applications*

Every company has low-priority yet time-sensitive information to share with its employees (a company picnic, a luncheon seminar, or a memo about parking lot maintenance, for example). This broadcast information is traditionally stored on paper and delivered through bulletin-board postings, internal mail, or e-mail. Bulletin boards and internal mail require labor to print, photocopy, and post or deliver their information.

E-mail is effective, but it forces noncritical information into the same mailbox as urgent messages and requests, often irritating users who receive large amounts of what they perceive as junk mail. Using Notes to create broadcast applications provides an alternative delivery method for noncritical, company-wide information. Stored in public directories and replicated throughout the company's Notes servers, these databases create an effective one-way information flow (from the sender to the recipients). Because most of the information in a broadcast application is read-only, Responses are usually not a part of the database.

Responses could be included however, to encourage people to share their ideas about a given broadcast topic. (A company picnic announcement, for example, might allow employees to compose a Response if they want to bring food items or refreshments.)

Some examples of broadcast applications include:

❖ **Internal News**. Moving company newsletters or departmental updates into broadcast databases can reduce internal photocopying and printing costs, allow information to be delivered faster, and allow the employees responsible for creating the materials to collaborate.

❖ **External News**. Storing information obtained from a clipping service or other outside source (an Internet mailing list, for example) in a broadcast database consolidates information and reduces multiple subscriptions to information services or lists.

❖ **Personal Announcements**. A broadcast database that allows anyone to post information they want announced company-wide (weddings, births, autos for sale) and centralizes this information into a monitored, non-intrusive, medium.

## Reference Applications

As businesses grow and mature, policies, procedures, and knowledge are documented. Some of this information may be printed as a book (an employee handbook, for example). Other information may be stored in a binder (telemarketing scripts or internal systems documents).

Aside from the obvious cost of maintaining the knowledge on paper (consider changes to an employee handbook after 1,000 copies just came in from the printer), costs also originate from distribution and creation.

Reference applications are Notes databases designed to support or replace existing printed reference materials. These databases can reduce the cost of preparation and distribution dramatically (if you make a change to the employee handbook, for example, it's updated company-wide when the next replication occurs). They also allow collaborative efforts in the creation of the documents. Sharing a Document on a Notes Server lets Jon enter original content, which can be embellished by Bob. After Bob finishes, Sally (who spells better than a computer) proofreads the work. Finally, Bruce (the boss), approves it to be distributed company-wide.

Some examples of reference applications are:

❖ **Business Policies**. A Business Policies database could contain travel and expense guidelines, on-line instructions for filling out company forms, or a guide to company benefits.

❖ **Knowledge Bases**. Examples of a knowledge base include a database of answers to commonly asked questions or a comprehensive collection of information about each of the company's products.

❖ **Document Library**. A document library could be a collection of white papers on technologies used by a manufacturing firm or a collection of standard contracts at a law firm.

## Tracking Applications

All businesses have information that they want to track and update on a daily basis. It may be a customer base where calls and correspondence to and from the customer are recorded, a shipping manifest where shipping information is added daily, or a project-tracking system where hours spent on a given project are recorded as they are worked. Generally, this kind of information requires input from multiple sources. Jack in sales may create the original customer document. Alice in support, however, will be the one on the phone with the customer next week when they discover that "some assembly required" means a degree in engineering and a six-year-old assistant.

Tracking applications are a challenge to businesses, because tracking different events usually requires a variety of software packages. (Examples include a network-based contact manager, a shipping-and-receiving program, or a project-management package.) While Notes isn't suited for real-time tracking applications, its flexible development structure combined with replication and security makes it a powerful tool to apply to a variety of less rapid transaction-oriented situations.

Tracking applications may be Documents alone or a combination of Documents and Responses. In some cases, a Document may have many different types of Responses. For example, a project database where the project information is stored in a Document and Responses for entering time spent, resources required, and project notes are all associated with the main Document.

Some examples of tracking applications are:

❖ **Employee Tracking and Evaluation**. In personnel, a tracking database can be used to track the interview, hiring, and ongoing performance of each employee.

❖ **Process Improvement Tracking**. In this example, a tracking database is used to record the ongoing status of process improvement initiatives across the company.

❖ **Help Desk or Customer Support Tracking**. Companies with telephone support departments or internal help desks can use Notes to track calls. Actions taken to support the Customer may be stored in Responses or with the main Document.

❖ **Workflow/Approval Applications**. This is a final, important example of how a business can use Lotus Notes. Workflow/Approval applications are Notes databases that use background tasks or Notes' built-in mail capability to route knowledge according to predefined rules. These applications can be complex, such as a "cradle-to-grave" human resources system that tracks information about each employee in the company and routes information based on calendar events or changes in performance to accounting and select supervisors. They can also be deceptively simple, such as a database that uses a background macro to send out reminders through electronic mail.

A Workflow application can be a combination of the other applications we've discussed to this point. As an example, imagine a Help Desk database (a tracking application) at a medium-sized company. The help desk supervisor reviews the database weekly and uses a specially designed view to determine the five most frequently asked questions for the week. After he reviews the questions, he forwards a sample question and answer for each of the top questions to a Help Desk Top 10 database (a broadcast application). Supervisors in the company use the Help Desk Top 10 database to look for trends in their departments and to help identify possible education needs in the company.

Some other examples of workflow applications include:

❖ A product-support database where problems and fixes are marked internal use only or public. If a posted problem and fix are marked public, they are automatically routed to another database. That database, in turn, is replicated out to customer sites.

❖ A company meeting database that allows employees to enter a meeting date and time, agenda, and a list of attendees. One day before the meeting, e-mail is sent to all attendees reminding them of the upcoming event along with the proposed agenda.

# Using Notes to Collect Information for Other Applications

After reading all the examples of standard ways that Notes can be used, it might be tempting to say that, in summary, businesses can (and do) use Lotus Notes for almost anything—which, based on what we've talked about so far, would be a reasonable assumption. But there are some applications that Notes, by its design, does not handle well.

For example, information that requires heavy numerical analysis isn't well served by Notes, nor is data that must be collected and analyzed in real time (such as a point of sale application that must decrement a master inventory database when a sale is made). Finally, information that is heavily dependent on relational linking and joins (accounting data, for example) isn't a strong application candidate for Notes.

However, because of replication, workflow, and other Notes features, Notes is a good method for collecting some of the data we've just discussed, with the ultimate destination of that data being another application. An example of this might be using Notes as a front end for some modules of an accounting application, such as payables management.

In such a scenario, expense reports could originate and move in Notes from user to user by mail enabling. The reports, when approved, would then be stored in an accounting package to be applied to the proper accounts in general ledger using a third-party tool.

# A Real-Life Example of How Lotus Notes Is Being Used

While the generic examples we've discussed up to this point more than illustrate the power of Notes as a tool to collect knowledge, I can't help feeling that people are bombarded with so many promises about technology today that most of them have become the "show-me" type. With that in mind, this section discusses how a software company uses Lotus Notes every day and ties the examples we've just reviewed to a business perspective.

## *Introducing Great Plains Software*

Great Plains Software (GPS) is a privately owned business headquartered in Fargo, North Dakota. Since the company began in 1981, the employees who comprise Great Plains have worked to fulfill a mission that is focused sharply on the people and businesses they serve: to improve the life and business success of partners and customers by providing superior accounting software, services, and tools.

Great Plains fulfills this mission by being a leading developer of accounting and financial management software. The company offers solutions ranging from integrated software for small businesses to powerful client/server applications for midrange corporations. Great Plains products include Great Plains Profit, Great Plains Accounting, Dynamics LAN, Dynamics C/S+ and Dexterity, the development environment used to create Dynamics products.

In addition to being a technology leader in the accounting software industry, Great Plains is also an innovative place to work. The company's steadfast devotion to its mission has made Great Plains a featured company in Jerry Jasinowski and Robert Hamrin's best-seller, *Making it in America, Proven Paths to Success from 50 Top Companies*. Meanwhile, the employee's shared values and relentless pursuit of their dreams has also resulted in Great Plains being featured in Robert Levering and Milton Moskowitz's best-selling book, *The 100 Best Companies to Work for in America*.

And, of course, standing next to Great Plains' support, service, and attitude are its products. Throughout its history, the company has won dozens of awards, including Editor's Choice Awards from *PC Magazine* and *Mac Week* for its Great Plains Accounting, Profit, and Dynamics products, and Best in Products, Support, and Overall distinction from *VARBusiness*. Of special interest to readers of this book is the Partner Beacon Award, given to Great Plains by Lotus Development Corporation in 1993 for the "Most Innovative Vertical Solution" (GPS' Integration Manager for Lotus Notes).

## How Great Plains Software is Using Lotus Notes

As you might gather from the last section, Great Plains Software is strongly committed to the success of its partners and customers. That commitment, combined with the belief that continuous learning and process improvement are a key to the success of any business today, creates an ongoing challenge for the men and women of Great Plains—how can they transfer the knowledge accumulated through the design, creation, and support of their products to partners and customers in a timely and efficient manner?

The answer is PlainsOnline; a set of Lotus Notes databases designed by Great Plains' Information Services Team to allow Great Plains and its partners to share up-to-date information by way of CompuServe's Enterprise Connect Service and AT&T's Network Notes.

When talking about PlainsOnline, there are two components I'd like to discuss:

1.  The technical implementation (because it simply wouldn't be possible without Notes)

2. The types of applications that comprise the PlainsOnline solution

Because I'm a computer geek at heart, I'll begin with the technical details. If you don't want to consider the technical implementation yet, I'll suggest that you skip to the section titled "Dynamics, Dexterity, Great Plains Accounting, and PlainsOnline Discussion Databases," and continue to the summary. When you reach the summary, consider coming back to this section and giving the technical stuff a try.

That said, let's consider the physical tools needed to share information between a company and its Partners using Lotus Notes. Figure 2.1 illustrates how PlainsOnline connects GPS and its network of partners.

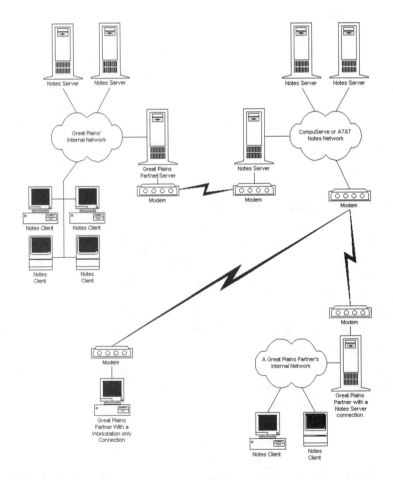

**Figure 2.1** *A conceptual view of how PlainsOnline connects Great Plains Software and its partners.*

Using Figure 2.1 to map the flow of information from GPS to its customers and partners:

1.  Information and knowledge move from GPS' internal Notes Servers to the external Notes Server via replication and workflow.

2.  The GPS external Notes Server connects to CompuServe and AT&T periodically to update replicas maintained by each service provider.

3.  Once CompuServe's and AT&T's databases are updated, customers and partners can connect and replicate it to their own Notes Servers or Notes Clients.

This arrangement allows GPS and its partners access to the knowledge and information GPS wants to share regardless of the size of their organization, 24 hours a day. The one person consulting business can use a single Notes client to connect and replicate, while larger organizations already using Notes internally can connect their servers to CompuServe or AT&T directly and replicate automatically. Along with replication, both CompuServe and AT&T allow Notes users connected to their system to transfer e-mail via Notes to any other user or server on their networks.

**NOTE**  Notes users can also send and receive e-mail through CompuServe's and AT&T's gateways to the Internet, MCI mail, and dozens of other systems.

Another thing to point out is that since AT&T and CompuServe are providing the connection, replication, and mail transfer services, Great Plains has the advantage of thousands of local access telephone numbers to its information around the world, as well as a solution that can be scaled to thousands of customers and partners. All things considered, the CompuServe and AT&T networks represent a very powerful way to move knowledge and information, which leads us to wonder what kind of knowledge and information Great Plains is sharing.

## *Dynamics, Dexterity, Great Plains Accounting, and PlainsOnline Discussion Databases*

These databases allow partners to communicate with Great Plains and with each other in a discussion format. Examples of how partners and customers use them include posting a topic designed to seek out other partners with experience approaching a particular problem, responding to a question posted by GPS to provide feedback about one of Great Plains' products, and participating in a discussion thread designed to help Great Plains set the direction for PlainsOnline in the future.

These discussion databases offer many advantages:

1. Since the conversations between partners, customers, and Great Plains are saved in the database, new users can review the database to see what issues have already been discussed and resolved before they post a question.

2. Because the database is open to virtually thousands of experts on Great Plains' products, the amount of knowledge that can be applied to a problem or question posted is the sum of the participants. This means that useful Responses can be given to almost any question that can be asked.

## Developer Links and PlainsOnline Address Database

The Developer Links and PlainsOnline Address databases are reference applications. Developer Links contains information about all of Great Plains' partners that can be filtered through a number of views, including views by geography, by product line, or by the types of services offered. Once a user locates a partner or customer she wishes to communicate with, she can use the physical address and telephone number in the Developer Links database to gather more information or use the PlainsOnline Address database to look up an e-mail address to request information electronically.

The Developer Links and PlainsOnline Address database offer the following advantages:

1. Replication allows information to stay up-to-date throughout the community of partners. Changing an address or a telephone in one place ensures that it will, over time, be updated in all locations.

2. Views and powerful search capabilities within Notes make it easy to locate Partners based on very specific criteria. For example, using full-text searching (which we'll discuss in depth in Chapter 6), a user can look for a partner located in Texas that has a point-of-sale application developed in Dexterity.

## The Partner Source Database

The Partner Source is an example of a broadcast application in Notes. It is designed to provide up-to-date information about Great Plains' products, strategy, and direction. Some examples of the information you might find in the Partner Source include class schedules for Great Plains University, competitive information, a copy of Great Plains' Schedule (a schedule for product releases over the next year) and the Strategy (a Document detailing future product directions).

Advantages offered by the Partner Source include:

1. Rich text fields allow the Partner Source to include graphics and formatting, making information easier to present and read (some files are distributed in Adobe Acrobat's PDF format, for example).
2. Replication ensures timely information is delivered throughout the Partner community.

## The PlainsOnline Support Database

The PlainsOnline support database is an internal tracking application designed to collect information about partner calls to Great Plains for support. When a new support request is received, information about the partner calling is automatically filled in from the PlainsOnline Address book.

By collecting information into a single database shared from a Notes Server, support personnel can use the database as a reference for troubleshooting problems, and management can have a comprehensive view of the types of calls being placed for support.

## The Dynamics and Dexterity TechKnowledge Databases

The Dynamics and Dexterity TechKnowledge databases are used by partners as reference guides to problems reported by customers to Great Plains Support along with solutions. I didn't include these two databases in our previous discussion of reference applications because they are also excellent examples of a workflow/approval application.

On Great Plains internal Notes network, support personnel compose a new problem/solution Document for the TechKnowledge database based on new calls. The Document is routed to the support person's supervisor, where it verified for accuracy. From there, the Document travels to the Design and Documentation group where it is edited to ensure that it communicates the problem and solution effectively. Finally, the Document is moved to the external Notes Server at Great Plains to be replicated to the CompuServe and AT&T networks.

## In Summary

While Notes isn't the ideal development environment for every application a business may use to solve problems, it is uniquely suited to five distinct classes of applications:

- ❖ **Discussion Applications**. Applications that take advantage of Response Documents to create links between main ideas and supporting information.

- ❖ **Broadcast Applications**. Applications that take advantage of rich text and replication to ensure timely, easy-to-read information is distributed.

- ❖ **Reference Applications**. Applications that take advantage of rich text, Views, and Notes' powerful search capabilities to make knowledge accessible.

- ❖ **Tracking Applications**. Applications that are generally combined with workflow to create automatic solutions to common business problems.

- ❖ **Workflow/Approval**. Any combination of the first four applications that automate the flow of information or knowledge throughout an organization.

In cases where Notes isn't the proper tool to store information, its replication and mail-enabled features may still make it an innovative way to collect information to be passed to another application.

Businesses that recognize Notes' strengths can create powerful tools in Notes that improve processes, streamline information, and increase the overall level of knowledge within an organization. Also, as you've seen from PlainsOnline, those benefits can extend beyond the organization to an entire industry.

# Chapter 3

# Using Notes to Locate Databases

## In this Chapter...

In this chapter, we'll discuss different elements of the Notes Client and illustrate how you can use them to locate databases on Notes Servers or on your local hard drive. We'll also work through the first of many step-by-step exercises designed for you to follow at your computer.

The topics we'll cover include:

- ❖ Exploring the Notes Client
- ❖ Exploring the Notes Workspace
- ❖ Finding out information about a Notes database
- ❖ Adding a Notes database to the Workspace as an icon
- ❖ About Documents and Using Documents
- ❖ Taking what we've learned step-by-step (Exercise 3.1)

# Before We Begin

1. I'm assuming in this and all subsequent chapters that you have Notes or Notes Desktop installed on your computer. If you do not have one of these packages installed, please refer to the installation instructions provided by Lotus or contact your company's Notes or e-mail administrator.

2. In addition to having one of the three versions of Notes installed on your computer, you will need the databases included with this book installed to follow the hands-on examples. If these databases are not already installed, please refer to the appendix in this book titled "Installing the Sample Applications that Ship with this Book."

3. Since Notes is a multiplatform tool (versions for Windows/NT/95, OS/2, Macintosh, Mac OS, and several flavors of UNIX exist as of this writing), and because the very nature of Notes makes it different things to different people, discrepancies will exist between your computer's screen and many of the illustrations presented here. As a point of reference, these illustrations were collected using Windows 95 and a beta copy of Notes, Release 4. If you are not familiar with Windows 95, you can use the appendix to this book entitled "The Appearance of the Notes Client on Different Operating Systems" to help translate elements of these screen shots to your own operating system.

4. In addition to using screen shots from Windows 95, I use keyboard and mouse sequences based on Windows/NT/95. While these key sequences work on many platforms the Notes Client runs on (for example, the key sequence **Alt+F** opens the File menu on all versions of Windows, OS/2, and most UNIX platforms), you may have to substitute different keyboard or mouse commands for your operating system (such as **Command+F** for the Macintosh or Mac OS).

5. I'd like to take a moment to clarify how I use certain terms in the step-by-step exercises:

   ❖ *Selecting* a menu item or Notes element means clicking the object one time with the left mouse button.

   ❖ *Highlighting* means using the mouse to click and drag over an object or range of objects so that they are "selected."

   ❖ *Right-clicking* means clicking once on an object with the right mouse button.

For example, the following sentence:

"Highlight the phrase 'Notes is neat' and select **Text, Text Properties...** from the main menu or right-click on the selected text and choose **Properties...** from the pop-up menu"

would mean place the mouse cursor before the word Notes, click and drag the mouse cursor over the sentence "Notes is neat," and then click once with the mouse button on the menu choice Text, followed by one click on the command **Text Properties...**; or after highlighting the text, click the right mouse button once on the area you just highlighted and choose Properties from the pop-up menu.

6.  At the time this book went to press, the Final Customer Ship of Notes, Release 4 was not available. While great effort has been made to ensure that screen shots and information in this book is as accurate as possible, discrepancies may exist between the illustrations presented here and the actual screens on your computer.

7.  Finally, I'd like to explain how this book uses the following three symbols:

This symbol is used to call attention to information that can help you avoid losing or damaging your data.

This symbol is used to give a paragraph special importance. The information next to it may be about a particularly useful feature, an important concept, or a special condition of which you should be aware.

This symbol is used to call attention to information that will help you perform an action more quickly, such as a keyboard shortcut or user suggestion.

## Exploring the Notes Client

In the first two chapters, you were introduced to Notes on a conceptual level. Now it's time to meet Notes "face-to-workspace."

Start Notes by selecting the **Notes** icon and pressing **Enter** or by double-clicking the **Notes** icon on your desktop. After launching Notes, you will see a screen similar to the one in Figure 3.1.

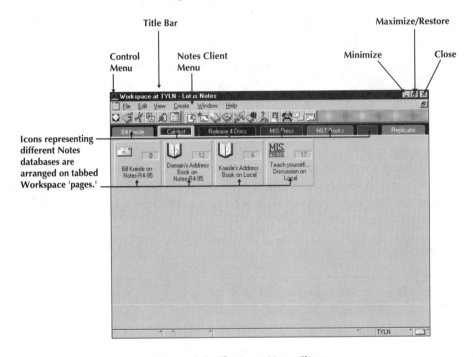

**Figure 3.1** *The Lotus Notes Client.*

As you can see from Figure 3.1, the main Notes application consists of many elements. There is a Notes Client window with its associated controls (menu, title bar, border, etc.) and a child window within it called the *Workspace.*

## Elements of the Notes Client We'll Discuss in Later Chapters

The Notes Client is a busy place. There are many buttons and beveled surfaces begging you to click them with the mouse or to otherwise activate them. Throughout this book, we will explore the entire Notes Client. To begin, however, we're going to confine our exploration primarily to the Workspace.

For the curious, impatient, or those readers who are just plain addicted to mousing around, Figure 3.2 details other elements of the Notes Client. The paragraphs following the illustration discuss what the elements labeled are and when we will cover them in this book.

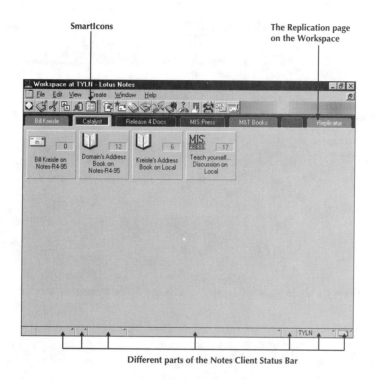

**Figure 3.2** *Areas of the Notes Client we'll discuss in later chapters.*

SmartIcons are used by Lotus to create user-defined shortcuts for commonly used menu commands (such as **File, Database, Open...** or **File, Exit Notes**). We'll discuss SmartIcons extensively in Chapter 11.

The tabbed page on the Workspace labeled *Replicator* is used to manage database replication, which we discussed earlier and will discuss again in greater detail in Chapter 8.

The additional information areas on the Notes Client status bar will also be covered throughout the book, based on the focus of the chapter.

# Exploring the Notes Workspace

The Workspace is where most of your interaction with Notes will occur. Its interface is designed to mimic tabbed pages that move to the front of the Workspace window when you click on them (drawing on the metaphor of opening a tabbed page in a datebook or binder). Database icons are stored on these tabbed pages, giving you a way to organize your information.

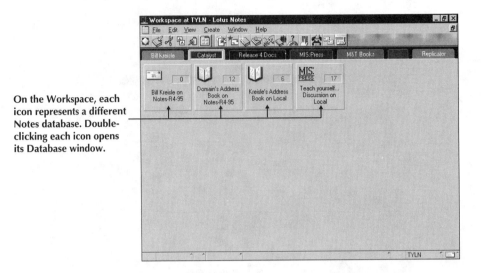

On the Workspace, each icon represents a different Notes database. Double-clicking each icon opens its Database window.

*Figure 3.3* *Databases are represented on the Notes Workspace by icons.*

You can move database icons on a Workspace page by clicking and dragging them from their current location to another area on the page. You can also move database icons to a different Workspace page by clicking and dragging them from their current location to the tab of the page where you want the database to go.

As you can see from Figures 3.1 and 3.3, each tabbed page can have a text label. What isn't illustrated by the two figures is the fact that you can also make each tab on the workspace a different color. You can change the text or color of a tab using any of the following actions:

❖ double-click the tab you wish to customize;

❖ select the tab with the mouse or arrow keys and press **Enter**;

❖ click the tab once with the mouse, then click the right mouse button over the Workspace and choose **Workspace Properties...** from the pop-up menu.

Any of these actions will cause the dialog box shown in Figure 3.4 to appear.

After selecting the **Tabs** page of the dialog box, information you type in the text box will appear on the tab, and the color you select from the drop-down list will become the tab's color when it is not the currently active page. After you have made the desired changes, close the Workspace Properties dialog box by clicking on the **Control Menu** icon in the upper-left corner of the dialog box and selecting **Close** or by pressing **Alt+F4** on the keyboard.

Of course, some of you won't close the Workspace Page Name dialog box until you click on the other tab in the dialog box—the one with an icon that looks like a lowercase *i* inside a circle. That dialog page is an information page, providing you with additional information and options for the Workspace that we'll discuss in Chapter 11.

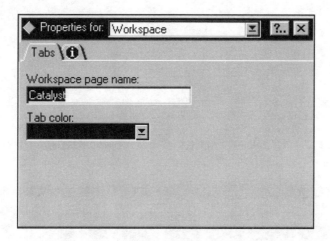

**Figure 3.4** *Use the Workspace Page Name dialog box to customize Workspace pages.*

## Adding and Removing Workspace Pages

You can add and remove tabbed pages from the Workspace by right-clicking on the Workspace and selecting **Create Workspace Page...** from the pop-up menu or by selecting **Create, Workspace Page...** from the Notes Client menu (see Figure 3.5).

This will cause a new tab to be added to the left of the currently selected page (see Figure 3.6). You can have up to 32 tabbed pages on the Workspace in Notes, Release 4.

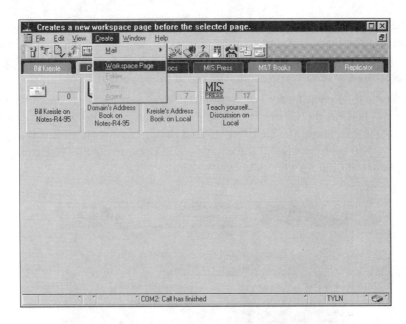

**Figure 3.5** *Adding a Workspace page using the* **Create, Workspace...** *command.*

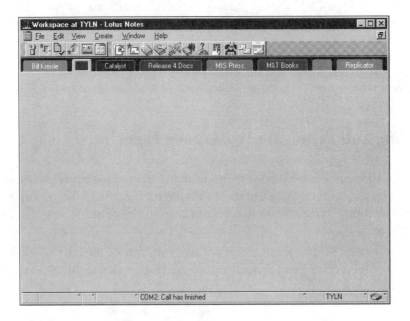

**Figure 3.6** *A new tabbed page on the Workspace.*

To delete tabs from the Workspace, select the page you want to remove and right-click on it. Select **Remove Workspace** page from the pop-up menu.

WARNING

There is no **Undo** command for a deleted Workspace page. Be sure you want to remove it before answering **yes** to the prompt shown in Figure 3.7

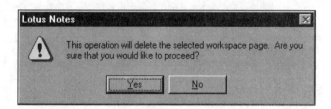

**Figure 3.7** *You will be prompted before Notes deletes any tabbed pages from your Workspace.*

SHORTCUT

You can also delete a tab from the Workspace by selecting it and pressing the **Delete** key.

## Changing the Texture of the Workspace

If you have a monitor that can display 256 colors and would like to "texturize" your Workspace, you can do so in Notes by selecting **File, Tools, User Preferences...** from the Notes Client menu to open the Preferences dialog box (see Figure 3.8).

From this dialog box, select **Textured Workspace** from the Advanced Options list to change the Workspace's appearance to be similar to Figure 3.9.

## Using the Workspace to Organize Your Information

There are a number of approaches to using the Workspace's tabbed pages. For example, one user, wanting to organize databases by department, may label the first tab **Administration**, the second tab **Executive**, the third tab **Accounting**, and so forth. Another user may use tabs to organize databases by how frequently he or she feels they need to be checked for new information, creating one tab called **Daily**, another called **Weekly**, a third called **Biweekly**, and so forth. A third user may organize databases by their location, labeling each tab with the name of the Notes Server where the databases on that page reside.

If you're new to Notes, you're probably not sure how you want to organize your databases yet. As you begin to use Notes in your daily life, however, you'll appreciate the ability to customize the Workspace to suit your needs.

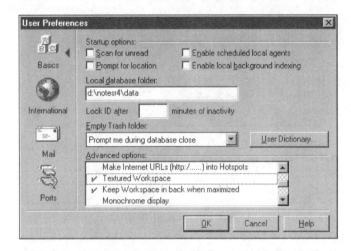

**Figure 3.8** *The Preferences dialog box.*

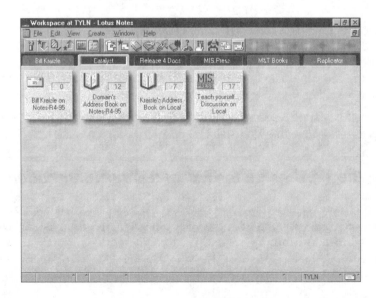

**Figure 3.9** *A textured Workspace.*

# Locating Databases

As I mentioned in the preceding section, the primary purpose of the Workspace is to organize Notes databases and to help manage replication. Notes organizes databases by using an icon to represent each different database you work with, as shown in Figure 3.3. When you're just getting started with Notes, your Workspace will not contain many icons. You can be sure, however, that regardless of the number of icons you currently have, there are more databases "out there" than you see on your Workspace. In this section, we'll discuss how to find them.

To locate new databases, use the **File, Database, Open...** command on the Notes Client menu, or press **Ctrl+O** while the Workspace is the currently active window. This command will open a dialog box similar to the one in Figure 3.10.

**Figure 3.10** *The Open Database dialog box*

This dialog box allows you to search for Notes databases on your local hard drive and any Notes servers to which you are connected. These servers and the word *Local* (representing your hard drive) will appear in the Server drop-down list.

Selecting **Local** or the name of a Notes Server in the Server list will connect your Notes Client with the desired location and fill the Database list with the names of any Notes databases or folders you can open for that location. You may be prompted for a password at this point.

Once you have established where you want to look for Notes databases, use the Database list portion of the Open Database dialog box or the Filename text box to begin your search. Each Notes database has a title (a descriptive name up to 25 characters), and a filename (the name that the operating system the Notes

Client or Server is running on uses to identify that particular database.) The Database list portion of the Open Database dialog box displays each database's title. When you select a database in the list, you will see the filename of the database displayed in the Filename text box.

Databases may also be stored in subdirectories on your Local drive or subdirectories on a Notes Server. As you can see in Figure 3.10, the Windows 95 version of Notes represents subdirectories with a folder icon and databases with an icon that looks like a book or binder. Double-clicking a subdirectory will fill the Database list portion of the Open Database dialog box with the names of any databases or additional folders it contains. To move up one folder or subdirectory, click on the **up-arrow** icon.

In addition to double-clicking the location, subdirectory, or up-arrow icon to navigate, you can also select any of those items by clicking them once and pressing **Enter** or clicking the **Open** button. Don't open any databases yet, though—there are still a couple of things I'd like to discuss with you regarding the Open Database dialog box.

You can use the **Browse** button on the Open Database dialog box to search for databases, similar to the way you might search for files in other applications such as a word processor or spreadsheet (see Figure 3.11).

***Figure 3.11*** *Searching for databases using the* ***Browse*** *button on the Open Database dialog box.*

# Finding out Information about a Database before Adding it to Your Workspace

When you're dealing with a large number of servers and databases, sometimes it is difficult to tell if a database is the one you want to use from its title alone. To find out more about a database before opening it or adding it to your Workspace, select it and click the **About...** button in the Open Database dialog box to see a brief description of the database.

The **About...** button gets its information from an optional document available to the database's designer or manager called an *About document.* I use the term *optional* because while every Notes database can contain an About document, that option may not have been exercised by the designer of the database you are looking at. If there is an About document, it will appear in a dialog box similar to Figure 3.12.

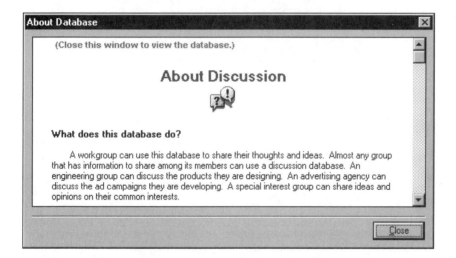

**Figure 3.12** *Clicking the* **About...** *button in the Open Database dialog box may provide you with information about a database before you open it.*

If there is no About document for the database you are looking at when you click the **About...** button, you will see a dialog box similar to Figure 3.13.

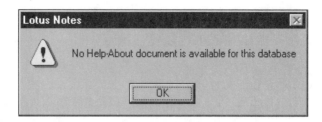

***Figure 3.13*** *If you click the **About...** button and the selected database does not contain an About document, you will see this message.*

It is also possible that you could click the **About...** button for a selected database and see a message like the one in Figure 3.14.

***Figure 3.14*** *If you are not in a Database's Access Control List, you will see this message.*

If you see the "You are not authorized..." message, it is because you are not listed in the selected database's Access Control List (ACL). As you remember from Chapter 1, the Access Control List determines who can do what with a specific database. To be given access, you must contact the database's manager and ask to be added to the database's ACL.

## Adding the Database to the Workspace

Once you have selected a server, reviewed the list of databases, and selected one you would like to look at, you can add the database to your Workspace by making sure it is selected in the Open Database dialog box and clicking the **Add Icon** button. This will create an icon representing the database on your Workspace. The Open Database dialog box will remain open, allowing you to navigate to another server or to make another selection from your current location.

# Opening the Database

After you have finished adding all the databases you want to have on your Workspace, close the Open Database dialog box by clicking the **Done** button. You can then open a database by double-clicking on the icon representing it or by highlighting its icon using the arrow keys and pressing **Enter**.

**SHORTCUT**

If you're going to add one database to your Workspace and open it immediately, you can save a few steps by clicking the **Open** button while the database is selected in the Open Database dialog box. Clicking this button is the same as selecting the database from the Open Database dialog box, clicking the **Add Icon** button, closing the Open Database dialog box, and double-clicking on the new icon.

# About Documents and Using Documents

So far, you've started Notes, looked at the Workspace, and learned how to add an icon to the Workspace using the **File, Database, Open...** command and the Open Database dialog box. Now that you've added a database to your Workspace and opened it for the first time, what do you do with it?

One of the first things to do is to see how the database's designer envisioned the database being used when it was created. How do we do that? We look for two special documents that are part of every Notes database: an About document (which we discussed earlier) and a Using document. Going back to our three-ring binder analogy from Chapter 1, the About document and the Using document are similar to two pages added to the binder that tell you a little bit about the binder (why it was created, who the intended audience is, etc.) and how you can use the binder to find or add information ("If you add a page to this binder, be sure to include the following information on every page...," for example).

In addition to being available from the Open Database dialog box, the About document appears the first time a database you have added to your Workspace is opened. If you have been following along on your computer as you have been reading, you probably have the About document for a database on your screen right now. If that's the case, press the **Esc** key to close the About document and keep pressing the **Esc** key until you are back at the Workspace.

Another way to see the About or the Using document is to select a database from the Workspace (click on it once using the mouse or select it using the Arrow keys), then choosing Help, **About This Database** or **Help**, **Using This Database** from the main menu (see Figure 3.15).

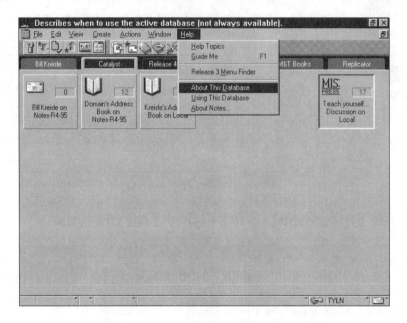

**Figure 3.15** *You can see the About and Using documents using commands from the Help menu.*

**NOTE**

You can also see the About document in a special Notes database called the *Database Catalog*. The Database Catalog is a Notes database that is maintained by one or more Notes Servers and is updated nightly. It contains a list of all databases on the Notes Servers in your *domain* (a term you can find in the glossary of this book), their locations, and a copy of each database's About document. It also contains the names of people or groups that have manager access to a Notes database (so if you aren't in the Access Control List for a database, you can find out whom you need to contact to ask for access). Since we're just getting started with locating databases in this chapter, we won't look at the database catalog in the following exercise, but you might want to remember it's there for future reference.

# Taking What We've LearnedbStep-by-Step (Exercise 3.1)

To summarize what we've covered so far, here's a step-by-step example for adding a Notes database to your Workspace and reading the About document. To complete this exercise, you should have the sample databases that were included with this book installed on your computer. If you do not have these databases installed, please refer to the appendix in this book titled "Installing the Sample Applications that Ship with this Book" before continuing.

## *Step 1*

Select the **File, Database, Open...** command from the Notes Client menu, or activate the Open Database dialog box by pressing **Ctrl+O** (see Figure 3.16).

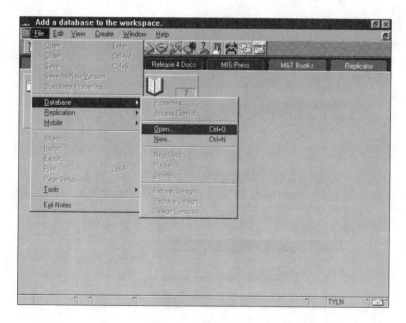

***Figure 3.16*** *Using the* ***File, Database, Open...*** *command.*

## *Step 2*

Select **Local** Servers from the drop-down list (see Figure 3.17).

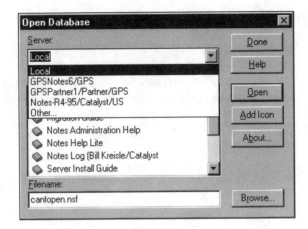

***Figure 3.17*** *Selecting **Local** means opening a database from your local disk drive.*

## Step 3

Select the **TYLN** subdirectory (click on it once with the mouse) from the list box in the Database list and click the **Open** button, or double-click the **TYLN** subdirectory (see Figure 3.18).

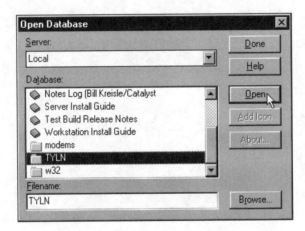

***Figure 3.18*** *Opening the TYLN subdirectory.*

## Step 4

Select the database called **teach yourself... Discussion** and click the **Open** button (see Figure 3.19).

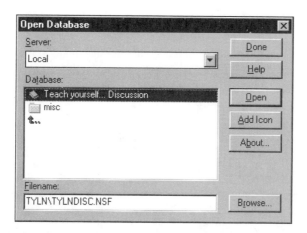

**Figure 3.19** *Selecting the **teach yourself... Discussion** database from the TYLN subdirectory on your local disk drive.*

The database is added to the current page of your Workspace, and since this is the first time you've opened the database, the About document is automatically displayed. Note that the About document is a Rich Text document, combining fonts and graphics (see Figure 3.20).

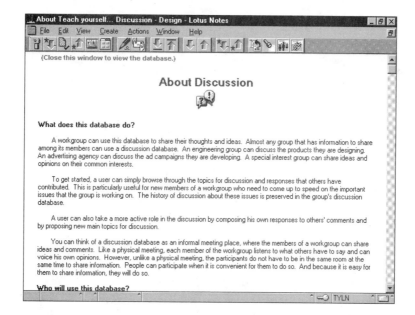

**Figure 3.20** *The About document for the teach yourself... Discussion database.*

## Step 5

After you have finished reading the About Document, close it by pressing the **Esc** key or by selecting **File, Close** from the Notes Client menu. You will see the teach yourself... Discussion database's default View (see Figure 3.21). We'll discuss Views in the next chapter.

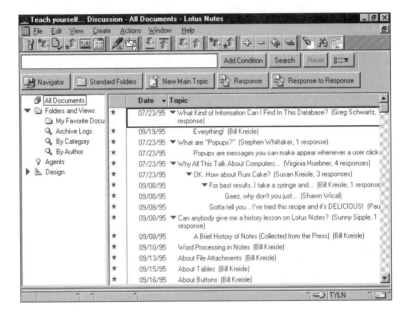

***Figure 3.21*** *The teach yourself... Discussion database's default View.*

## Step 6

Select **Help, Using This Database** from the main menu to open the teach yourself... Discussion database's Using document (see Figure 3.22).

## Step 7

After you have read the Using document, press the **Esc** key to close it or select **File, Close** from the main menu to close it. Select **File, Close** again to exit the default View and return to the Workspace. You will see the teach yourself... Discussion icon on your Workspace page (see Figure 3.23).

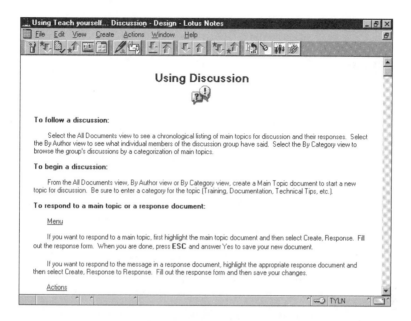

**Figure 3.22**  *The Using document for the teach yourself... Discussion database.*

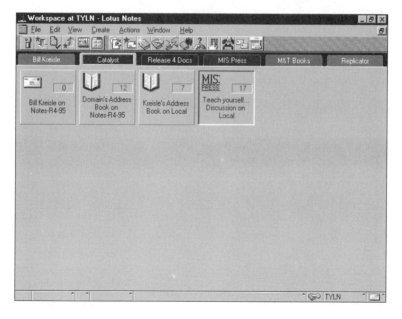

**Figure 3.23**  *The teach yourself... Discussion icon has been added to the Workspace.*

# In Summary

Here's what we learned in this chapter:

❖ Notes uses the Workspace to organize databases.

❖ The Workspace consists of tabbed pages. You can add or delete tabs from the Workspace by right-clicking the tab and selecting **Create Workspace Page...** or **Remove Workspace Page...** from the pop-up menu.

❖ Each database is represented on the Workspace by an icon.

❖ Icons are added to the Workspace using the **File, Database, Open...** command.

❖ Notes Databases can be added to the Workspace from the local hard drive, from multiple Notes Servers in a network, or from Notes Servers that you connect to remotely using a modem.

❖ Each database may contain additional information in two special documents: the About document and the Using document.

❖ You can see the About document a number of ways:

❖ It is displayed the first time you open a database.

❖ It can be viewed by clicking on the **About...** button in the Open Database dialog box.

❖ It can be read by selecting the database on the Workspace and choosing **Help, About This Database...** from the main menu.

❖ You can see the Using document by selecting **Help, Using This Database...** from the menu while the database is open or while it is the current selection on the Workspace.

# Chapter 4

# Using the Database Window to Locate and Track Documents in a Notes Database

## In this Chapter...

As you recall from Chapter 3, the first time you add a database to your Workspace and double-click its icon to open it, you see the database's About Document. After closing the About Document, the next part of the database you'll see is called the *Database Window*. As the name implies, the Database Window provides the user with a window into the contents of a databease.

This chapter discusses the Database Window and its elements, paying particular attention to an element called the *View pane* and its contents, *database Views*.

Lastly, we'll discuss features in Notes that are designed to help you know when new Documents are added to a database or when a Document you've already read has been changed.

This information is covered by the following sections:

❖ The Database Window

❖ The View pane and Database Views

❖ How Views display Response documents

❖ How Views categories

❖ Reading Documents

❖ Locating unread Documents in Views

❖ Controlling unread indicators

❖ The Navigator pane

## The Database Window

As its name implies, the Database Window is used to look inside a Notes database to see the Documents stored within. It is composed of three elements, which, in keeping with the window metaphor, are referred to by Lotus as *panes*—a Navigator pane, a View pane, and a Document Preview pane. Figure 4.1 illustrates the Database Window and its panes.

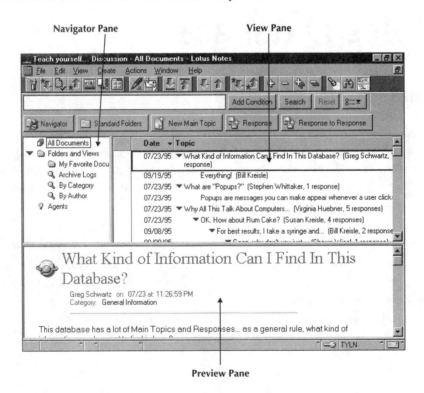

**Figure 4.1** *A Navigator, View, and Preview pane complete the database window.*

**NOTE** When you open a Database Window, all three panes may not be visible. We'll learn the commands to hide or move some of these panes later in this chapter.

The Navigator pane, View pane, and Preview pane are designed to work together to help you quickly locate information that is stored in a Notes database:

1. The Navigator pane allows you move between different Views in a Notes database and to collect Documents from different Views into folders.

2. The View pane organizes the documents in the database according to the view currently selected in the Navigator pane.

3. The Preview pane allows you to highlight a Document in a Notes View and preview its contents.

Figure 4.2 illustrates how the Navigator, View, and Preview panes of the Database Window work together.

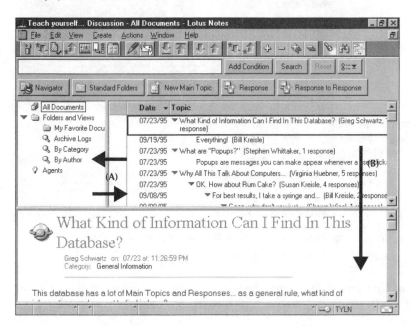

**(A)** The Navigator Pane allows the user to select different Database Views for display in the View Pane.

**(B)** The Preview Pane displays the Document currently selected in the View Pane.

***Figure 4.2*** *How the panes of the Database Window work together.*

Each pane in the Database Window can be resized by clicking and dragging the gray bar that separates it from the other panes (Figure 4.3).

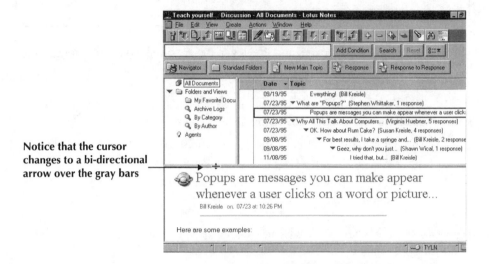

**Notice that the cursor changes to a bi-directional arrow over the gray bars**

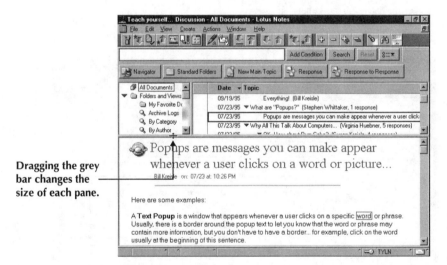

**Dragging the grey bar changes the size of each pane.**

***Figure 4.3*** *Click and drag the gray bars that separate the panes in the Database Window to resize them.*

You can click and drag the gray bar(s) separating the panes to the edges or bottom of the Database Window to hide a particular pane. In Figure 4.4, the vertical bar separating the Preview pane from the Navigator and View panes is moved to the bottom of the Database Window.

**By dragging the separator between the Document Preview Pane and the Navigator and View Panes to the bottom of the window, we can hide the Preview Pane.**

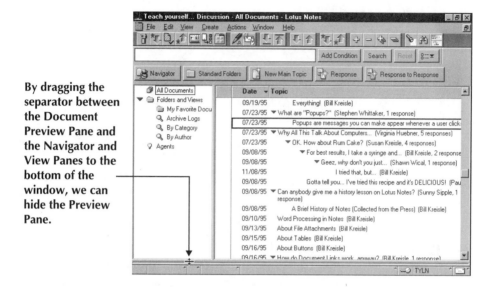

***Figure 4.4*** *Click and dragging a gray bar to the edge or bottom of the Database Window hides one or more panes.*

You can also use commands from the Notes Client menu to hide and show different panes in the Database Window:

1. **View**, **Document Preview** to toggle between displaying and hiding the Document Preview pane.

2. **View**, **Show** to change between the default Folders Navigator and any custom Navigators in the database.

Of the three panes in the Database Window, the most important pane you'll work with is the View pane. The reason for this is that the View pane is used to display all of a database's different views.

## The View Pane and Database Views

Going back in time and space for a moment, let's compare what we learned in the previous chapter to our three-ring binder analogy:

❖ You've been to the library and looked at the binders there.

❖ You've read the first page or two of a few binders to decide which binder you want to read.

❖ You've checked out a book.

That translates to the following in Notes:

❖ You've connected to a Notes Server or your local hard drive and selected a database to open.

❖ You've gotten some information about the database by looking at the About Document.

❖ You've decided to add the database's icon to the Workspace and opened the database.

What's the next step? Well, going back to our analogy, after taking the book off the shelf and deciding to read it, you'd probably review the table of contents or the index so you could go directly to the information you're looking for. What's the equivalent in a Notes database to a table of contents in our binder? Notes Views.

## What Makes Database Views So Important?

Views are your primary means of navigating through a Notes database. They help you find existing information quickly and provide you with a tool to locate Documents that have been added or changed in a Notes database since the last time you read it.

You access views in a Notes database through the View command on the main Notes menu and through the Navigator pane, a special portion of the Database Window that we'll talk about later in this chapter.

Since Views are created by a database's designer, the contents of the drop-down menu you see when you select the View command and the choices you see in the Navigator pane will be different with each database. Even if some databases contain Views that share the same name (two databases with a View called Main View, for example), they may present information differently once they are selected.

Because Views are so flexible, I believe that how well you understand them translates into how well you can use them to find information. With that in mind, I'll spend the next few paragraphs covering Views from a conceptual level before we get into any step-by-step examples.

Sounds like a long talk about computer science is coming up, doesn't it? Not to worry—you're halfway home if you think of Views as the table of contents and indexes in our binders. You're three-quarters of the way home if you can imagine those tables and indexes automatically changing whenever a Document is added to or changed in the binder.

The rest of the job is knowing how Views display Documents and Responses (the pages of our binder and the Post-It Notes we've attached to them) and how Notes Views use Categories.

## How Views Display Responses

If you go back to my comparison of Response Documents in a Notes database to Post-It Notes on the pages of a binder, it isn't difficult to imagine the challenge that Responses would create for a typical table of contents (Figure 4.5). They are actually different Documents from the page they are attached to, yet the fact that they are attached to the page means that they are somehow related to the original Document's content. How could a table of contents display that?

One way would be to group Responses directly below their parent Document (Figure 4.5).

**Chapter 1**

| | |
|---|---|
| **About Basketweaving for Fun and Profit** | 1 |
| Bill's Response to the First Chapter | 1.1 |
| Bob's Response to the First Chapter | 1.2 |
| Jon's Response to Bob's Response | 1.2.1 |
| Deneen's Response to the First Chapter | 1.3 |
| **Types of Baskets you can Weave** | 3 |
| **Your First Basket!** | 6 |
| Carie's Response to Your First Basket! | 6.1 |
| **The Cross-Over-The-Thingy Weave** | 8 |
| **The Pushed-Under-The-Other-One Weave** | 10 |

**Chapter 2**

| | |
|---|---|
| **Your Second Basket!** | 12 |

***Figure 4.5*** *How a traditional table of contents in a book might incorporate the concept of a Response Document.*

A second approach might be to have two tables of contents, where Responses are separate from their parent Documents (Figure 4.6).

**Chapter 1**

**Chapter 2**

**Responses**

**Figure 4.6** *Another example of how a traditional table of contents in a book might incorporate the concept of a Response Document.*

A third approach might be to have a single table of contents that treats every Document in the database the same, whether it is a Response Document or a parent Document (Figure 4.7).

**Chapter 1**

**Chapter 2**

**Figure 4.7** *How a traditional table of contents would handle Responses if they were treated the same as any Document in the binder.*

Not coincidentally, these methods are similar to how Notes approaches displaying Responses and Documents in its Views. The first method discussed is what Lotus calls a *Response Hierarchy View.*

Response Hierarchy Views are commonly used in discussion applications. Main topics are the original Documents in the database, and comments from others about the main topic are Responses. Because the Responses are closely related to the content of the parent Document, it makes sense to group them next to each other.

Figure 4.8 shows you how a Notes View displays Documents and Responses in a discussion database and compares it to what we discussed earlier in this section.

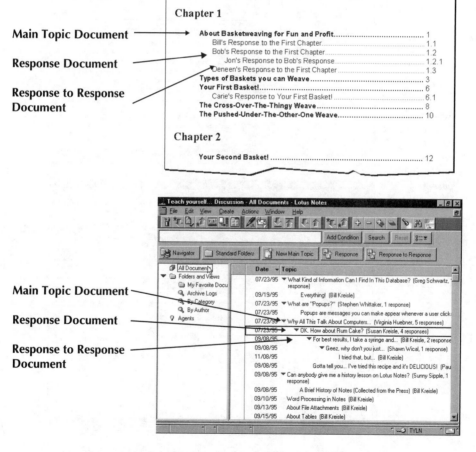

**Figure 4.8** *A View of a discussion database where Responses are associated with their parent Documents.*

As you can see, our paper approach and the approach Notes takes to grouping Responses with Documents is similar. One difference between the Hierarchy View in a Notes database and a paper table of contents is that Responses in the Notes View can be updated automatically as new Documents and Responses are added or deleted. Another difference is that Responses in the Notes View can be "collapsed" under their parent Documents, as illustrated in Figure 4.9.

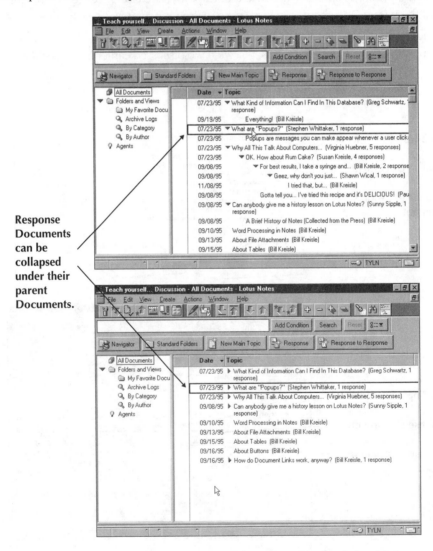

**Response Documents can be collapsed under their parent Documents.**

***Figure 4.9*** *Response Documents can be collapsed under their parents.*

The second method used by Views to display Documents (where Responses are separated from the Documents they are associated with) is what Lotus refers to as a *Responses Only View*. In a Responses Only View, there would be pages in the table of contents dedicated to listing only where all of the Post-It Notes in the binder are located. This listing might be sorted by the name of the person who added the Post-It Note to the binder, or possibly by the date the Post-It Note was added. However, it wouldn't be a requirement of these pages that you know which main Document each Post-It Note is attached to.

As an example of when you may want to have Responses separated from their parent Documents, imagine a tracking application (say, a project-tracking database). In this database, the amount of time spent on a project each day is recorded as a Response to a main project Document. At week's end, a View is used to sort the hours spent by each person across multiple projects and create a status report. Since we're interested only in the total number of hours spent by each person, a Responses Only View with Documents sorted by person and date allows us to create this type of report.

Figure 4.10 shows a Notes View from a project-tracking database and compares it to the paper version we discussed earlier in this chapter. In the View responses are separated from their parent Documents, grouped logically on a value stored in each Response's fields.

The third method a view can use to display Documents is what Lotus calls a *No Response Hierarchy View*. Going back to our example of a Response Hierarchy View in a discussion database, imagine a second View for this discussion database, designed to group Documents together based on the name of the person who created them (all Documents are treated the same). In this View, it wouldn't matter if the Document was a main topic or a Response, you'd want everything created by the same person grouped together.

Figure 4.11 shows you a No Response Hierarchy View in a discussion database and compares it to what we discussed earlier.

Which brings up one more point about Views—you can have many different Views in a singe Notes database. This is analogous to selecting the right tool for the right job—different types of Views provide you with a window on the information you need in the way best suited to help you find it. In our project-tracking database, for example, we'd certainly want more than a Responses Only View that gave us the total number of hours spent by person. We'd also want to have a Response Hierarchy View that showed an entry for our project Document and then displayed Responses containing hours spent on a project together.

## Chapter 1

## Chapter 2

## Responses

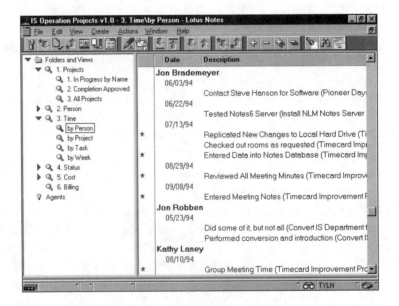

**Figure 4.10** *Responses can be separated from their parents using a Responses Only view.*

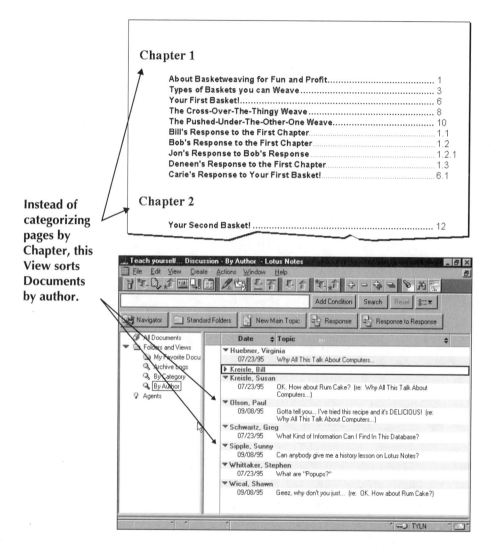

**Figure 4.11** *A No Response Hierarchy view in a discussion database.*

# How Views Use Categories

The second item we need to cover before moving to our step-by-step exercises is how Views use Categories, Categories group Documents together in a View based on common field values. In our ever-versatile binder analogy (metaphors in my books work hard for their money), Categories would be similar to the separators in an index. Let's look at the following index from another book I'm currently working on as an example.

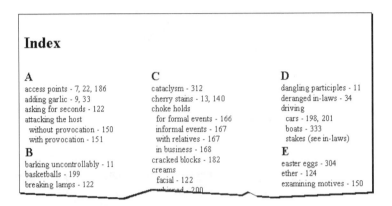

*Figure 4.12  A sample index page from a book.*

In Figure 4.12, A, B, C, D, and so on are equivalent to Categories in a Notes View—they group items together based on a common value contained in each Document, making it easier to navigate items in the list. When moved from the traditional printed medium to Notes, Categories add a number of features not possible in a traditional index:

❖  Because they are part of a View, Categories can be updated automatically. If a new category is added to the database (using Figure 4.12 as reference, adding an entry that starts with an *A* would be a good example), a new Category appears in the View.

❖  Categories can be collapsed to allow for faster navigation between Documents in a Notes database.

Let's take a moment to compare our book index (Figure 4.12) with a Notes View that uses Categories to index its Documents (Figure 4.13)..

The View in Figure 4.13 is not part of the sample database included with this book. It is from a database I designed specifically to help illustrate the concept of categories.

NOTE

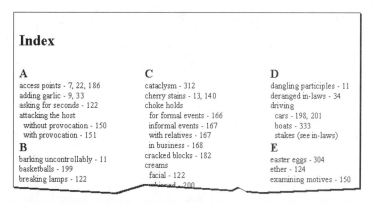

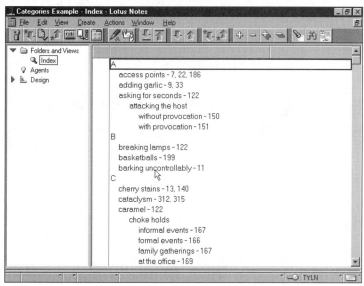

**Figure 4.13** *How Figure 4.12 might compare to a Notes View.*

One of the first things you will notice is that when our index became a Notes View, the three short columns became one long one. That's how Notes displays Documents in a View—as one long list. Because of this, scanning down to the letter *E* to find a Document involves scrolling past a number of Documents that you are not looking for. However, where Notes loses to the paper medium in that it uses a single column, it gains on paper considerably in that Categories are collapsible. That means that since each letter in the index is a Category, the View can be collapsed so that it looks like Figure 4.14.

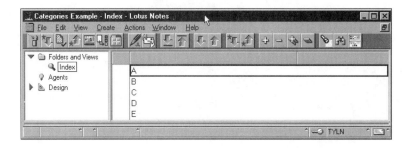

**Figure 4.14** *Our Notes View with the Categories collapsed.*

That shortens the View, making it easier to locate a specific topic. Another feature of Categories in Notes Views is that you that you can have selected Categories expanded, and others collapsed. Figure 4.15 shows us the same Notes View we've been looking at in Figures 4.13 and 4.14 with Category D expanded and the other Categories collapsed.

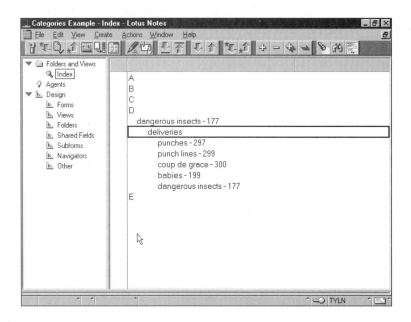

**Figure 4.15** *You can expand a single Category in a View and see the Documents beneath it.*

Another advantage a Notes View using Categories has over a traditional paper index or table of contents is that Categories can be nested. Nesting means that expanding one Category can open several subcategories and opening a subcategory can display even more subcategories, eventually leading to Documents. That would be similar to an index that grouped all the entries for the letter *A* under one category and then grouped all the pages that contained a particular word beginning with *A* under a subcategory. Figure 4.16 illustrates a Notes View that has nested Categories.

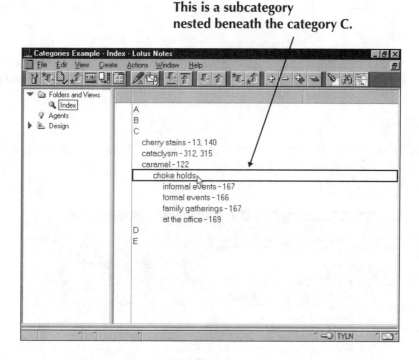

**This is a subcategory nested beneath the category C.**

***Figure 4.16*** *A Notes View that uses nested categories.*

# Taking What We've Learned Step-by-Step (Exercise 4.1)

In this exercise, we're going to open several Views in a Notes database, and see how what we've discussed up to this point applies to each View we look at. To begin, let's take a look at the All Documents View from the Teach yourself... discussion database included on the disk that came with this book.

> If you haven't installed the Teach yourself... discussion database already, please see the appendix in this book titled "Installing the Sample Applications that Ship with this Book" before continuing. You might also want to review the Exercise 3.1 if you aren't sure how to add the Teach yourself... Discussion database's icon to your Workspace.

**N O T E**

## *Step 1*

Open the Teach yourself... Discussion database from the Workspace by double-clicking on its icon or by selecting its icon using the arrow keys and pressing **Enter**.

## *Step 2*

Select **View, Show, Folders** from the main menu to be sure that the Folders Navigator pane is opened. In the Navigator pane, click on the View named All Documents (Figure 4.17).

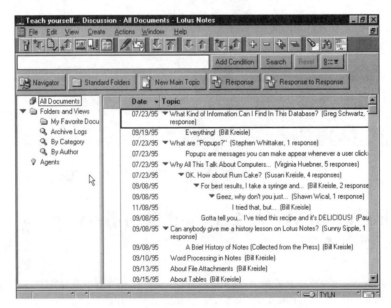

***Figure 4.17*** *The Navigator pane and the*
*View pane of the Teach yourself... discussion database.*

The All Documents View is a Response Hierarchy View. It contains Documents and Responses, and it groups Responses with their parents. Next, notice that a Notes view can sort the Documents it displays on almost any value in its Documents. You will notice that this View is sorted by date. If you look closely, you'll also notice that only the dates for the main Documents are used for sorting. Notes gives database designers a great deal of control over how they want to display information.

## Step 3

Staying in this same database, let's change to another view by selecting **View, by Author** from the main menu (Figure 4.18) or by expanding the Folders and Views item in the Navigator pane and clicking the **By Author View** (Figure 4.19).

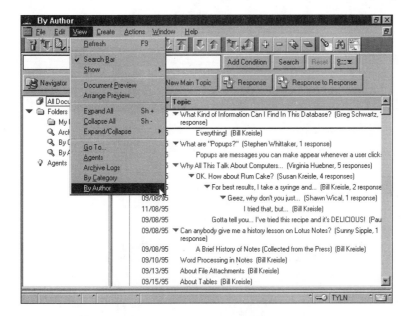

***Figure 4.18*** *Using the **View** command from the Notes Client menu to open the View titled **by Author**.*

If you compare the screen shots of the Teach yourself... Discussion database's Main View (Figure 4.17) to the By Author View (Figure 4.19), you will notice that the By Author View organizes the Documents in the database according to the name of the Document's author without regard for associating Responses with their parents. This is an example of a No Response Hierarchy View. The author names are used as Categories.

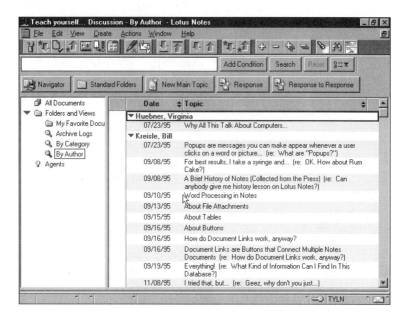

**Figure 4.19**  *Using the Folders and Views item in the Navigator pane to open the View titled **by Author**.*

## Step 4

Take a moment to explore the different ways to expand and collapse categories:

First, collapse the entire View so that only the Categories (in this case, author names) are visible by selecting **View, Collapse All** from the Notes Client menu. Figure 4.20 illustrates the collapsed View.

Next, expand the entire View so that all of the Documents in the View are visible by selecting **View, Expand All** from the Notes Client menu.

Finally, use these different keyboard, mouse, and menu commands to expand and collapse individual categories in a View:

1. Double-click a Category name.

2. Press **Enter** while a Category is selected.

3. Choose **View, Expand/Collapse, Expand Selected Level +** from the main menu.

4. Use the *twisties* (small triangles to the right of the category), by clicking them with the mouse.

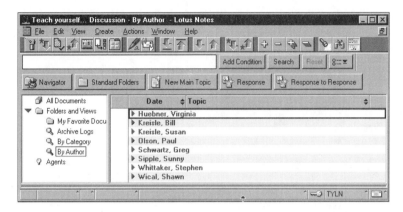

**Figure 4.20** Using the **View, Collapse All** command to see only top-level Documents or Categories.

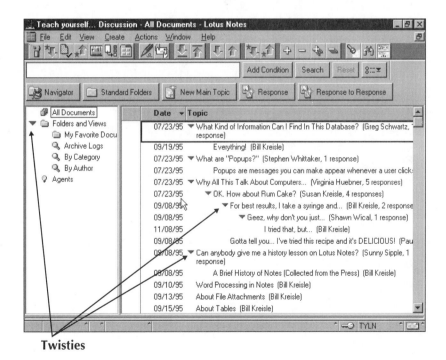

**Figure 4.21** Twisties.

If your keyboard has a numeric keypad, you can also use the plus (+)] or minus (-)]keys on it to expand and collapse the currently selected category, and **Shift +** or **Shift -** to expand and collapse all categories.

## Step 5

Finish the exercise by closing the Teach yourself… Discussion database.

## Reading Documents

Earlier in this chapter, we discussed the idea that Responses could be collapsed under their parent Document. With the exception of double-clicking the parent Document or selecting the parent Document and pressing **Enter**, the commands you just learned to expand and collapse Categories will expand and collapse Response Documents as well.

Why won't double-clicking or hitting Enter on a selected Document work? Once you have used a View to locate a Document you want, selecting it and pressing **Enter** or double-clicking the Document opens it for reading and editing.

If, once a Document is opened, it contains more information than can fit in the current window, you can use the **Up/Down/Left/Right Arrow** keys, the **Page Up/Page Down** keys, or the mouse combined with the window's scroll bars to move to other parts of the Documents.

After you have read a Document, you can close it by pressing the **Esc** key, or by selecting **File, Close** from the main menu.

## Taking What We've Learned Step by Step (Exercise 4.2)

In this exercise, we'll open the Teach yourself… Discussion database again and use the Main View to locate and read specific Documents.

## Step 1

Open the Teach yourself… Discussion database and the All Documents View.

Select **View, Expand All** from the Notes Client menu to ensure that all categories are expanded.

Move your selection to the first Document in the View, which is titled "What kind of information can I find in this database?" (Figure 4.22).

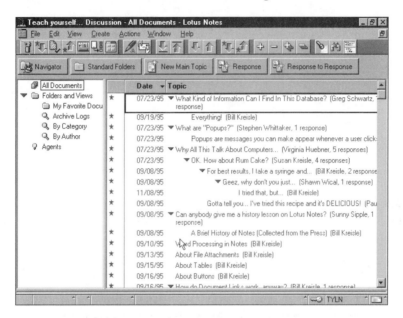

***Figure 4.22*** *The first Document in the All Documents*
*View of the Teach yourself... Discussion database.*

The key sequence **Ctrl+Home** will take you to the first Document or category in a View, and **Ctrl+End** will take you to the last Document in a View.

**SHORTCUT**

## Step 2

Open the Document by double-clicking the Document with the left mouse button, select the Document and press **Enter** or choosing **File, Open** from the Notes Client menu (Figure 4.23).

## Step 3

Close the Document (Select **File, Close** from the Notes Client menu or press the **Esc** key). Move the selection to the next Document in the View, which is a Response to the Document we just read titled "Everything!" (Figure 4.24). Open this new Document and after reading the information in the Document, close it to return to the All Documents View.

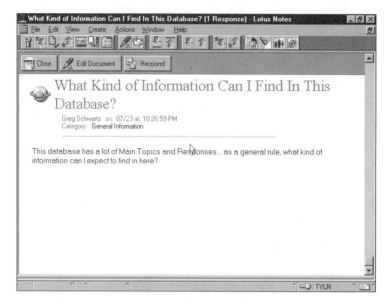

**Figure 4.23**  *The contents of the first Document in the All Documents View of the Teach yourself... Discussion database.*

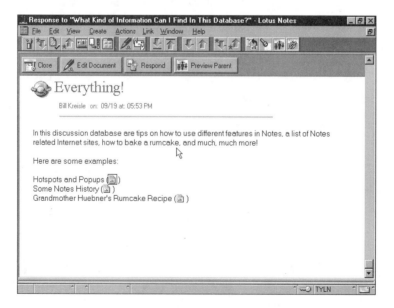

**Figure 4.24**  *The contents of another Document in the All Documents View of the Teach yourself... Discussion database.*

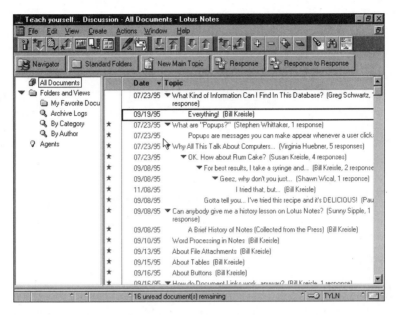

***Figure 4.25*** *The All Documents View of the Teach yourself... Discussion database.*

## Step 4

Finish the exercise by closing the Teach yourself... Discussion database.

# Using Views to Keep Track of Read and Unread Documents

Compare the screen shot in Step 1 (Figure 4.22) to Step 3 (Figure 4.25). Do you notice anything different? If you're related to Sherlock Holmes, you may have noticed that the small stars that appear to the left of the "What kind of information can I find..." Document and its Response in Figure 4.22 are missing from Figure 4.25.

You noticed that? Good for you! Since you're obviously related to the great detective, here's another question: All we did is open the two Documents that no longer have stars next to them and close them again. Why would the stars disappear?

Did you say that the stars disappeared because opening and closing the two Documents meant that from Notes' point of view (no pun intended), we read them? You're correct! So here's one more question: Why would Notes care if we read those two documents?

Because Notes is nosy?

Well, you were on a roll until that one.

Since Notes databases are designed to be shared on a server, over time, hundreds of Documents may accumulate in a database. With that in mind, keeping track of Documents that you have and have not read is an important function—it allows you to quickly go to new or changed information in a database without having to reread Documents. Depending on choices made by the designer of the View you are using, Notes helps you accomplish this in a number of ways:

1.  It displays a small star next to Documents you have never opened.

2.  It makes unread Documents appear in a different color from Documents that you have read in the View.

3.  It does both.

As I mentioned earlier, how Notes Views display unread Documents is up to the database's designer, so two Views in the same database may display unread Documents differently.

Unread indicators are an optional feature, so a database designer may choose not to display unread Documents indicators at all. If this happens, there are still a number of ways to know if there are unread Documents in a database that don't involve the database designer in question and a sharp stick.

At the Workspace, use the **View, Show Unread** command to add a small window to each database's icon that displays the number of unread Documents in each database (Figure 4.26).

Once you've discovered that a database contains Documents you haven't read, select the database and use the **Edit, Unread Marks, Scan Unread** command to go directly to any unread Documents in the database (Figure 4.27).

---

You can also open any database View and press the **Tab** key to move to each unread Document in a View.

**SHORTCUT**

---

In addition to these options, there are also SmartIcons designed to help you navigate between unread Documents in a View. We'll talk about SmartIcons in Chapter 11.

**Selecting Show Unread from the View menu causes a small rectangle to appear on each database icon containing the total number of unread documents in each database.**

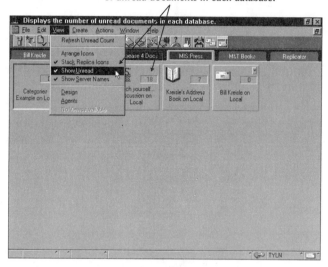

**Figure 4.26** *Tracking unread Documents from the Workspace using the* **View, Refresh Unread Count** *command.*

**Selecting Scan Unread from the Edit, Unread Marks menu opens the first unread document in the selected database.**

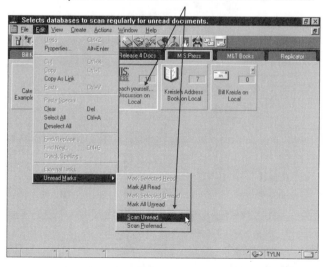

**Figure 4.27** *Using the* **Edit, Unread Marks, Scan Unread** *command.*

# Controlling Read/Unread Indicators

As you can see from the number of commands designed to help you locate unread Documents, unread indicators are an important part of using Notes effectively. The reason for this is simple. As you begin to work with more and more databases, you won't be able to keep track of what you have and haven't read in each database. (In addition to tracking when new Documents are added, unread indicators also tell you when Documents you have already read have been edited.)

Another aspect of unread indicators we need to discuss is controlling them. In our example, we opened a small discussion database (about 14 entries). It is easy to imagine that we will read every entry in this database, setting our unread indicator to zero. Once we have done this, new entries in the discussion will be easy to find using the View or the Workspace.

Imagine however, that the discussion database we used for an example contained several hundred entries. Knowing that we won't have time to read every entry in the database, we might skim through topics locating ones that interest us. This will cause the total number of unread Documents to decrease, but we'll never get it to zero because we don't have time to read everything. Does that mean we have to remember how many unread Documents there are in each database and compare the number of unread today to the number of unread yesterday to see if anything new has been added? Fortunately, the answer is no. Notes provides four commands you can use to control unread indicators in each database:

❖ Mark All Read

❖ Mark Selected Read

❖ Mark All Unread

❖ Mark Selected Unread

All four of these commands are available by selecting **Edit, Unread Marks** from the Notes Client menu. Here's how they work.

The **Mark All Read** and **Edit, Mark All Unread** commands mark every Document in a database read or unread. This will change the number displayed in the unread count window on the database's Workspace icon to zero (because there will be no unread Documents in the database) or to the total number of Documents in the database (because all of the Documents will be unread).

The **Mark Selected Read** and **Mark Selected Unread** commands, on the other hand, allow you to select one or more Documents in a Notes database and change them to display as read or unread Documents. To use these two commands, we need to answer one quick question: how do you select multiple Documents in a Notes database?

## Taking What We've Learned Step-by-Step (Exercise 4.3)

In this exercise, we'll learn how to mark multiple Documents in a Notes database so we can use the **Mark Selected Read** or **Mark Selected Unread** command on a specific group of Documents in a Notes database.

### *Step 1*

Open the Teach yourself... Discussion database's All Documents View and select **View, Expand All** from the Notes Client menu.

Select **Edit, Unread Marks, Mark All Unread** to mark all Documents in the database as unread. A small star will appear next to every Document in the left-most column of the Main View (Figure 4.28).

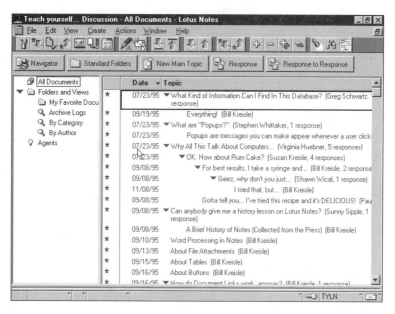

**Figure 4.28**  *The All Documents View of the Teach yourself... Discussion database after selecting **Edit, Unread Marks, Mark All Unread** from the Notes Client menu.*

## *Step 2*

Hold down the **Shift** key and click on a Document with the mouse. A small checkmark will appear to the left of the Document. This means it is selected (Figure 4.29).

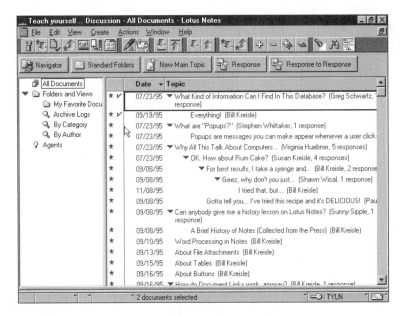

***Figure 4.29*** *Documents with checkmarks to their left are selected.*

 If instead of the checkmark appearing, the Document opens, you double-clicked instead of clicking once. Press **Esc** to close the Document and try again.

**N O T E**

You can also use the **Up/Down Arrow** keys to move to a Document and press the **Spacebar** to select it.

If you want to remove a Document from a selected group, use the **Spacebar** to deselect it. You can also **Shift+** click the Document using the left mouse button.

 You can also click the left mouse button on the leftmost column of any View to select/deselect the Document.

**SHORTCUT**

## Step 3

After you have selected one or more Documents, choose **Edit, Unread Marks, Mark Selected Read** from the Notes Client menu (Figure 4.30).

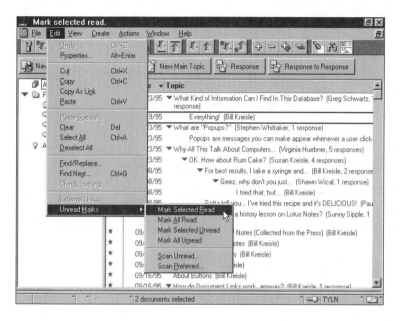

***Figure 4.30*** *When multiple Documents are selected, the **Edit, Unread Marks, Mark Selected Read** command will affect each Document in the selection.*

Notice that the stars beside the selected Documents disappear and the selected Documents are displayed in a different color than the rest of the Documents in the database.

## Step 4

Take a moment to experiment with the other two commands—**Edit, Unread Marks, Mark All Read** and **Edit, Unread Marks, Mark Selected Unread**.

## Step 5

Complete the exercise by closing the Teach yourself... Discussion database.

# Navigators

Navigators are an important step forward in usability for Lotus Notes. However, to someone who wants to explain things as thoroughly as possible to a new user, they also present a tremendous challenge.

You see, a Navigator provides a way to move between Views in a Notes database. It also provides a way to go to a specific Document in Notes (just as a View does). In addition, it provides a way to go to Views in other Notes databases or even other Navigators. Finally, it allows the user to work with Folders (supersets of the Views in a Notes database).

But there isn't a uniform, consistent way the Navigator accomplishes all of this. Nearly everything that makes up a Navigator's function is up to its designer.

So...where do we start?

I suggest we start at the same place we did when we approached defining Notes. We will start with a simple sentence that we'll expand on in the rest of this section. Here's the short definition:

Navigators combine Views, Folders, and visual indicators to make locating Documents more intuitive for users.

Working from this definition, it becomes clear that, first and foremost, the purpose of a Navigator is to help you locate Documents. You can see the Navigators in a database using the **View, Show** command on the Notes Client menu. You will see at least one Navigator, called *Folders*, as well as the names of any Custom Navigators on the View, Show submenu..

## *Working with the Folders Navigator*

The Folders Navigator is created by Notes with every database. Figure 4.31 illustrates the Folders Navigator in the Teach yourself... Discussion database.

As you can see from this illustration, the Teach yourself... Discussion database's Views are located in two places. The All Documents View is above the Folders and Views section of the Navigator, while the By Category and By Author Views are within the Folders and Views section. Clicking on a View in either location causes the selected View to appear in the View Window.

**The Folders Navigator**

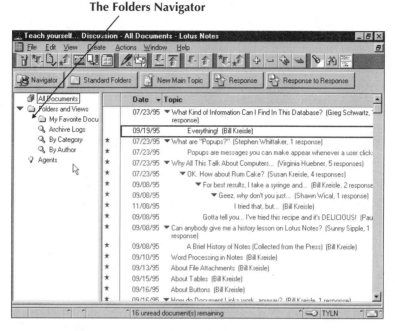

**Figure 4.31** *The Folders Navigator in the Teach yourself... Discussion database.*

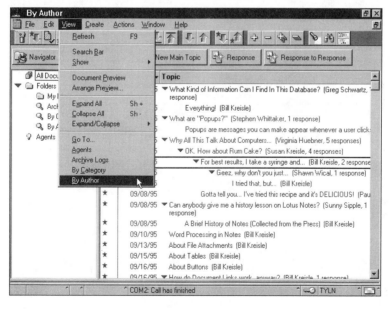

**Figure 4.32** *The All Documents View from the Folders Navigator can only be selected from the View command on the Notes Client menu using* **Go To...** .

In addition to using the Folders Navigator to see all the Views in a Database, you can also use it to organize a database's Documents into Folders. As I mentioned earlier, a Folder is a superset of a database's Views—it collects placeholders for your Documents from multiple Views.

Placeholders? Let's work with a Navigator in a step-by-step exercise to help explain.

# Taking What We've Learned Step-by-Step (Exercise 4.4)

In this exercise, we're going to open the Folders Navigator, then walk through creating and using a Folder.

## Step 1

Open the Teach yourself... Discussion database.

Select **View, Show, Folders** from the Notes Client menu (Figure 4.33).

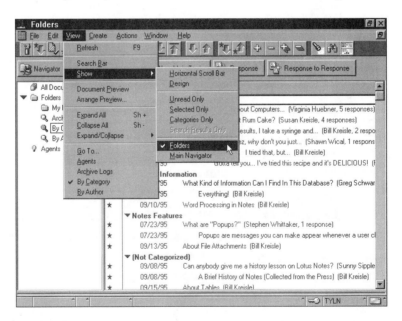

***Figure 4.33*** *Selecting the Folders Navigator using the* ***View, Show*** *command.*

## *Step 2*

Expand the Folders and Views heading so that you can see the Views and Folders beneath it by clicking on the twistie to the left of the heading or by double-clicking the heading.

Select the **by Category** View (Figure 4.34).

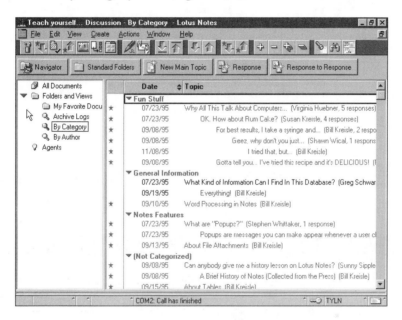

**Figure 4.34** *The **by Category** View of the Teach yourself... Discussion database.*

Select **My Favorite Documents** Folder in the Folders Navigator (Figure 4.35).

## *Step 3*

Open the All Documents View and select the first two Documents in the View using **Shift +** click or the **Spacebar**. Select **Actions, Move to Folder** from the Notes Client menu (Figure 4.35 and 4.36).

Select **My Favorite Documents** from the Move to Folder dialog box, and click the **Add** button (Figure 4.37).

Notice that the checkmarks next to the first two Documents in the All Documents View are gone after issuing the **Actions, Move to Folder** command.

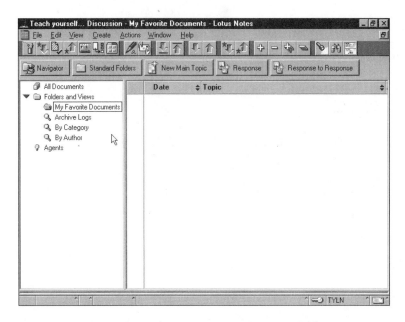

**Figure 4.35** *The My Favorite Documents Folder.*

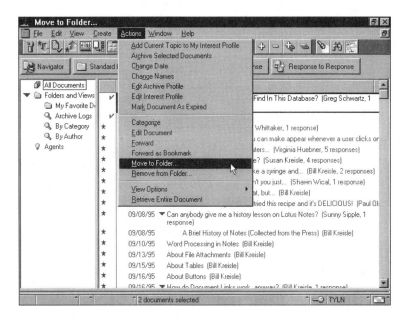

**Figure 4.36** *Using the **Actions, Move to Folder** command after selecting the first two Documents in the All Documents View.*

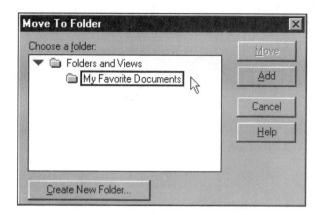

**Figure 4.37**  *The Move to Folder dialog box.*

**SHORTCUT**

You can also move Documents to Folders by clicking and dragging the Documents from the View pane to the desired Folder in the Navigators pane.

**N O T E**

There are options in this dialog box that we won't discuss in this exercise. For more information about the options in the **Move to Folder** dialog box, open it again later using the **Actions, Move to Folder** command and clicking the **Help** button.

## Step 4

Expand the Folders and Views heading in the Folders Navigator. Click **My Favorite Documents** and you will see the two documents you marked in the All Documents View (Figure 4.38). Click once on the second Document in the View and press the **Delete** key. Notice that a small trash can appears to the left of the Document.

## Step 5

Open the All Documents View again. Notice that the trash can appears to the left of the second Document in the View (Figure 4.39).

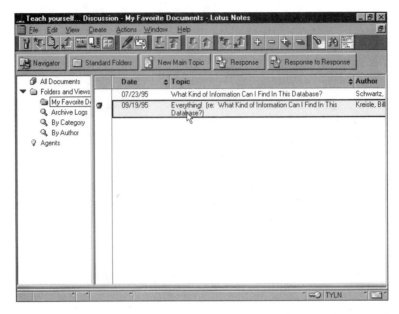

**Figure 4.38** *The contents of the My Favorite Documents Folder.*

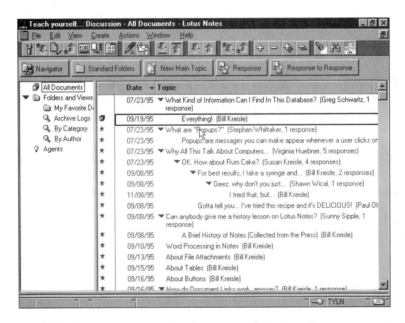

**Figure 4.39** *The Document marked for deletion in the My Favorite Documents Folder is the same Document that appears in the All Documents View.*

## Step 6

Complete the exercise by closing the Teach yourself... Discussion database and answering "No" to the prompt (Figure 4.40).

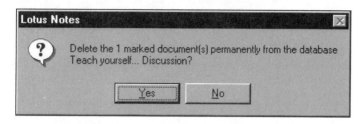

***Figure 4.40*** *The Delete Document dialog box.*

This brings us back to placeholders. When you move a Document to a Folder, the word *move* is misleading as you can see from our exercise. It was the same document in both places. This is a useful feature in Notes because it means the same Document can be visible in different Views (think about the Views in the Teach yourself... Discussion database, for example). It also means that the same Document can be stored in multiple Folders.

## *Working with Custom Navigators*

As you can see from the previous exercise, the Folders Navigator is a very versatile tool designed to help you locate Documents. The versatility of the Folders Navigator pales beside the flexibility a Custom Navigator provides database designers and users.

You can see a Custom Navigator in the Teach yourself... Discussion database by selecting **View, Show, Main Navigator** from the Notes Client menu.

As you can see from Figure 4.41, the views we're used to seeing in the Folders Navigator are represented in the Main Navigator as icons. Clicking on an icon or the text next to them in the Main Navigator will open the selected View in the View Pane.

**NOTE**

While it is not covered in great detail here, remember that Navigator isn't limited to moving between Views. Any spot on a Custom Navigator can be made to open a View, represent a Folder, open another Navigator, or even run an Agent.

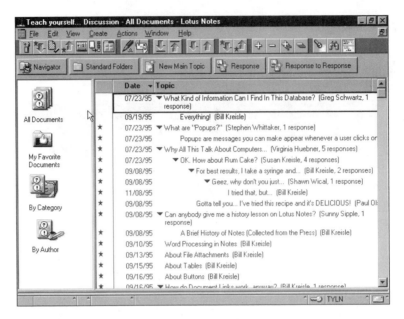

**Figure 4.41** *A Custom Navigator.*

# The Document Preview Pane

The Document Preview pane is designed to perform a single task; preview Documents. As such, I have only a couple of things to add to what you've already read about the Document Preview pane in this chapter.

First, I'd like to add that it can move. The Document Preview pane can be moved around the Database Window by selecting **View, Arrange Preview...** from the Notes Client menu and selecting the location for the Document Preview pane from the Preview Pane dialog box (Figure 4.42).

Figures 4.43 and 4.44 show the Document Preview Pane in the other two possible locations. Notice that the Navigator Pane stays "anchored" in the upper left corner, while the View Pane moves with the Document Preview pane.Second, I'd like to point out that in addition to clicking the gray separator and dragging it to the edge of the screen, you can toggle the Document Preview pane on and off using the **View, Document Preview** command from the Notes Client menu.

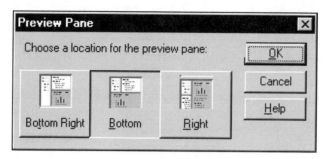

*Figure 4.42* *You can move the location of the Document Preview pane in the Database Window using the **View, Arrange Preview...** command on the Notes Client menu.*

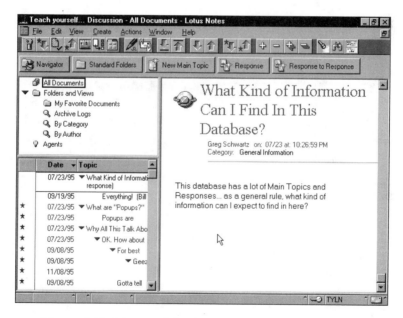

*Figure 4.43* *Selecting **Right** from the Preview Pane dialog box.*

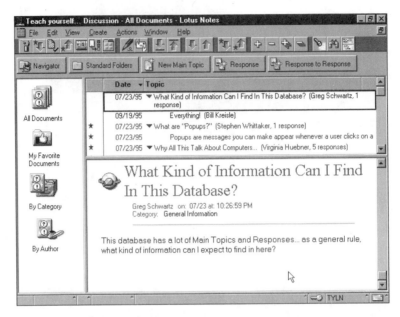

**Figure 4.44** *Selecting* **Bottom Right** *from the Preview Pane dialog box.*

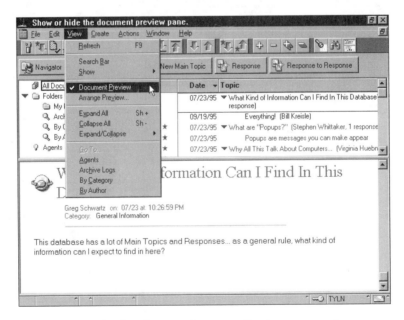

**Figure 4.45** *The View, Document Preview command.*

# In Summary

❖ The Database Window is designed to help you locate Documents in a Notes database quickly and effectively. It is composed of three elements, or panes:

  1. The View pane

  2. The Document Preview pane

  3. The Navigator pane

❖ Of the three panes of the Database Window, the most important element is the View Pane, because it displays the contents of database's Views.

❖ The View is the primary window into a database. Some Views are accessed from the View command on the Notes Client menu. Other Views must be accessed through a Navigator or the **View, Go To...** command.

❖ If a Notes database contains Response Documents, Views may display them directly beneath their parent Document or in a manner unrelated to their parent (as if they were main Documents themselves).

❖ As you use Notes databases, Notes keeps track of the Documents you have and have not read in each one. You can display the number of unread Documents in a database by selecting **Edit, Unread Marks, Show Unread** from the workspace's main menu.

❖ Most of the time, you can use a database's Views to locate unread Documents. Occasionally, you may need to use the **Tools, Scan Unread, Selected Databases** command or the Tab key in a View to locate unread Documents.

❖ You can control unread indicators using the following menu commands:

  **Edit, Unread Marks, Mark All Read**

  **Edit, Unread Marks, Mark Selected Read**

  **Edit, Unread Marks, Mark All Unread**

  **Edit, Unread Marks, Mark Selected Unread**

❖ A Navigator organizes Views and Folders visually. All databases have a default Navigator known as the **Folders Navigator**.

❖ Navigators can be selected using the **View, Show** command on the Notes Client menu.

❖ A Folder is designed to contain Documents collected by the user from different Views. Documents are not actually moved to Folders—deleting a Document from a Folder deletes if from all other Folders and Views.

❖ You can select one of three different locations for the Document Preview pane using the **View, Arrange Preview...** command on the Notes Client menu, and you can toggle the Document Preview pane on and off using the **View, Document Preview** command.

# Chapter 5

# Adding Information to Notes Databases

## In this Chapter...

In Chapter 4, we learned how to use Notes to locate Documents. Next, we'll learn how to edit the Documents we've located and how to add new Documents, including Responses.

Before delving into these new steps, however, we'll revisit the topic of Access Control Lists (because the level of access you have governs how you can contribute information to Notes), and introduce Fields, Forms, and Labels.

Here's the outline for this chapter:

❖ Understanding the Access Control List

❖ Determining your privileges in a database

❖ Fields, Labels, and Forms

❖ Editing existing Notes Documents

❖ More about Fields

❖ Adding Documents

# Understanding the Access Control List

The purpose of the Access Control List (ACL) is to control who does what with a Notes database by allowing users different privileges. These privileges are associated with different levels of access.

You can assign seven basic levels of access in a Notes database:

1. *No Access* means no privileges in the database—you cannot even add it to your Workspace. In Figure 5.1, user Angela Ralph has No Access privileges.

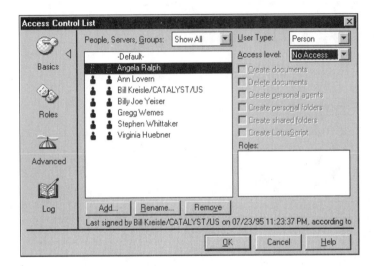

***Figure 5.1*** *A user with No Access privileges.*

2. *Depositor Access* includes the privilege to add the database to a user's Workspace and to add information but not open any Documents in the database for reading. (An example of when someone may use Depositor Access is a suggestions database where anyone should be able to enter a suggestion but not read other suggestions once they are entered.) In Figure 5.2, user Billy Joe Yeiser has Depositor Access privileges.

3. *Reader Access* gives you the privilege of adding the database to your Workspace and reading the Documents contained in the database you've added. Users with Reader Access are not allowed to edit or

delete existing Documents. This is a common level of access for broadcast or reference applications where Documents are published for an entire organization. In Figure 5.3, user Virginia Huebner has Reader Access privileges.

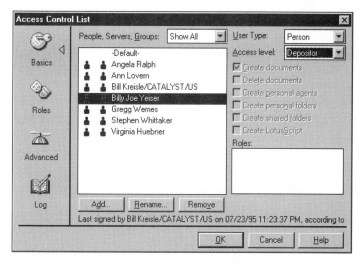

**Figure 5.2** *A user with Depositor Access privileges.*

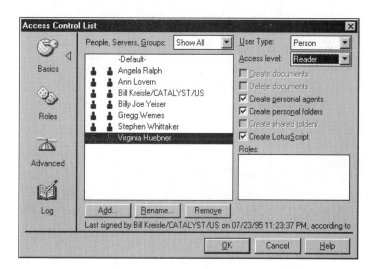

**Figure 5.3** *A user with Reader Access privileges.*

With Reader Access, a database manager has the option to allow individual users the ability to create personal Agents, Folders, and LotusScript.

Also notice that while Reader Access is a higher level of access than Depositor, one privilege Depositors have that Readers do not is the ability to create new Documents.

**NOTE** You may have Reader Access to a database but still be unable to see all Documents in the database due to an option exercised by the database's designer called a *Reader Names Field,* which we'll discuss later in this chapter.

4. *Author Access* gives users the privilege to add a database to their Workspaces, read the Documents contained within it, and typically, to compose new Documents and edit Documents that they have previously created. Author Access is often used in discussion applications, where participants should be able to create main Documents and Responses as well as edit the Documents they create. Authors cannot edit Documents created by others.

In Figure 5.4, user Ann Lovern has Author Access privileges.

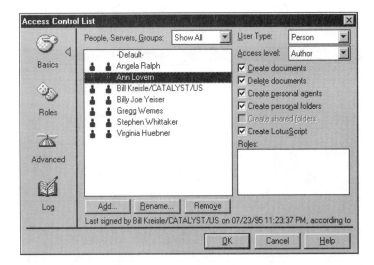

***Figure 5.4*** *A user with Author Access privileges.*

With Author Access, a database manager has the option to allow the creation of personal Folders, Agents, and LotusScript, as well as decide whether a specific user should be allowed to create or delete Documents.

5. *Editor Access* gives a user the same privileges as Author Access, but it adds the ability to make changes to any Documents (their own and those composed by other people). In a discussion application, for example, you may want to appoint one person as a database monitor. The monitor is responsible for ensuring that Documents added to the discussion do not contain profanity or otherwise upsetting material. Giving a user Editor access allows them to alter the contents of Documents created by any other user. In Figure 5.5, user Gregg Wemes has Editor Access privileges.

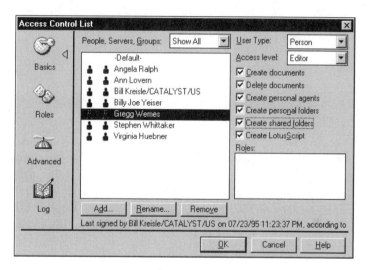

**Figure 5.5** *A user with Editor Access privileges.*

With Editor Access, a database manager has the option to allow the creation of personal Folders, Agents, and LotusScript, as well as the creation of shared Folders. The database manager can also decide if a particular user should be allowed to create or delete documents.

6. *Designer Access* gives the user the same privileges as an editor and adds the ability to create and modify the design elements of a database, including Views, Forms, Navigators, the About and Using Documents, Agents, LotusScript, and, the Database's Icon. Typically, a database will have only one or two users as Designers. In Figure 5.6, user Stephen Whittaker has Designer Access privileges.

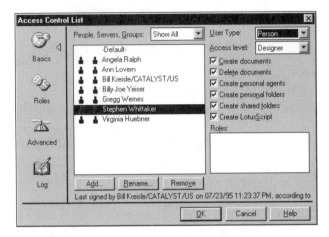

**Figure 5.6** *A user with Designer Access privileges.*

With Designer Access, a database manager has the option to allow the creation of personal Folders, Agents, and LotusScript, as well as the creation of shared Folders. The database manager can also decide if a specific user should be allowed to create or delete documents.

7. *Manager Access* includes the privileges of Designer Access as well as the ability to add and delete other users from the Access Control List. A database's manager is also the only user authorized to delete the database completely from a Notes server. Since this is the only level of access that can modify the Access Control List, every database must have at least one manager. In Figure 5.7, user Bill Kreisle has Manager Access privileges.

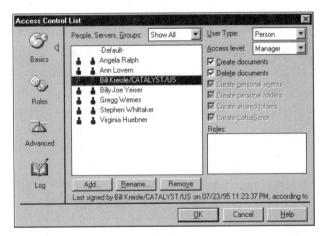

**Figure 5.7** *A user with Manager Access privileges.*

Notice that users with Manager Access can still be restricted from creating or deleting Documents.

# Determining Your Privileges in a Database

As you can see, Notes can get pretty specific as to what you can do with one of its databases. Until now, the step-by-step examples we've worked with depended on your having Author privileges or higher to the examples database. Since Editor Access is the default access level in the Teach yourself... Discussion database, it didn't matter if you knew about the ACL when you were working with the examples.

**NOTE**  The default access in a database's ACL specifies what privileges should be given to a user who isn't specifically named in the ACL or in one of the groups in the ACL. For example, you aren't in the ACL for the Teach yourself... Discussion database, but since the default access is Editor, you have Editor privileges.

In this chapter's examples, however, you must have sufficient access to perform the tasks presented. (Translated: If you want to follow along with the examples, you should use the Teach yourself... Discussion database or one in which you have Editor Access or higher.)

There are several ways to determine what level of access you have in a database. The first is trial and error. For example, try to open the database. If you are in a group that is set to No Access or if you are not named specifically in the database with some level of access, you will see the dialog box shown in Figure 5.8.

***Figure 5.8***  *If you do not have sufficient access to open a database,
you will see this dialog box.*

If you can add the database to your workspace or open it, then you have at least Depositor Access. If you open a View and see Documents, you have at least Reader Access. There is, of course, a more structured approach to determining your privileges in a database. You have to use the first method (trial and error) to get to it, however.

Once you have the database icon on your workspace (meaning you have to try to open it before you know if you have any access at all), select it and choose **File, Database, Access Control** from the main menu. This will open the Database Access Control List dialog box (similar to Figure 5.9).

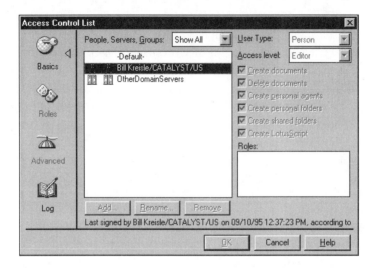

**Figure 5.9** *The Database Access Control List dialog box.*

This dialog box will allow you to select your name from the list and see what level of access you have been assigned.

**NOTE**

One problem with using this technique for determining your access is that Notes administrators frequently control access by creating groups of people and including the name of the group in the list instead of each individual's name. That means if you don't know which groups list you as a member, you won't know for sure what level of access you have. If you cannot tell what level of access you have from the Access Control List, a third method to determine what level of access you have is to select the database and click the access level indicator on the Notes Client as illustrated in Figure 5.10.

This will open a dialog box indicating your access level. (Figure 5.11) It will not indicate any options that may be exercised by the database manager for a particular level of access, however. (Meaning that if you have Author Access, but the database manager removed the privilege of deleting documents, this dialog will simply indicate Author Access.)

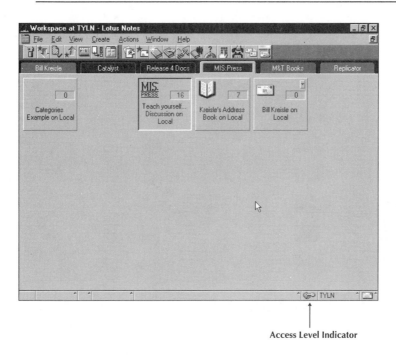

Access Level Indicator

***Figure 5.10*** *The Access Level Indicator on the Notes Client*

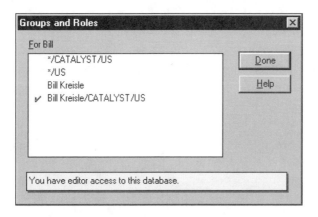

***Figure 5.11*** *The Groups and Roles dialog is opened when you click on the access level indicator.*

You can also see what your Access Level is "at a glance" by looking at the type of Icon currently being displayed on the Access Level Indicator while you have a database open, as illustrated in Table 5.1.

**Table 5.1** *Determining your Access Level to a Database from the Icon Displayed on the Status Bar while the Database is Open*

| Icon | Access Level |
|:---:|:---|
| | Manager Access |
| | Designer Access |
| | Editor Access |
| | Author Access |
| | Reader Access |
| | Depositor Access |

# Fields, Labels, and Forms

The next thing we need to discuss before we start adding information to our Notes database is how Notes uses Fields, Labels, and Forms. (We'll start with Fields, and I'll sneak Labels and Forms in on you toward the end of this section, so stay on your toes.)

Fields contain everything you type, paste, attach, or import into a Notes database. They are arranged on Forms and enhanced by Labels. I've put off talking about Fields until this chapter because they break my ever-useful binder analogy—I can't think of an effective way to illustrate a Field when you're picturing a loose-leaf binder full of pages.

You see, the problem is this: to be represented correctly in our binder analogy, a Field would have to somehow translate to a part of each page in the binder. Sort of like an area on the page where you're only supposed to put a certain type of information. Like a page number, or a title, or a header... or a footer... hmmm... (maybe the binder analogy can be stretched one more time!).

OK, work with me, here. Let's pretend that Figure 5.12 is a page from one of the binders in our original library.

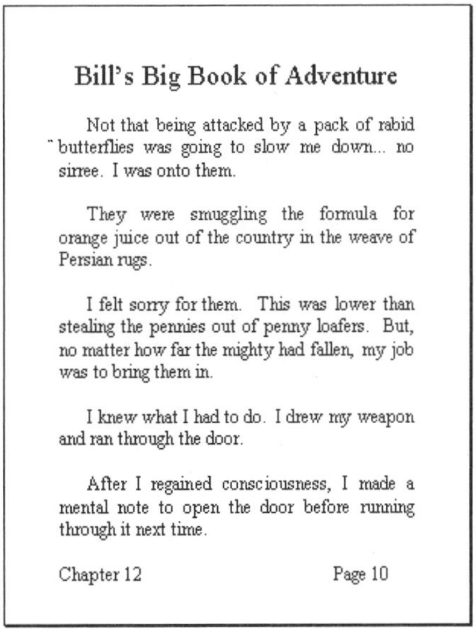

**Bill's Big Book of Adventure**

Not that being attacked by a pack of rabid butterflies was going to slow me down... no sirree. I was onto them.

They were smuggling the formula for orange juice out of the country in the weave of Persian rugs.

I felt sorry for them. This was lower than stealing the pennies out of penny loafers. But, no matter how far the mighty had fallen, my job was to bring them in.

I knew what I had to do. I drew my weapon and ran through the door.

After I regained consciousness, I made a mental note to open the door before running through it next time.

Chapter 12                Page 10

***Figure 5.12***  *A page from a book.*

The format of the page in the illustration is similar to what you might see on the page of a book. The top of the page is reserved for the title of the book. Most of the page is an area intended to contain text or pictures, while the bottom of the page has an area designed to tell us what chapter and page number we're currently reading. Every page in the book will look like this page (more or less). Going back to our illustration, let's give each area of the page a specific name and purpose (Figure 5.13).

The areas we defined that will change from page to page (the body, the chapter number, and the page number) are the same in concept as Fields in Notes. The other areas (such as the title of the book and the words *chapter* and *page*) are the same on every page. They're the same in concept as Labels in Notes.

Because the page itself is now a collection of predefined areas for changing information (Fields), and a collection of constant text (Labels), the page is now the same in concept to a Form in our Notes database.

To put it another way, in our binder, a predefined layout, combined with information printed in each defined area, makes a page. In Notes, the Form (when combined with Fields and Labels) composes a Document.

So thanks to the ever-versatile binder metaphor (I'm going to run for office using that analogy, just wait and see), we've covered Fields, Labels, and Forms. That means we're ready to move on.

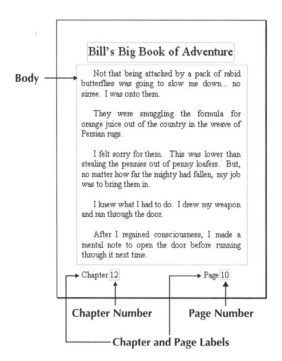

**Figure 5.13** *A book's page follows a predictable Form.*

# Editing Existing Notes Documents

One of the first ways we can add information to a Notes database is by editing existing Documents. Editing a Document consists of four steps (which I'll present as a list here and cover in more detail later in the chapter with a step-by-step example):

1.  Select the Document you wish to edit using a database View, Folder, or Navigator.

2.  Open the Document for editing by choosing Edit from the menu that appears when you right-click the Document, by selecting the Document choosing **Actions, Edit Document** from the Notes Client menu, or by pressing **Ctrl+E**.

3.  Make changes by moving to the desired Field(s) in the Document and entering or editing its contents.

4.  Save changes and close the Document by selecting **File, Save** from the Notes Client menu followed by **Actions, Close** (or by pressing **Esc** after you have finished editing and answering yes to the prompt.)

These steps can be compared to steps for our binder. If you were going to edit a page, you'd have to turn to the page, go to the area you wanted to edit, make your changes, and return the binder. In Notes, that is the same as opening a View, putting the Document in edit mode, moving to a Field, making changes, and saving your work.

## Taking What We've Learned Step-by-Step (Exercise 5.1)

Let's look at the four steps required to edit an existing Notes Document from a hands-on perspective by editing a document in the Teach yourself... Discussion database.

### *Step 1*

Open the Teach Yourself... Discussion database, and select the **By Author View** from the View menu. Expand Category, Bill Kreisle. Select the Document titled "Word Processing in Notes" (Figure 5.14).

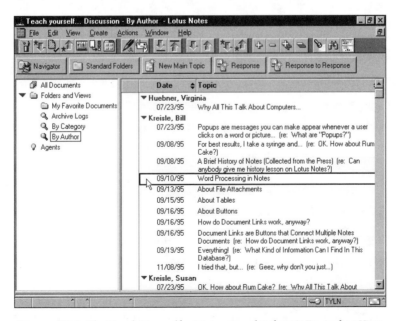

***Figure 5.14*** *The Teach Yourself... Discussion database's By Author View.*

## *Step 2*

Open the Document titled "Word Processing in Notes" for editing by doing one of the following:

1. Click on the Document with the right mouse button and select Edit from the menu.

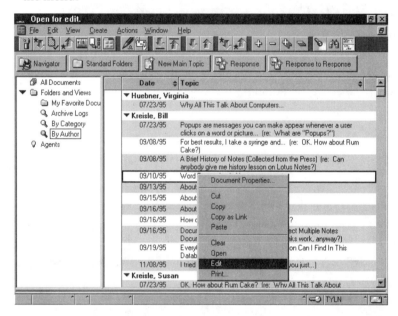

**Figure 5.15** *Opening a Document for editing using the right mouse button menu.*

2. Select the Document and choose **Actions, Edit Document** from the Notes client menu.

3. Select the Document and press **Ctrl+E** to open the Document in edit mode.

## *Step 3*

A small blinking vertical bar (the insertion point) is positioned in the first Field of the Document. (Editable Fields are flanked by small brackets on the upper-left and lower-right corners as shown in Figure 5.17).

Use the **Up/Down Arrow** keys to move the insertion point to the Field containing the text, "A Notes Rich Text Field provides users with extensive…" (Figure 5.18).

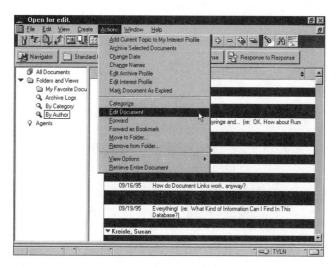

**Figure 5.16** *Opening a Document for editing using the Action menu on the Notes Client.*

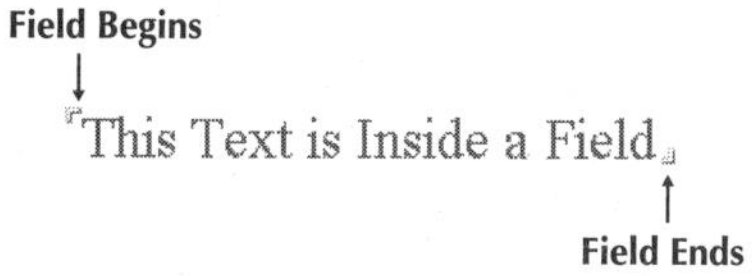

**Field Begins**
↓

⌈This Text is Inside a Field⌋

↑
**Field Ends**

**Figure 5.17** *Fields are delimited by small brackets.*

**The Insertion Point**

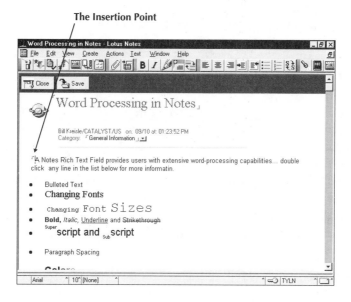

**Figure 5.18** *The "Word Processing in Notes" Document, opened for editing.*

## Step 4

Correct the spelling of the word information at the end of the first paragraph. Save your changes and close the Document using one of the following:

Select **File, Save** followed by **Actions, Close** from the Notes Client menu.

Press **Esc** and answer **Yes** at the dialog box shown in Figure 5.19.

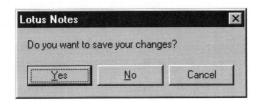

**Figure 5.19** *The Save Changes dialog box.*

Congratulations, you're an editor!

## Pop Quiz (worth 100 points)

Assuming that the database containing the Document you edited is on a server, what do you think will happen to the unread indicator for that Document for the other users accessing that database?

If you said it would change to unread for those users, add 100 points to your score. Your editing will flag the Document as unread to other users.

## Back to the Fields

As you saw in Figure 5.17, Fields are often represented by a tiny pair of brackets on the Document you are editing. You can navigate among Fields by clicking them with your mouse (placing the cursor in the Field you clicked) or by using the **Up/Down Arrow** keys to move the cursor from Field to Field. Not all fields are editable. Some are calculated based on the values entered in other Fields or the action being performed. In Figure 5.18, the line in the Document that reads "Bill Kreisle/CATALYST/US on 9/10 at 01:23:52 PM" is a combination of calculated fields and labels designed to inform users who created the Document and when it was created.

Let's go back to the binder and page example we used to introduce Fields (Figure 5.12) for a moment. Just as the predefined areas of the page are intended to hold different types of information (page number, chapter number, body text), Fields on a Form can be a combination of the following types:

❖ *Number Field.* Designed to hold numbers, including integers and decimals. Number Fields can be formatted to display currency symbols, thousands separators, and scientific notation. Alphabetic characters (*a,b,c...*) cannot be saved in Number Fields.

❖ *Time Field.* Designed to hold time and date values. Time Fields may be formatted to accept a variety of date-time values (01/01/95 12.00.00 AM, 1-1-95, or 12.00 AM, for example).

❖ *Text Field.* Designed to hold text and numbers. Text Fields can also contain lists, delimited by characters specified by the database's designer. For example, a Text Field for favorite colors might consider Red, Black, Green to be a list of three values if the comma is a specified delimiter.

❖ *Rich Text Field.* Designed to hold formatted text, numbers, pictures, file attachments—just about anything.

❖ *Keyword Field.* A Text Field with a predefined list of values that you choose from. (For example, a Keyword Field called *state* that is part of an address may only allow two letter abbreviations of the 50 states to be selected from its list.)

❖ *Names Field.* Designed to hold a list of user, server, or group names. These are most frequently used to collect lists of addressees for Documents in a workflow.

❖ *Author Names Field.* Designed to hold a list of user, server, or group names that can edit a Document if they have Author Access.

❖ *Reader Names Field.* Designed to hold a list of user, server, or group names that can read a Document. Only those users, servers, or groups specified in the Reader Names field will see the Document in Views, Folders, or Navigators. If a Reader Names field is blank, it is assumed that everyone should have access to read the Document.

Some Fields react differently when you try to enter information into them. A Keyword Field, for example, is a list. If you try to type information into a Keyword Field, and you happen to type a letter that is the first letter of a word in the list, then that word will appear. (In a state Keyword Field example, typing A would make AL appear in the Field.) If you type a letter that isn't the first letter of a keyword, you hear a beep.

Pressing **Enter** in a Keyword Field makes a dialog box containing the predefined values for that Field appear. Pressing **Enter** in any other Field type inserts a new line in the Field (whether it belongs there or not).

Which makes things a little confusing, if you ask me. Here you are, all excited about entering information into Notes, and now you learn Lotus' dark secret. How can you tell what information belongs in what field? Use this list.

❖ *Number Field.* The only way you'll notice a number Field has an illegal value (that is, something that isn't a number) is if you try to save a Document with letters where numbers should be and you get the error shown in Figure 5.20.

***Figure 5.20*** *If a Number Field contains text instead, you'll see this dialog box.*

Fortunately, database designers know about this problem, so number Fields are next to Labels like "time (in minutes)" or "cost," to help you recognize when numbers should be used instead of text.

❖ *Time Field.* Like numbers, you'll probably only notice a Time Field when you type something that doesn't belong and try to save the Document (Figure 5.21).

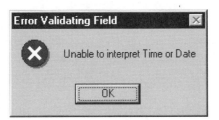

***Figure 5.21*** *The error you'll receive if Notes can't convert what you've entered in a Time Field into a time/date value.*

One tricky thing about time Fields is that dates are entered differently depending on your operating system and its default date settings. (If you're running Notes for Windows, for example, you most likely will enter a date as 1/1/95. On OS/2 or the Mac OS, however, the date may require a format of 1-1-95.)

❖ *Text Field.* Text Fields can hold letters or numbers and won't generate an error if either are entered into it when you save your Document. One thing to remember about a text Field, however, is that it is a "plain" Field. You can't apply formatting to the text (make it bold or italic for example), and you can't insert pictures in or attach files to a Text Field. To determine if you're in a Text Field, place your cursor inside the field and select Text from the Notes Client menu. You will notice that all the formatting choices (such as bold and italic) are dimmed for Text Fields.

❖ *Rich Text Field.* If you select **Text** from the main menu and see formatting options enabled such as bold and italic, you're in a Rich Text Field. That means you can import and attach files, paste pictures, or do whatever else you may think of (pretty much).

Here's a thought. A Rich Text Field can hold a Notes database! (So, if you create a database and put another database in a Rich Text Field in one of its Documents and save it, and then put that database in a Rich Text Field of another database, and then put that database...)

❖ *Keyword Field.* As I mentioned earlier, the "gotcha" in Keyword Fields is finding them. Any time you start typing and Notes starts complaining, you're probably in a Keyword Field. Pressing **Enter** while you're in a Keyword Field will provide you with a list of legal keywords and, possibly, a box to allow you to enter new keywords (Figure 5.22).

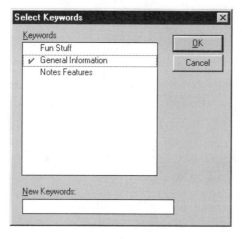

***Figure 5.22*** *The Select Keywords dialog box.*

With Release 4 of Notes, a Keyword Field may also have a small box to the left of its first bracket that is not only an indicator of a Keyword Field, but also a mouse shortcut (clicking the box opens the Select Keywords dialog box).

*Figure 5.23* *A visual indicator that Category is a Keywords Field.*

However, that small box is an option that may or may not be used by the database's designer.

Well, that wasn't as much fun as some of the other stuff we've learned, but it's important information that we can say we've added to our list. In addition, it better prepares us to move on to the next section.

## Adding Documents

With the Access Control List, Fields, Forms, and editing under our belts, it's time to explore another way to add information to a Notes database—composing new Documents.

You compose a new Document in Notes by selecting a database to add a Document to and then using the Create command on the Notes Client menu. Under the Create menu will be a list of Forms you can use to compose new Documents. Like Views, the Forms in this menu represent choices made by the database's designer. So what you see when you select **Create** from the Notes Client menu will vary depending on the database that is selected.

It also means that two databases may use the same Form name ("Response") for example, but the Forms will contain different Fields and Labels. Figure 5.24 illustrates the Create menu from two databases.

As you can see from Figure 5.24, the Teach yourself... Discussion database allows you to create Documents using three types of Forms: Main Topic, Response, and Response to Response. The standard Notes Mail Database allows you to create Documents using the Memo, Reply, Reply with History, and Workflow Forms.

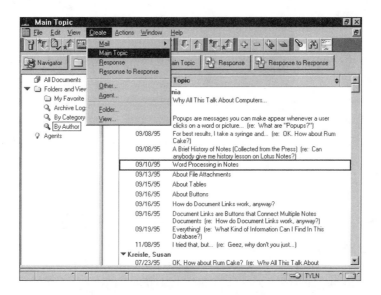

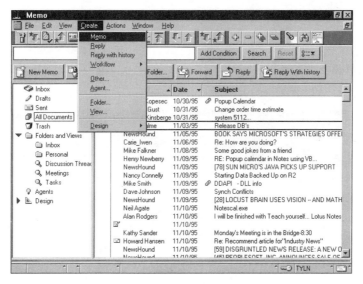

**Figure 5.24** *Different databases will have different Forms available from the Create menu.*

As we did earlier for editing documents, let's look at the steps required to add a Document to a database briefly and then work with the steps later in a hands-on exercise:

1. Select the database where you will add information.

2. If you are composing a Response Document, open a View and highlight the Document that will be the parent to the Response. If you are composing a main Document, skip this step.

3. Choose **Create** from the Notes Client menu, and select the name of the Form you wish to use to add a Document to the database.

Note that Step 2 in these instructions is a conditional statement. It requires different actions depending on whether you are composing a Response Document or a main Document in the Notes database. The following exercises will cover both options.

# Taking What We've Learned Step by Step (Exercise 5.2)

In this exercise, we'll add a Main Topic and Response to the Teach yourself... Discussion database.

## *Step 1*

Select the Teach yourself... Discussion database and choose **Create, Main Topic** from the Notes Client menu (Figure 5.25).

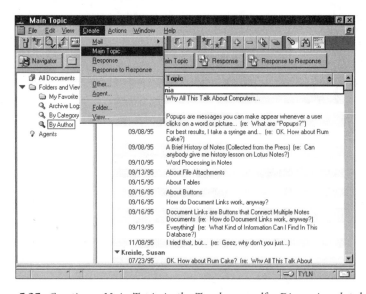

***Figure 5.25*** *Creating a Main Topic in the Teach yourself... Discussion database.*

## *Step 2*

A new window called *Lotus Notes—New Topic* will open. Enter "Using Rich Text Fields" into the first field in the form. Use the **Down Arrow** key to move to Category Field and press **Enter**. Select **General Information** from the key-words list and click **OK**.

***Figure 5.26*** *Adding information to the Main Topic Document's Fields.*

Use the **Down Arrow** key again to move to the body of the Main Topic Document.

## *Step 3*

Type "Could someone show me some of the things I can do with a Rich Text Field, please?" in the Main Topic Document's body Field (Figure 5.27).

## *Step 4*

Save your changes by pressing **Esc** and answering **Yes** to the prompt, or by selecting **File, Save** followed by **Action, Close** from the Notes Client menu.

Select **View, By Author** from the main menu. Locate and expand your name in the **By Author View** to see your new Document.

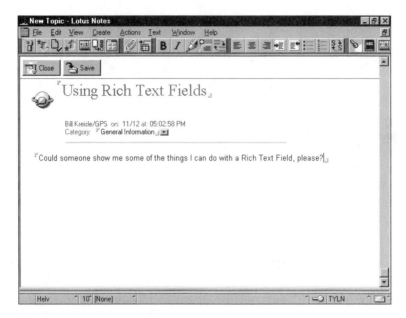

**Figure 5.27** *Adding Information to the new Main Topic Document.*

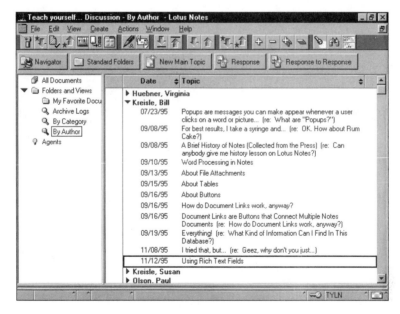

**Figure 5.28** *Locating the Document you just added to the Teach yourself... Discussion database.*

# Taking What We've Learned Step by Step (Exercise 5.3)

In this exercise, we're going to respond to the topic we just entered into the Teach yourself... Discussion database. We're also going to work with formatting text in a Rich Text Field.

## *Step 1*

If it's not still open from the previous exercise, open the Teach Yourself... Discussion database. Select **View, Show, Folders** from the Notes Client menu, and select the **All Documents View**. Click once on the **View** pane to change focus to the View, and press **Ctrl+End** to move to the bottom Document in the View (Figure 5.29).

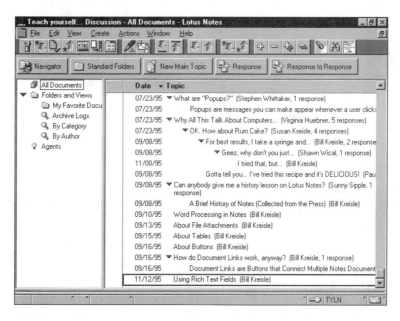

**Figure 5.29** *The Document created in Exercise 5.2 in the All Documents View.*

## *Step 2*

Leaving the Document we created in Exercise 5.2 highlighted in the All Documents View, select **Create, Response** from the Notes Client menu or click the **Response** button on the Action Bar.

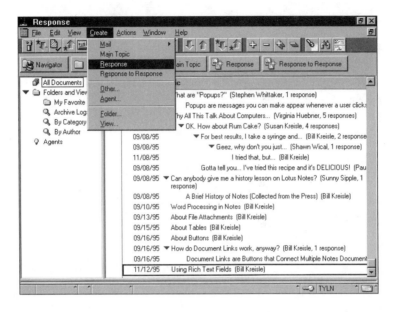

***Figure 5.30*** *Creating a Response to the Document we created in Exercise 5.2.*

## Step 3

Enter the Response text similar to Figure 5.31. To change the fonts of your Response to look like the example, highlight the text you want to change by clicking and dragging with the mouse, then choose **Text** and the appropriate menu command from the Notes Client menu.

## Step 4

Save your changes by pressing **Esc** and answering yes to the prompt or by selecting **File, Save** followed by **File, Close** from the Notes Client menu.

In the Main View, our Response will appear immediately after the main topic we composed in Exercise 5.2.

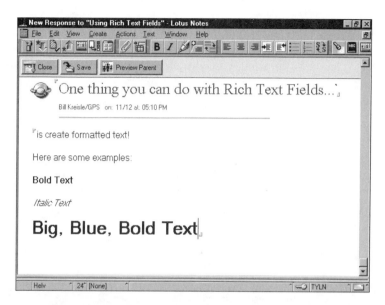

**Figure 5.31** *Adding information to a Response Document.*

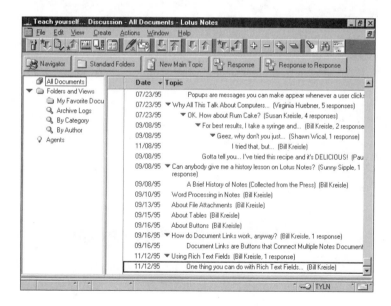

**Figure 5.32** *The New Document and Response created in Exercises 5.2 and 5.3 both appear in the All Documents View.*

# Layout Regions and Dialog Boxes

So far, we've learned the primary way to enter data into Notes is to use Forms, which are a collection of Fields and Labels. Fields are areas that are enclosed in half-brackets, and may require a specific value in them such as numbers, dates, or preselected keywords. With Notes Release 4, there two more ways a designer can use to ask you for data—Layout Regions and Dialog Boxes.

Layout Regions are a special area on a Form designed to organize fields and labels in a manner similar to a dialog box. Like standard forms, different field types can be used in a layout region; your best clue as to what field type is expected will come from the labels the designer provides you with and the error messages you receive when trying to save. Figure 5.33 illustrates a Layout Region on a Notes Form.

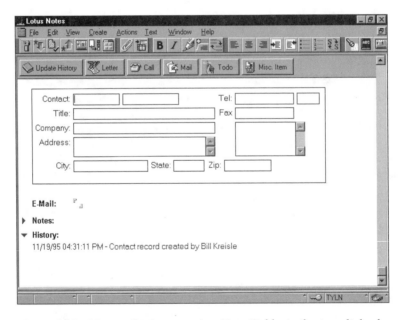

***Figure 5.33*** *A Layout Region organizes Notes Fields similar to a dialog box.*

# Summary

We've covered a lot in this chapter:

❖ Access Control Lists (ACLs) affect your ability to open, read, edit, or add Documents to a Notes database. There are seven levels of access control. A database manager has a number of options with each access level to tailor it more finely to his application.

❖ Forms organize Fields and Labels into Documents. Fields are variable areas that you fill in on each Document—they can be designed to hold numbers, time values, text, rich text, or predefined keywords. Labels are constant from Document to Document. They are generally used to explain what should be entered into a Field.

❖ To edit a Document in Notes, select the Document from a View, Folder, or Navigator and put it in edit mode by selecting **Action, Edit Document** from the Notes Client menu, or by pressing **Ctrl+E**. Once this is completed, you can use the mouse or **Up/Down Arrow** keys to move to the Field you wish to edit and make your changes. Save changes by selecting File, Save from the main menu, or by pressing **Esc** and answering **Yes** to the "Save Changes?" prompt.

❖ To add a Document to Notes, choose **Create** from the Notes Client menu combined with the name of the Form you wish to use to create the Document. If you are composing a Response Document, you should select the Document that will be the new entry's parent before selecting the Create command.

# Chapter 6

# More Ways to Add Information to Notes Databases

## In this Chapter...

When we discussed editing and composing Documents in the Chapter 5, we focused primarily on entering information into Text, Rich Text, Number, and Date Fields. In this chapter, we're going to expand on the things that we can add to Rich Text Fields, including File Attachments, Embedded Objects, Tables, and Buttons. While we're talking about Buttons, we'll cover a special type called a *Document Link*.

Next, we'll look at copying and pasting information in Notes databases, followed by a discussion on deleting Documents from Notes.

Here's the outline for this chapter:

❖ File Attachments

❖ Embedded Objects

❖ Tables

❖ Buttons

❖ Document, View, and Database Links

❖ Copying and pasting into Fields

❖ Copying and pasting into Views

❖ Deleting Documents

## File Attachments

File Attachments are copies of files that can be stored in a Notes database. They are contained in Rich Text Fields on a Document, and are represented as an icon with the file's name. Figure 6.1 illustrates a File Attachment in a Rich Text Field.

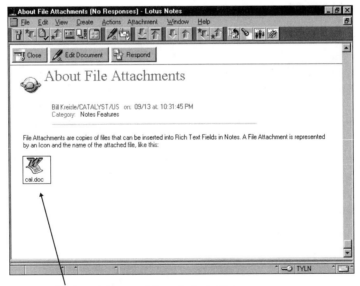

A copy of the Word for Windows file
cal.doc is attached to the Rich Text Field
of this Document.

***Figure 6.1*** *File Attachments are represented by an icon combined with the file's name.*

To attach a file to a Document, use the **File, Attach...** command from the Notes Client menu to open the Creqate Attachment(s) dialog. (See Figure 6.2.)

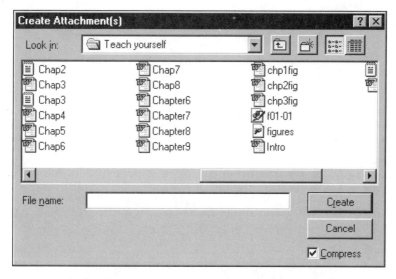

**Figure 6.2** *The Create Attachment(s) dialog box.*

**The File, Attach...** command is only available when you are editing a Document and have the cursor in a Rich Text Field.

N O T E

From the Create Attachment(s) dialog, you can select the drive, directory, and name of the file you want to attach to your Notes Document. Clicking on the **Compress** check box inserts the file using compression, meaning it takes up less space in the database. Clicking the **Create** button inserts a copy of the selected file.

To eliminate confusion, this command is inserting a copy of the file you select from the Create Attachment(s) dialog box. The file will still exist in its original location. After clicking the Create button, the file will exist in its original location and a copy of it will be inserted into the doucument's Rich Text field.

N O T E

If you want to insert more than one File Attachment at a time using the Create Attachment(s) dialog box, you can do so by typing the name of the files in the File Name list box separated by a space, or by holding down the **Ctrl** key and clicking on the name of each file you want to insert.

SHORTCUT

You can delete a File Attachment from a Rich Text field by clicking on it once and pressing the **Delete** key. Before the file is deleted, Notes will display the prompt shown in Figure 6.3.

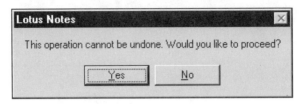

**Figure 6.3** *Deleting a File Attachment from a Rich Text Field will generate this message.*

This prompt is telling you is that after you delete the File Attachment, you cannot use the **Edit, Undo** command to get it back.

If you double-click a **File Attachment** icon in a Rich Text Field, you will see the Attachment Properties information tab (Figure 6.4).

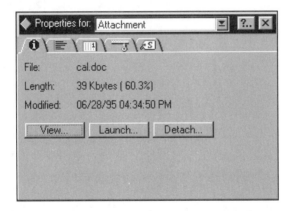

**Figure 6.4** *Double-clicking a* **File Attachment** *icon will open the Attachment Properties information tab.*

You can also view the dialog box in Figure 6.4 by right-clicking the **File Attachment** icon and selecting Attachment Properties from the pop-up menu (Figure 6.5).

Going back to Figure 6.4, you'll notice that the information page of this dialog box gives you the name of the file, the size of the file, and information about when the file was originally created. The dialog box page also contains View, Detach, and Launch buttons.

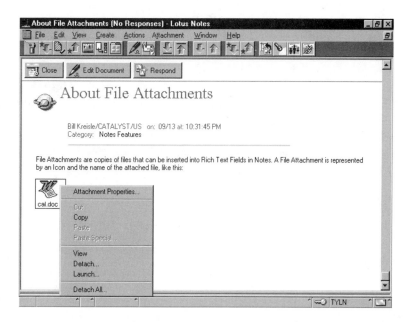

**Figure 6.5** *The Attachment Properties command on the right-click menu.*

Clicking **Detach** makes a copy of the file at a location you specify. If you checked the Compress box when you stored the attachment, it will be automatically decompressed when it is written back to disk.

Clicking **Launch** makes a temporary copy of the file on your local hard drive and launches the application associated with the file's extension. What this means is that if you attach and save a Microsoft Write file, when another Windows user double-clicks on the attachment and selects the **Launch** button, she will launch the Microsoft Write and a copy of the file automatically. When the second user closes Write, the temporary copy of the file created on her computer will be deleted.

There are few important things to note concerning the Launch button:

1. Different computers may have different applications associated with the same file extension. As an example, you create a Microsoft Word Document called MYFILE.DOC and insert the file into Notes as an attachment. Another Windows user, who favors WordPerfect, may double-click on your extension and select **Launch**, only to discover that WordPerfect wasn't the application that created the file.

2.  The Launch button may not work on files that were attached by a Notes user on a different platform. For example, a Microsoft Word for the Macintosh user creates a file called MYFILE and attaches it to a Document. A Windows user who has Microsoft Word for Windows installed double-clicks on the attachment and clicks the **Launch** button. Because the file MYFILE has no extension, Notes may respond with the dialog box shown in Figure 6.6:

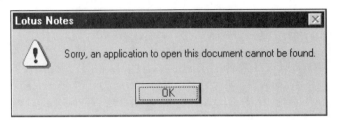

**Figure 6.6** *Launching a file with no extension or an extension not recognized by your operating system will generate this message.*

3.  Some extensions (exe, bat, app, or cmd, for example) are considered programs by Windows, OS/2, and UNIX. Selecting **Launch** on a file with one of these extensions will actually run the selected program!

---

WARNING

Never launch an attachment with an EXE, BAT, COM, or CMD extension if you aren't 100% sure of what the program will do and are reasonably sure you know the person who composed the Document. A malicious user could make an attachment called SMILE.BAT or something else equally innocent-sounding that erases your hard drive!

---

4.  Detaching a file makes a copy of the attachment on your hard drive, but it does not remove the attachment from the Document (just as attaching a file makes a copy in the Notes Document but does not remove the original file).

    Depending on the type of file attached, clicking **View** may open Notes' built-in viewing utility. This utility is designed to allow you to look at files created with programs you may not have on your computer. It is especially useful for viewing attached image files (Figure 6.7).

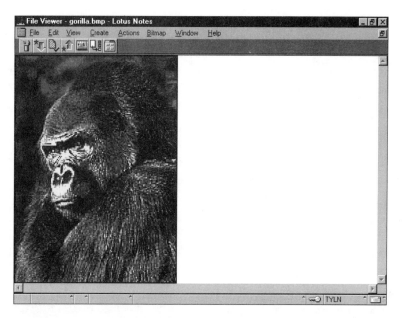

***Figure 6.7*** *Using Notes' built-in viewer to examine attached files.*

# Embedded Objects

Embedded Objects are special types of File Attachments. They are files that become a part of your Notes Document. The difference between an Embedded Object and an attached file is that changes made to an Embedded Object by its associated application are stored in the Notes database, while changes made to attached files are made to temporary files on a local hard drive. One way to think of the difference between working with Embedded Objects and File Attachments would be comparing it to working with an original page of a book versus working on a photocopy. Whatever you do to the original page will be available to the next person who reads it, while what you do to the photocopy is never seen by the book's next reader.

Why would you use Embedded Objects instead of File Attachments? Imagine that you are one of three people asked to edit a Document that was created in Microsoft Word and stored in a Notes Document. If the Document was stored as a File Attachment, you would double-click the Document's icon, select **Launch**, and work with the temporary copy. When you finished making your changes, if you wanted the next person who was supposed to edit the document to see your suggestions, you would have to save the file to your local hard drive and attach the new file to the Document, next to the original. The next editor would have to launch the original and your document to see if you're suggesting the same changes she would and create a third file and attach it to the Document.

If the Document was an Embedded Object, however, you could double-click on the Document, and it would automatically launch the associated application (there is no Detach or View option for Embedded Objects). After you finished editing, your changes would be saved in the Notes Document. (Meaning that the next person who double-clicks on the Embedded Object would see your changes because they were stored within it.)

You can insert an Object into a Rich Text Field by placing your cursor at the desired location in the field and choosing **Create, Object...** from the main menu. This will open a dialog box similar to Figure 6.8, which lists the different Objects that are registered with your operating system.

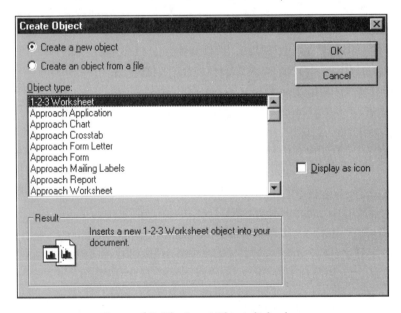

***Figure 6.8*** *The Insert Object dialog box.*

The types of Objects you can insert will vary from one machine to another.

**N O T E**

From the Insert Object dialog box, select the type of Object you want. If the **Create New** radio button is selected, whatever Object type you select will be a new Object within the Rich Text Field. If the **Create from File** radio button is selected, you will be given a dialog box to locate the file you wish to insert into the Rich Text Field as an Object. You can use the Display as Icon checkbox to display the Object you are inserting as an icon. If you do not select this checkbox, the Object you insert will appear in the Rich Text Field much the same as if it were being viewed by the application used to create the Object. Figure 6.9 illustrates a Microsoft Chart inserted into a Rich Text Field as an icon and in its native format.

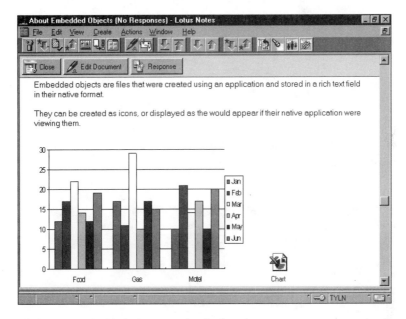

***Figure 6.9*** *An Embedded Object can be displayed as an icon or in its native format.*

You can delete an Object from a Document in the same way you can delete a File Attachment—select it by clicking on it once, and press the **Delete** key. You will see the "Operation cannot be undone. Would you like to proceed?" message we discussed earlier in this chapter.

**N O T E**    Objects are still a relatively new technology on some operating systems, and Objects that work seamlessly across platforms are definitely work in progress. While there are times when storing a file as an Object might make sense, make sure you can live with the consequences of working with a new technology (meaning an occasional failure of epic proportions).

# Tables

Tables can be inserted into Rich Text Fields by positioning the cursor at the desired location in the field and choosing **Create, Table** from the Notes Client menu. This will open a dialog box similar to the one shown in Figure 6.10.

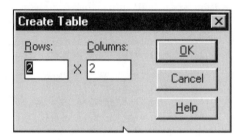

***Figure 6.10*** *The Create Table dialog box.*

Using the Create Table dialog box, you can specify the number of row and columns desired. If you aren't sure how many rows and columns you will need you can make changes to the table later. Figure 6.11 illustrates a table in a Rich Text Field.

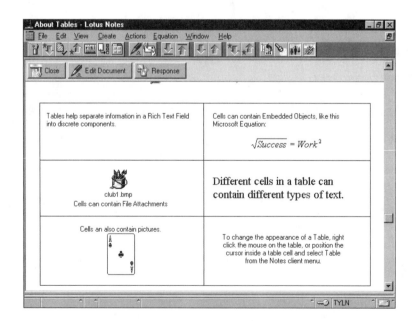

***Figure 6.11*** *A table inserted in a Rich Text Field.*

While you are editing a table, you can use the **Tab** key to move from one cell to the next. To make changes to a table after it has been inserted, position the cursor inside one of the table's cells and select the Table command from the Notes Client menu. You can also right-click anywhere on the table to open the Properties dialog box and choose **Table** from the drop-down list (Figure 6.12).

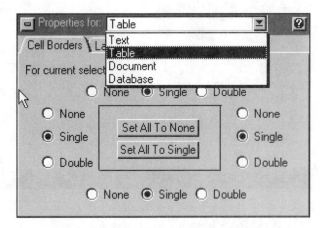

**Figure 6.12** *Changing a Table's Properties using the right mouse button and the Properties dialog box.*

To quickly add another row to a table, press the **Tab** key while you are in the last cell of the table.

SHORTCUT

# Taking What We've Learned Step-by-Step (Exercise 6.1)

In this exercise, we will compose a Document in the Teach yourself... Discussion database, and insert a Table, File Attachment, and Embedded Object into the Rich Text Field of the Document we create.

## *Step 1*

Select the **Teach yourself... Discussion** database and choose **Create, Main Topic** from the Notes Client menu. Enter "Exercise 6.1" in the first Text Field, and position the cursor in the Rich Text Field at the bottom of the form (Figure 6.13).

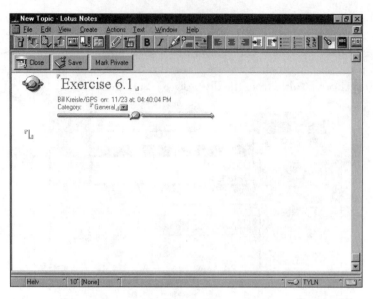

***Figure 6.13*** *Getting ready by creating a new Document in the Teach yourself... Discussion database.*

## *Step 2*

Choose **Create Table...** from the Notes Client menu. Dimension the table as 1 row by 2 columns and choose **OK**.

***Figure 6.14*** *Inserting a 1 row by 2 column table.*

## Step 3

Position your cursor in the first cell of the table, and select **File, Attach...** from the Notes Client menu. If you are running Notes on Windows (et al.) or OS/2, enter "c:\config.sys" in the File Name text box. If you are using another operating system, select a text file from your local hard drive using the Drive, Directory, and File Name list boxes.

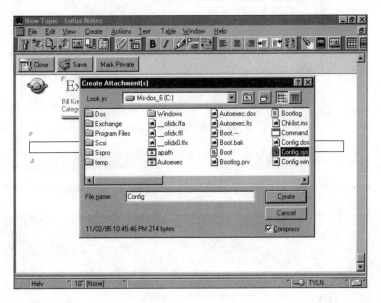

***Figure 6.15*** *Inserting a File Attachment into the first cell of the table.*

## Step 4

Use the **Tab** key to move to the next cell in the table. Choose **Create, Object...** from the Notes Client menu. Create a new Embedded Object using an associated application (Figure 6.16).

Notice that after you click **OK** to Create the Object, a heavy box appears around the new Object and the Notes Client menu choices change to reflect actions that you can take on that Object's type (Figure 6.17). This is an example of in-place editing— a component of the Object Linking and Embedding (OLE) standard, version 2.0.

## Step 5

Click outside of the newly created Object onto the second cell in the Table to close the Object and restore the Notes Client menu to its normal state (Figure 6.18).

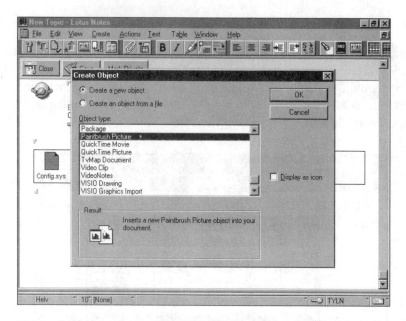

**Figure 6.16** *Creating an Embedded Object in the second cell of the Table.*

**Figure 6.17** *The Notes Client menu changes to reflect options you can use with the type of Object you chose to Create.*

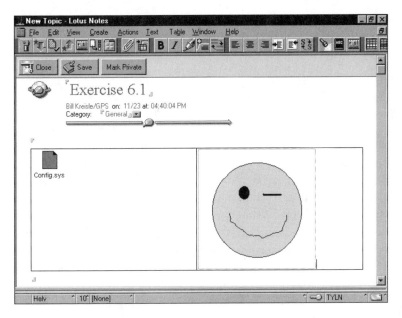

**Figure 6.18** *Click outside of an Embedded Object to*
*return control of the menu to the Notes Client.*

## Step 6

Complete the exercise by saving the new Document and closing the Teach yourself... Discussion database.

As you can see, the Rich Text Field is an important part of Notes (and if you think this is powerful stuff, wait until you see the next section).

## Buttons

Buttons in a Notes Document are designed to work the same way as buttons on, say, your radio. If you push one, something happens. How Notes accomplishes this is by allowing you to store mini-programs called *Agents* with each button that you (or the database's designer) create. When you click the button (or select the button using the **Arrow** keys and press the Spacebar), the action stored with it will execute.

Another important feature of Buttons is that they can be stored in Forms as well as Rich Text Fields. As you recall, Forms organize a Document's Fields and Labels—

every Document composed by the same form will have common Fields and Labels. By allowing Buttons to be stored in forms, every Document composed can have the same Buttons as well. This allows the database's designer to automate or simplify the process of creating or navigating Documents created by a specific form.

As an example, imagine a Notes database of purchase orders. Documents are composed in that database using a form with Fields for the order date, the bill-to address, the ship-to address, the items ordered, payment terms, and shipping terms. Since the bill-to address is often the same as the ship-to address, the database designer creates a Button called "Same as Bill To" on the Purchase Order Form, too. When the user clicks the "Same as Bill To" button, an Agent runs that copies the information from the bill to address fields to the ship -o address fields, saving time for the person entering the order.

**NOTE**    Since Buttons are the first thing I've mentioned that can be stored on a Form besides Fields, you might have the impression that they are the only thing we've discussed up to this point that can be included on a Form. Basically, anything that can be stored in a Rich Text Field can be stored inside a Form, including File Attachment, Embedded Objects, or pictures. Pictures, Buttons, and Tables are the items you'll find used in forms most often.

Because inserting Buttons means understanding Notes' Agent languages (a topic we won't cover in this book because of the amount of space I'd have to devote to discussing it could easily make another book) this section is devoted primarily to how you can use Buttons as opposed to creating them yourself. (Although in Exercise 6.1 you will use Notes' Agent language to create a Button so we can use it later in the exercise.)

"Big deal. Point at the Button and click," you're probably saying to yourself. "What else is there to know?"

For the most part, you're right. There, are, however, a couple of other things I'd like to mention:

1.  Buttons are similar to File Attachments with EXE, CMD, BAT, APP, or COM extensions. When you start them, something's going to happen. If you're not sure what a Button does or you don't recognize the name of the person who inserted it into a Document, don't click on it until you can find out more about it.

2.  You can delete Buttons from a Rich Text Field by selecting them and pressing the **Delete** key.

**WARNING**

Unlike File Attachments and Objects, Buttons are activated by clicking on them once. That means to select a Button to delete it, you have to place the cursor before the Button, and click and drag over the Button. You can also select a Button to be deleted by placing the cursor before the Button, holding down the **Shift** key, and using the **Right Arrow** key to move over the Button.

# Taking What We've Learned Step-by-Step (Exercise 6.2)

In this example, we're going to get a minimal introduction to one of the Notes Agent languages (@Functions) as we insert a Button into a Rich Text Field. As with the previous step-by-step example, we'll use the Teach yourself... Discussion database to compose our Document.

## Step 1

Open the Teach yourself... Discussion database and choose **Create, Main Topic** from the Notes client menu. Enter "Exercise 6.2" in the first field of the new Document and position the cursor in the last field on the Form.

Select **Create, Hotspot, Button...** from the Notes Client menu (Figure 6.19).

This will cause several things to happen. A Button will appear in the Rich Text Field, the Properties dialog box will open, set to Properties for Button, and the Document window will split, showing an area to program what action the button should take when it is clicked (Figure 6.20).

## Step 2

In the Properties For Button dialog box, select the first tabbed page and enter the text "Message from our Sponsor" in the Button Label text box.

In the action area make sure the **Formula** radio button is selected, and enter: @Prompt([OK]; "MIS:Press" ; "Be sure to look for our other Teach yourself... books the next time you're in the bookstore!")

in the text box beneath the radio button (see Figure 6.21).

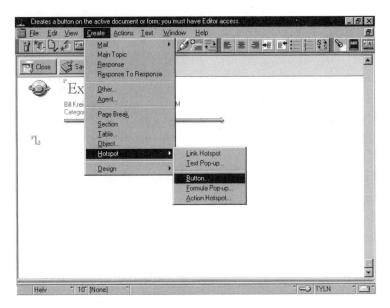

**Figure 6.19** *Creating a Button in a Rich Text Field.*

**The properties dialog with Properties for Button selected.**

**Newly created button**

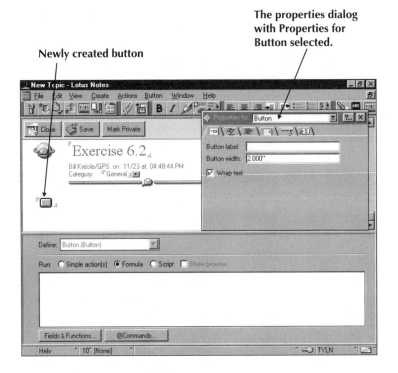

**Figure 6.20** *Different areas that appear when the **Create, Hotspot, Button...** command is issued from the Notes Client menu.*

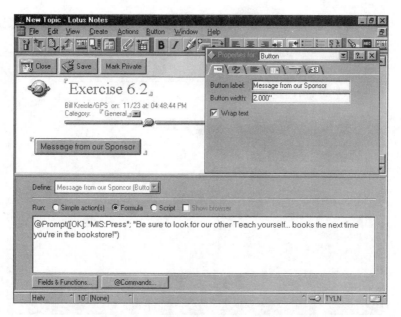

***Figure 6.21*** *Adding a label to a Button and entering the Button's formula.*

**NOTE**

It's important to enter the formula exactly as it appears above, paying attention to the use of parentheses, brackets, semicolons, and quotation marks.

Click outside the button on the Document to close the action area of the Document Window, and close the Properties For Button dialog box.

## *Step 3*

To examine the code behind the button again, hold down the **Ctrl** key and click the button, or use the **Up/Down/Right/Left Arrow** keys to highlight the button. Then, choose **Button, Edit Button...** from the Notes Client menu.

Click on the Document to close the action area of the Document Window.

## *Step 4*

Click the "Message from our Sponsor" Button. You will see the MIS:Press dialog box (Figure 6.23).

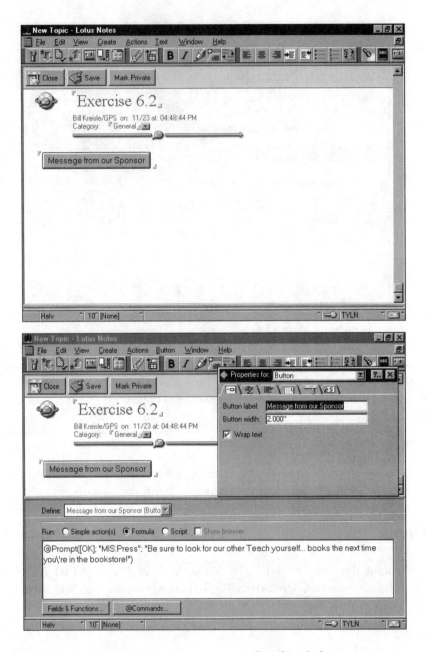

**Figure 6.22** *Examining the action a Button will perform before executing it.*

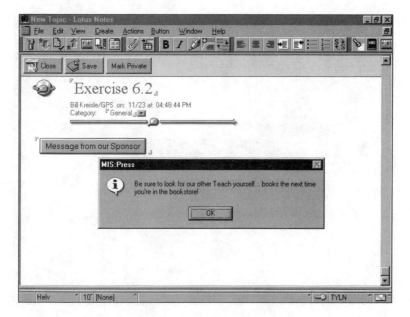

***Figure 6.23*** *The MIS:Press dialog box.*

Click **OK** to close the MIS:Press dialog box.

## Step 5

Using the mouse, click on the space in front of the "Message from our Sponsor" Button and drag the mouse over the Button to select it without launching it. Press the **Delete** key or select **Edit, Clear** from the Notes Client menu to remove the Button from the Document.

## Step 6

Complete the exercise by closing the Teach yourself... Discussion database. You do not need to save your changes unless you want to refer to this Document later.

This is a very basic example of using a Button in a Rich Text field—it simply opens a message box to display text. However, an experienced database developer can make Buttons powerful extensions to Notes.

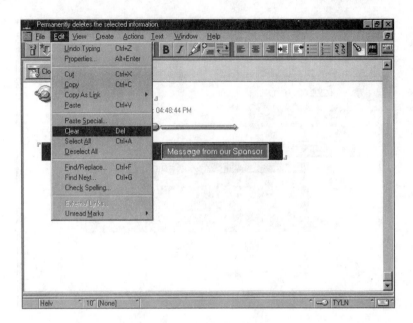

**Figure 6.24** *Deleting a Button from a Rich Text Field.*

## A Quick Look at @Prompt

While I said I wouldn't get deeply involved in the Notes macro language, I'd like to briefly cover the @Function we just used in our example (just in case you're curious). If you aren't interested in this part, feel free to skip to the next section of this chapter, "Document Links."

What we entered in the Formula box of the Insert Button dialog box was:

@Prompt([OK];"MIS:Press";"Be sure to look for our other teach yourself... books the next time you're in the bookstore!")

@Prompt is the name of a Notes @Function (pronounced "at-Prompt" and "at-Function"). As you saw in the step-by-step example, @Prompt creates a message box. What is contained in the message box @Prompt creates is determined by the *arguments* passed with the @Prompt function. Arguments are separated by semicolons. Looking at the preceding example, you can see that there are three arguments for @Prompt. All three arguments are grouped together by a set of parentheses.

The first argument, [OK] is one of several arguments the Notes Developer's Reference tells us we can use with the @Prompt function. It determines what kinds of Buttons will be displayed at the bottom of the Message box. For example, another first argument that could be used with @Prompt is [YESNO], which displays a Yes button and a No button at the bottom of the message box.

The second argument "MIS:Press" is the text that will be displayed in the message box's title bar.

The third argument "Be sure to look for our other Teach Yourself... books the next time you're in the bookstore!" is the text that will be displayed in the message box when it is opened.

As you saw earlier, @Prompt combined with our three arguments, produces the result shown in Figure 6.25:

**Figure 6.25** *An example of the @Prompt Function.*

# Document, View, and Database Links

Another type of Button you can insert into a Rich Text Field is called a *Link*. There are three different types of Link buttons you can insert: Document Links, View Links, and Database Links.

Document Links work as their name implies—they link Documents together. Here's how it happens: imagine that you've just finished reading a book called *Teach yourself... Lotus Notes*. After you finish the book you become so excited about Notes that you read more books and work with Notes a little bit on your own. Before you know it, you're a Notes evangelist!

To help others discover the "Gospel of Notes," you maintain a discussion database where you answer questions others have about Notes and provide tips to make life with Notes easier in general. As you're reviewing today's questions, you see that someone new has asked a question about Document Links.

The person who entered the question didn't notice that earlier in the discussion database, someone else had asked the same question. Of course, you realize that Notes is a little bit overwhelming to new users, so you don't mind answering the question again. However, since you're a Notes guru, you know you don't have to retype your answer—you can make a Document Link instead.

You compose a Response to the new user's question and in the Response enter the text "Document Links are connections between Documents in a Notes database. To learn more about Document Links, double-click here->." After you enter the text, you go to the discussion's All Documents View and select the Document you originally composed to answer another user's question on the same subject. While the original message is selected, you choose **Edit, Copy As Link, Document Link** from the main menu (Figure 6.26).

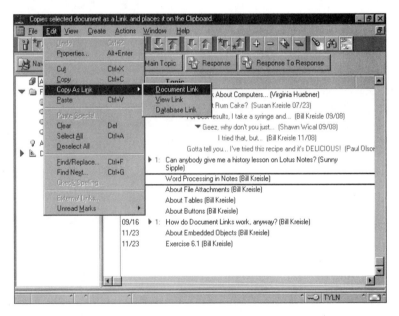

***Figure 6.26*** *To make a Document Link, select a Document and choose* ***Edit, Copy As Link*** *from the Notes Client menu.*

SHORTCUT

You can also right-click the document in the View and select **Copy as Link** from the pop-up menu.

You return to the new Document your composing, and insert the Document Link after the "click here->" text by choosing **Edit, Paste**. What you get is something similar to Figure 6.27.

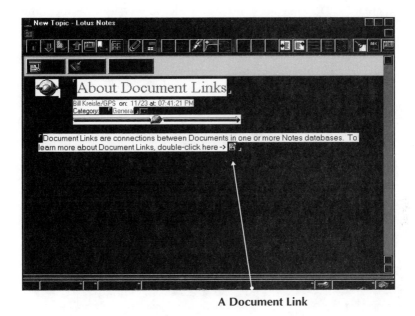

**A Document Link**

***Figure 6.27*** *A Notes Document containing a Document Link.*

When the user who asked the new question about Document Links checks the discussion database again, he will find your Response. When he double-clicks on the **Document Link** you've inserted into the Response, he will be taken to the original message you composed about Document Links earlier in the discussion database.

Of course, allowing you to save time and energy by avoiding retyping Documents is a useful feature of Document Links, but it's just a hint of their power. Document Links make creating reference materials easier by allowing you to create review points for users throughout the material. Take, for example, this book. I introduce a concept early on, and when I mention the concept again, I often copy some of the original information from an earlier chapter into the current one to give you a quick review. With Document Links, I could simply leave a bookmark that would take you back to the related information.

Document Links can also link Documents in different databases. Suppose you have two Notes databases, one for customer names and addresses and another for orders. Whenever you wanted to associate a new order with a customer in your database, instead of retyping the customer's name and address, you could create a "DocLink" from the new order to the customer Document.

# Taking What We've Learned Step-by-Step (Exercise 6.3)

In this lesson, we'll use the Teach yourself... Discussion database to recreate our earlier example of how you might create and use Document Links.

## *Step 1*

Open the Teach yourself... Discussion database. Select **Create, Main Topic** from the Notes Client menu. Enter "How do Document Links work, anyway?" in the new topic's first field. Close the Document and save your changes.

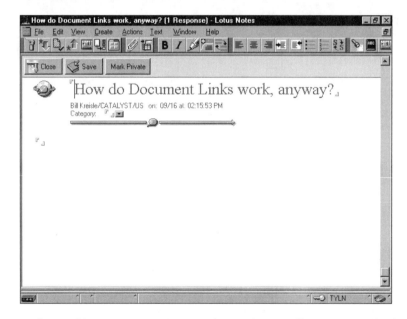

**Figure 6.28** *Adding a new Main Topic to the Teach yourself... Discussion database.*

## Step 2

Select the Document we just composed from the All Documents View, and choose **Create, Response** from the Notes Client menu (Figure 6.29).

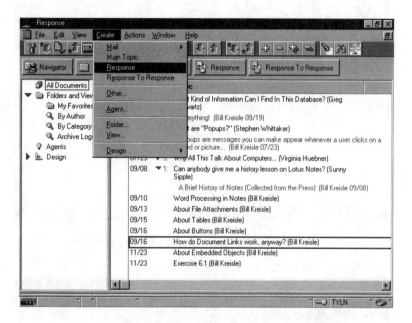

***Figure 6.29*** *Adding a Response to the new Main Topic.*

Enter "Document Links are Buttons that connect multiple Notes Documents" in the topic field. Move the cursor to the last field in the Form. Add the text "Like this..." (Figure 6.30)

## Step 3

Select **Window, 2. Teach yourself... Discuss...** from the Notes Client menu (Figure 6.31).

This will bring the window containing the All Documents View to the top of the Notes Client. Select the Response Document "Everything!" near the top of the All Documents View (Figure 6.32).

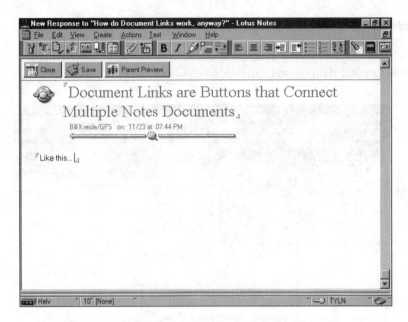

**Figure 6.30** *Adding a Response to the new Main Topic.*

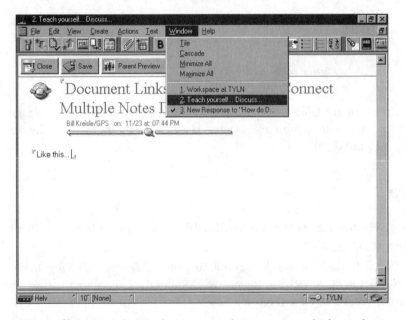

**Figure 6.31** *Using the Window command to navigate multiple windows.*

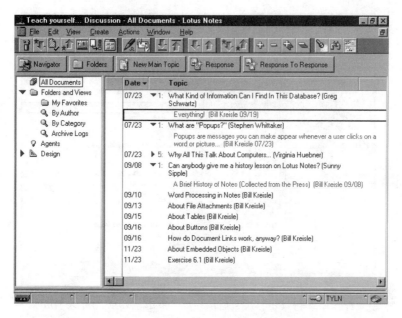

**Figure 6.32** *Selecting a Document to create a Document Link with.*

## Step 4

While the "Everything!" Response is selected, choose **Edit, Copy as Link** from the Notes Client menu (Figure 6.33).

The message "DocLink copied to clipboard..." will appear in the status area at the bottom of the Notes Client (Figure 6.34).

## Step 5

Select **Window, 3. Response to "How do Docu...** from the menu to bring the window containing the new Response Document to the front of the Notes Client (Figure 6.35a and 6.35b).

## Step 6

Place the cursor in the bottom field of the Response at the end of the sentence "Like this..."

Choose **Edit, Paste** from the main menu. The Document Link will appear in the Rich Text field along with the text you typed earlier (Figure 6.36).

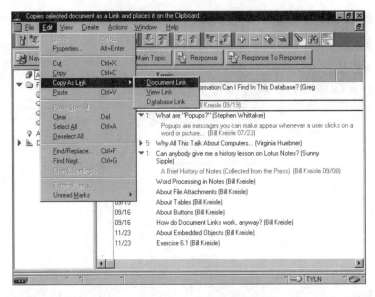

**Figure 6.33** *Copy the selected Document as a Document Link.*

**Figure 6.34** *The Status Bar will indicate that you have copied the Document as a Link.*

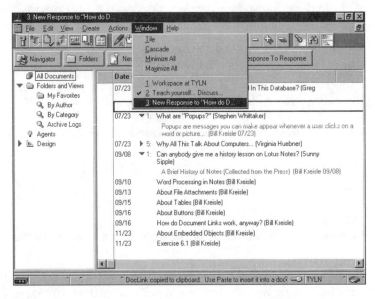

**Figure 6.35a** *Returning to the Response Document to insert the new Document Link.*

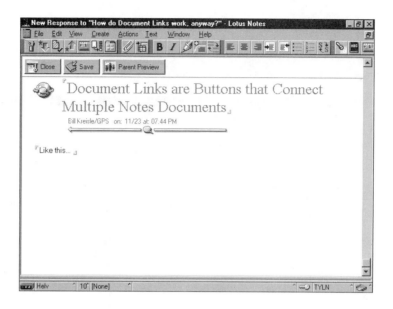

**Figure 6.35b** *Returning to the Response Document to insert the new Document Link.*

The newly inserted
Document Link

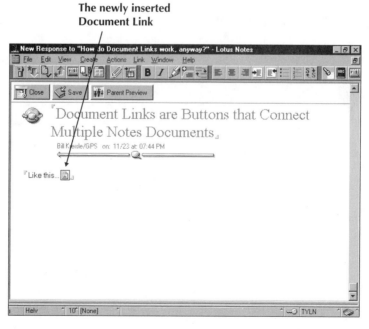

**Figure 6.36** *The Document Link is pasted into the Rich Text Field of the Response.*

## *Step 7*

Double-click the on **Document Link**. The "Everything!" Response will appear as the front window of the Notes Client (Figure 6.37).

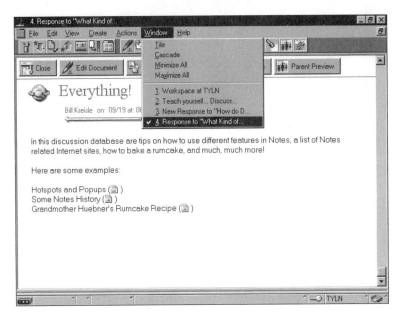

**Figure 6.37** *Double-clicking on the **Document Link** opens the Document specified by the Link button.*

Notice that the "Everything" Response becomes a choice on Notes Client's Window menu. Take a moment to explore the other Document Links in the "Everything!" Response. Close all Windows and the Teach yourself... Discussion database to complete the exercise.

View Links and Database Links work similarly, except that what appears when you double-click on them is the linked View or database.

To create a View Link, open a Notes database to the View you wish to link to and select **Edit, Copy As Link, View Link** from the Notes Client menu (Figure 6.38).

As with the Document Link, a message will display on the status bar of the Notes Client indicating that the Link to the selected View was successfully copied (Figure 6.39).

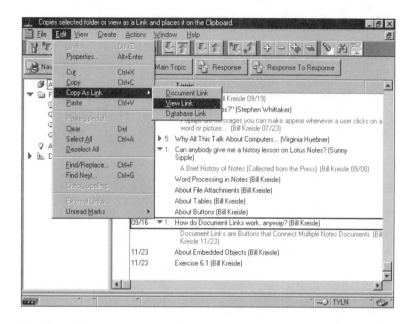

*Figure 6.38* Creating a View Link.

*Figure 6.39* The status bar's message that a Link to the View has been copied.

Finally, Database Links are created by selecting a database on the Workspace and choosing **Edit, Copy as Link, Database Link** from the Notes Client menu (Figure 6.40).

As with Document Links, you can also create a Database Link using the right mouse button menu. Right-click on the Database and select **Copy as Link** from the pop-up menu.

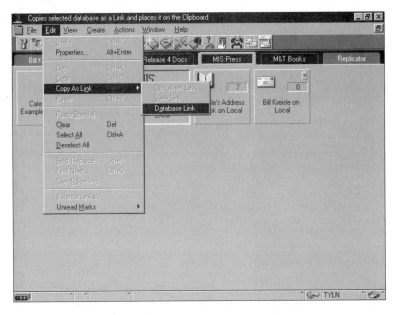

**Figure 6.40** *Creating a Database Link.*

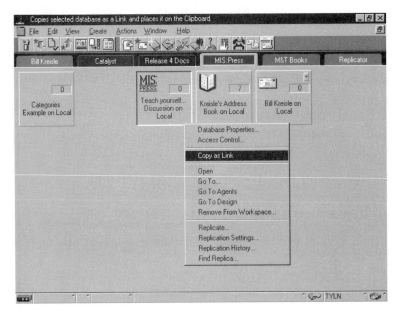

**Figure 6.41** *Using the right mouse button menu to create a Database Link.*

# Copying and Pasting Information in Notes

As you can see, Link buttons are another powerful feature of Notes—they allow you to reference information without retyping it. Of course, Links aren't the only way to reference existing information without retyping it. You can also copy information from a Document to a clipboard file and paste it into another one.

How you select information in Notes to copy to the clipboard file depends on where you are (in a Document or a view) and what you are doing (reading or editing):

❖ If you are reading a Document, you can select information by clicking and dragging the mouse over the area you want to copy, or by choosing **Edit, Select All** from the menu to select the entire Document.

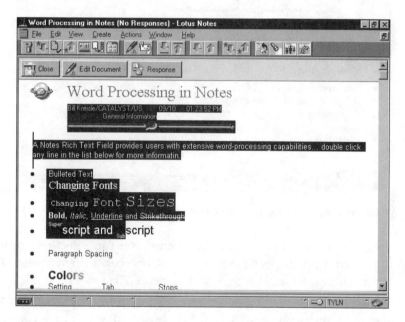

***Figure 6.42*** *Selecting information to copy while reading a document.*

❖ If you are editing a Document, you can select information by clicking and dragging the mouse over the information in a field you wish to copy, or by choosing **Edit, Select All** from the main menu to select the entire contents of the current field.

An important difference between copying information from a Document in Read Mode versus a Document in Edit Mode is that you can only copy information from the currently selected field while you are in Edit Mode. While you are in Read Mode, you can copy information from multiple fields simultaneously, but you can only paste what you've copied into a single field (Figure 6.43).

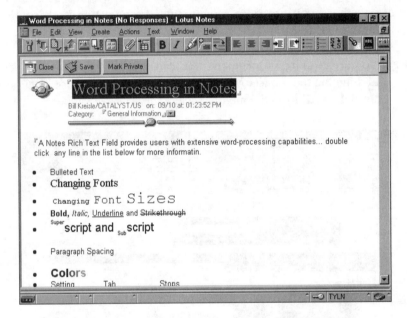

**Figure 6.43** *Selecting information to copy while editing a document.*

If you are using a View to navigate Documents, you can select one or more Documents from the View using the mouse or Spacebar, or by choosing **Edit, Select All** from the main menu to select all Documents (Figure 6.44).

Once you have selected the information you wish to copy, choosing **Edit, Copy** from the main menu copies it to the clipboard. After you have copied the information, choosing **Edit, Paste** from the menu reinserts it into the currently active view or the currently selected field of a Document. Where you can paste the information depends on where you got it from.

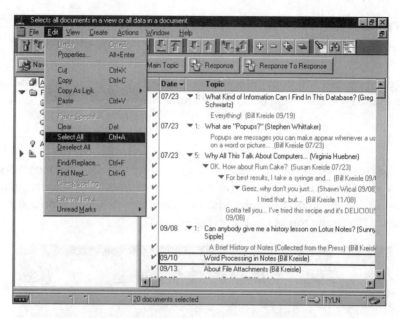

***Figure 6.44*** *Selecting Documents to copy from a View.*

❖ If you copied information from a Document in edit or read mode and you selected formatted text, attachments, Buttons, Tables, or labels to be copied, the information can be pasted only in a Rich Text field.

❖ If you selected text, numbers, or dates from the Document, they can be pasted into Text, Number, or Time Fields.

❖ If you copied one or more Documents from a View, you can only paste them into the database from a View. There are some important things to remember when copying and pasting Documents at the View level.

**N O T E**

Since Documents are created using a Form, and different Forms are stored in each Notes database, you may have problems copying Documents at the View level from one database and pasting them into another.

If you copy a Response Document from a view and do not copy the parent Document, the Document currently selected in the View when you paste the Response into it will become its parent.

# Taking What We've Learned Step-by-Step (Exercise 6.4)

In this exercise, we will copy information from a Document in read mode and paste it into a Rich Text Field on a new Document.

## *Step 1*

Open the Teach yourself... Discussion database to the All Documents View. Select **View, Expand All** from the Notes Client menu to be sure that all Documents and Responses are visible, then open the Response titled "Everything!" near the top of the View (Figure 6.45).

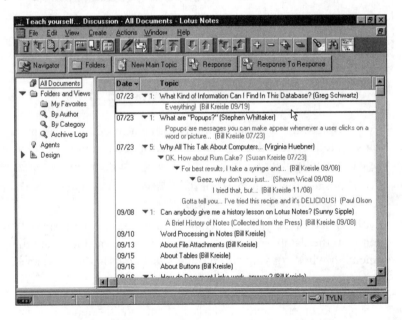

***Figure 6.45*** *The Response Document "Everything!"*

## *Step 2*

Experiment with selecting information by clicking and dragging the mouse over the Document. Choose **Edit, Select All** from the menu to highlight the entire Document (Figure 6.46). Choose **Edit, Copy** from the menu.

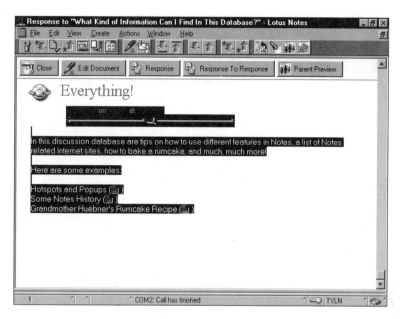

**Figure 6.46** *Selecting the entire Document to be copied.*

After selecting the information you wish to copy, you can also right-click on the selected area and choose **Copy** from the pop-up menu that appears.

SHORTCUT

## Step 3

Close the Document using the **File, Close** command. Create a new Document by selecting **Create, Main Topic** from the Notes Client menu. Place the cursor in the last field on the form, and choose **Edit, Paste** from the Notes Client menu (Figure 6.47).

Notice how formatting, labels, text, and pictures are all pasted into the field.

You can also paste information into a field by placing the cursor in it, right-clicking the mouse on the Document and selecting **Paste** from the pop-up menu.

SHORTCUT

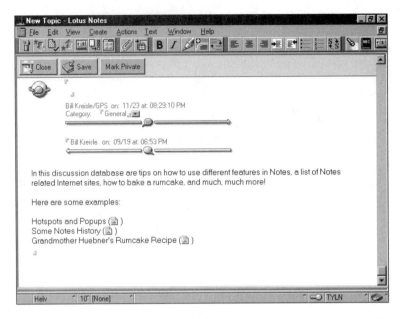

**Figure 6.47** *Pasting the contents copied from the previous Document into a new Document.*

## Step 4

Place the cursor in the first field on the form and select **Edit Paste** from the main menu (Figure 6.48).

Notice the message that appears when you try to paste labels, attachments, Tables, or other Objects into a text field.

---

N O T E

As you saw in the previous exercise, when you copy information to the Notes clipboard file, it can be pasted multiple times. Information copied to the clipboard remains on the clipboard until you close Notes or until you select and copy another Document or field.

---

## Step 5

Close the new Document and leave the Teach yourself... Discussion database open to the All Documents View for Exercise 6.5. You do not need to save the Document unless you want to refer to it personally later.

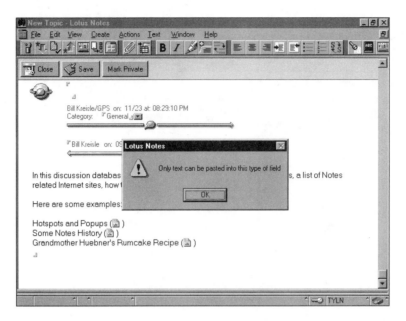

**Figure 6.48** *If you try to paste information into a Text Field that contains Pictures, File Attachments, or Embedded Objects, you will see this message.*

# Taking What We've Learned Step-by-Step (Exercise 6.5)

In this exercise, we will copy a Document from the Main View of the Teach yourself... Discussion database and paste the copy into the View.

## *Step 1*

Select the Response Document "Everything" from the All Documents View of the Teach yourself... Discussion database. Choose **Edit, Copy** from the Notes Client menu (Figure 6.49).

## *Step 2*

Choose **Edit, Paste** from the menu (Figure 6.50). Notice that a second Document labeled "Everything!" appears in the All Documents View as a

Response to Response Document (meaning the Response "Everything!" is the new Document's parent).

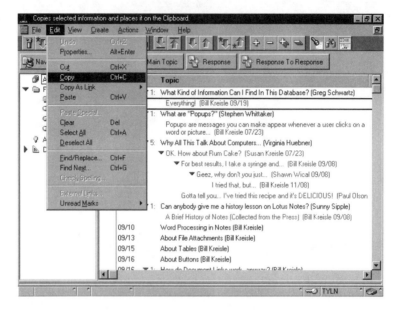

**Figure 6.49** *Copying a Document from the All Documents View.*

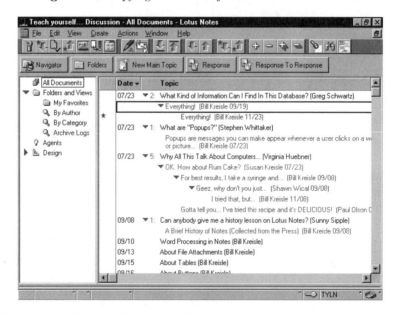

**Figure 6.50** *Response Documents are associated with whatever Document is selected when they are pasted into a View.*

## Step 3

Select the parent Document "What kind of information... " at the top of the All Documents View and choose **Edit, Paste** from the Notes Client menu. Notice that another "Everything!" response is added to the parent Document (Figure 6.51).

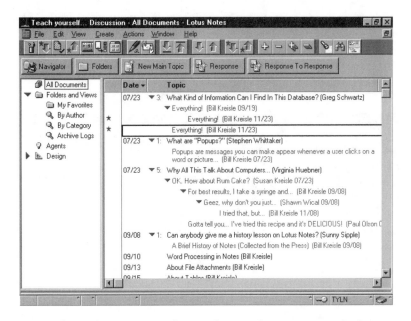

***Figure 6.51*** *The same Document can be pasted into a View multiple times.*

## Step 4

Close the Teach yourself... Discussion database to complete the exercise.

# Deleting Documents

After covering how to paste additional copies of Documents into a Notes database, it seems only fitting to mention how to delete them as well.

You delete information in Notes using the **Edit, Clear** command. Similar to the **Edit, Copy** and **Edit, Paste** commands we just discussed, the results of the **Edit, Clear** command depend on where you are (in a Document or a view) and what you are doing (reading or editing) when you call it.

If you are reading a Document, selecting **Edit, Clear** from the menu will mark it for deletion, and move you to the next Document in the view.

If you are editing a Document, selecting **Edit, Clear** from the menu will delete either selected information in a field, or, if no text is selected, the character to the right of the cursor in a field.

From a Notes View, choosing **Edit, Clear** marks the selected Document(s) in that view for deletion.

What does "marked for deletion" mean? Documents marked for deletion will have a small trash can next to them in any view, as illustrated in Figure 6.52:

**Documents marked for deletion in a Notes Database will have a small trash can to their left in any View.**

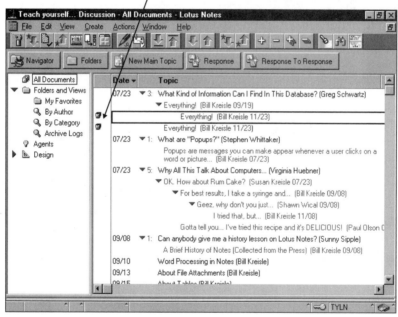

***Figure 6.52*** *A Notes View with Documents marked for deletion.*

While you remain in the Notes database, the deletion marker can be toggled on and off by selecting a Document and choosing **Edit, Clear** from the menu or pressing the **Delete** key. Documents marked for deletion will be removed from the Notes database the next time the current view is refreshed, or when the database is closed. Before the Documents are deleted, you will be prompted with a dialog box similar to the one in Figure 6.53.

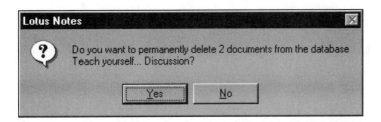

**Figure 6.53** *If a Notes database contains Documents marked for deletion, you will receive a prompt similar to this when the database is closed.*

Once Documents are deleted from a Notes database, there is no way to recover them without access to a backup copy of the database or a replica of the database that has not received the deletions.

WARNING

# In Summary

Rich Text Fields are a powerful part of Notes—they expand the ways you can add information to include, File Attachments, Embedded Objects, Tables, Document Links, View Links, Database Links, and Buttons.

❖   File Attachments are copies of files. They are represented in a Rich Text field by an icon combined with the file's name.

❖   Double-clicking on a **File Attachment** allows you to detach a copy of the file, to launch the attached file, or to view the contents of the attached file using Notes' built-in viewer. If the file has an EXE, BAT, CMD, COM, or other extension that indicates it is executable, the program will be run. If the file has an extension associated with another program, the associated program will be run with a copy of the file as its contents. If you edit the contents of a File Attachment, you must save the attachment as a new file, and reattach it to the Document if you want to share it with others.

❖   Embedded Objects are files that are "embedded" in a Rich Text field by the application that created them. Embedded Objects can appear in their native format in a Rich Text Field or they can be displayed as icons.

Double-clicking on an **Embedded Object** launches the application that created it with the embedded information as its contents. Unlike a File Attachment, the embedded information is stored in the Rich Text Field when the associated application is closed.

❖ Document Links connect Documents in the same or different databases. To navigate to the related Document, double-click the Button that represents the link. You create a Document Link by selecting the **Edit, Copy as Link, Document Link** command from the main menu.

❖ View and Database Links work the same way Document Links do, only they connect users with Views and databases instead of Documents.

❖ Buttons allow users to launch mini-programs called Agents. You can delete Buttons from a Rich Text Field by selecting the Button and choosing **Edit, Clear** from the Notes Client menu. If you receive a Document containing a Button, and you are unsure if you should launch it, holding down the **Ctrl** key and clicking on the Button will cause the Button option to appear in the Notes Client menu. Choosing **Button, Edit Button** from the menu will display the actions the Button is supposed to perform when clicked.

You can copy and paste information in Notes a number of ways:

❖ While reading a Document, you can select a range of information by clicking and dragging the mouse over it and selecting **Edit, Copy** from the main menu to move it to the clipboard.

❖ While editing a Document, you can select a range of information in a single field of the Document by clicking and dragging over it and selecting **Edit, Copy** from the main menu.

Depending on what you've copied while you were reading or editing, you can paste the information into a field of another Notes Document or into other applications (such as a word processor).

From the View level, you can copy and paste entire Documents. You can mark Document for deletion from a Notes database while you are reading them or at the view level. Documents marked for deletion will be removed when you refresh the View that contains the Documents or when you close the database and answer yes to the confirmation dialog box. Once you have deleted a Document from a view, it cannot be recovered. While you are editing a Document, you can only delete information from one field at a time.

# Chapter 7

# Using Plain- and Full-Text Searching to Locate Information

## In this Chapter...

While locating Documents using Views is efficient, there are times when you may want to find Documents that meet special criteria within a View. This is done in Notes using Plain Text and Full Text searching, which we'll cover in this chapter following this outline:

❖ What is plain and full-text searching?
❖ Plain-text searching via the **Edit, Find** command
❖ Full-text searching via the search bar

# What is Plain- and Full-Text Searching?

You're sitting at your desk when the phone rings. You answer, only to find yourself standing in the center ring of the Career Circus. Your boss is trying to print a presentation at the last minute before he flies to the stockholders' meeting and something "isn't right." You wonder why he's calling you instead of Joan, the resident network expert.

"Joan's out of town today," he begins. Your heart sinks. You wanted to be the ringmaster in the Career Circus, but there's the distinct possibility that today you're going to be the tightrope walker (or worse, the clown) instead. As he describes his problem he mentions something you immediately recognize as an opportunity, "I had this problem last week...."

Aha! Joan uses Notes to keep track of all of her customer calls! All you have to do is open the Help Desk database and you're set. You select **View, Calls by Technician** from the Help Desk database. You're going to walk the tightrope to thunderous applause.

Suddenly, reality smacks you in the face with an aluminum skillet. There must a thousand Documents here... how are you going to find the one you need before it's your turn to start talking? (And, just out of curiosity, how does Joan manage to help so many people in a week?)

Fortunately, you've just finished reading a book about Lotus Notes from MIS:Press. You take a calming breath (it says so right in the book). You execute a command from the Notes Client menu. You execute one more command. Bingo! There's the call from last week. You open the Document and read Joan's solution to the boss. He tries it. It works. You say "No problem," as you think to yourself, "So *that's* how Joan helps so many people..."

Wondering what commands made you a star? They were the ones that allow you to perform what Lotus calls *Plain-Text Searching* and *Full-Text Searching*.

## *Plain-Text Searching via the Edit, Find Command*

Plain-text searching is available in any Notes database, and it can be used from a View or in a Document to find words located in any Document's fields. You start a plain-text search by opening a View or a Document, then choosing

**Edit, Find** from the Notes Client menu. This will open the Find dialog box, pictured in Figure 7.1.

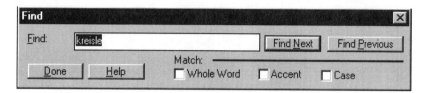

***Figure 7.1*** *The Find dialog box.*

From the Find dialog box:

1. Enter the word or part of a word you want to search for in the Find text box.

2. Select the **Match: Case** check box if you want to find only words or phrases that exactly match the ones you enter.

3. Select the **Match: Accent** check box if you want to search for words that use accented characters (*O* circumflex, *E* umlaut, etc). To specify an accented character, you must enter a special series of keystrokes, which will differ depending on your operating system. The on-line help in Lotus Notes, which you can access by clicking the **Help** button on the Find dialog box, contains more information about entering special characters.

4. Select the **Match: Whole Word** check box if you want to find words of phrases spelled exactly like the ones you enter. If this option is not selected, variants of the word will be included in the search results. For example, if **Match: Whole Word** is not selected, entering *contain* in the Find text box and clicking **Find Next** or **Find Previous** would return *contain, contains, containing, contained,* and so forth.

What you see after clicking the **Find Next**, **Find Previous** button depends on whether you are in a Document or a View. If you are in a Document, the **Find** command takes you to the first occurrence of the value you are searching for, as illustrated in Figure 7.2.

Clicking **Find Next** or **Find Previous** at the View level moves you forward or backward in the view to Documents that contain the text you're searching for (Figure 7.3).

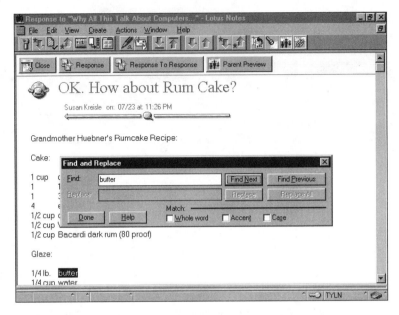

**Figure 7.2** *Executing the **Edit, Fin**d command in a Document.*

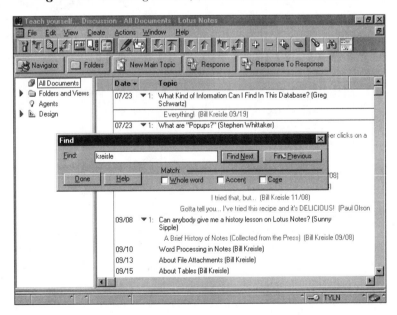

**Figure 7.3** *Executing the **Edit, Find** command in a View.*

# Full-Text Searching via the Search Bar

Full-text searching can be thought of as "industrial strength" searching. You can use full-text searching to locate information in any field of a Notes database by building complex queries from the search bar. Some examples of complex queries are:

- ❖ All Documents containing the word *Trek* but not the word *Star*.
- ❖ All Documents containing *Copy* and *Macintosh* in the same paragraph.
- ❖ All Documents containing the words *Shortcut* and *Key*.

Besides complex queries, full-text searches also support the use of wildcards. Wildcards are placeholders you can use in words or sentences to allow a variety of combinations to be true. The two wildcard characters that Notes supports for full-text searching are *\** and *?*. The asterisk is used to denote any value, any length. The question mark is used to denote any value with a fixed length. What does that mean? Let's look at some examples of wildcard searches:

comp*

This argument will return *computer, compost, compensation, complex*, or any other word beginning with *comp* as a match, no matter how long the word is.

compute?

This argument will return *computes, computed*, or *computer* as a match. The word *computers*, however, would not be returned, as there is only one question mark in the argument. Using *compute??* would return *computers*.

Full-text searching can be performed only on databases that are full-text indexed. A *full-text index* is a collection of files that Notes builds on your local hard drive or a Notes Server for each full-text indexed database. Full-text indexes make searching more powerful, but there's something you'll want to consider before creating one for every database you work with. A full-text index increases the size of a Notes database by a considerable amount. As illustrated by Table 7.1:

**Table 7.1** *Determining How Big a Full-Text Index Will Be*

| Database Size | Percentage text | Index size with word breaks only (50% of text) | Index size with word, sentence, and paragraph breaks (75% of text) |
| --- | --- | --- | --- |
| 8 MB | 75% (6 MB) | 3 MB | 4.5 MB |
| 8 MB | 50% (4 MB) | 2 MB | 3 MB |
| 8 MB | 25% (2 MB) | 1 MB | 1.5 MB |

**NOTE**

With Notes, Release 4, it is possible to perform full-text searches against database that do not have a full-text index created for them, however, this option may not be available depending on how your Notes Network is administered.

If the database is located on a Notes Server, it also increases the amount of work that server has to perform to keep each index up-to-date.

You create a full-text index by selecting a database icon and choosing **File, Database Properties** from the Notes Client menu, and then clicking the **Full Text** tab of the Properties for Database dialog box. Figure 7.4 illustrates the Full Text tab of the Properties for Database dialog box.

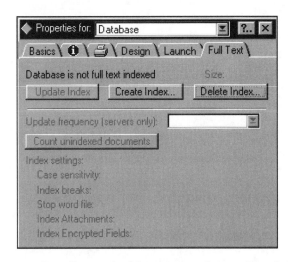

**Figure 7.4** *The Full Text tab of the Properties for Database dialog box.*

**NOTE**

To create a full-text index on a Notes Server you must have Designer Access or greater in the database you are creating it for.

To create a new full-text index, click the **Create Index...** button. To update an existing full-text index, click the **Update Index** button. To delete an existing full-text index, click the **Delete Index...** button.

The **Create Index...** button opens the **Full Text Create Index** dialog box, illustrated in Figure 7.5.

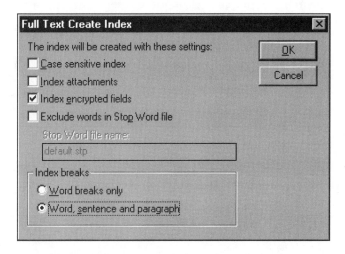

***Figure 7.5*** *The Full Text Create Index dialog box.*

The choices in this dialog box affect the size of the index that is created and determines how full-text searching can be performed later. Referring to Figure 7.5, selecting the **Case Sensitive Index** check box will allow users to base searches on the exact case they entered in a query. This option will increase the size of your index by about 5 to 10 percent.

Selecting the **Index Attachments** check box will allow you and other users to locate documents based on words or phrases contained inside the files attached to them. Obviously, this won't work with every type of attachment (bitmaps, for example). In a database that contains text files or word processing documents as attachments, however, it is very useful. How much this option will increase the size of an index depends on the number of attachments in the database and each attachment's size.

Encrypted fields are rich text fields that Notes scrambles so that only users with a specified identification or password can read them. Selecting **Index Encrypted** fields in this dialog box allows you to search for words or phrases in them.

N O T E

We don't discuss encryption in this book. You can find more information about it in the Notes Help database and the manuals Lotus provides with the Notes software.

Selecting the **Exclude Words in Stop Words File** checkbox will cause Notes to exclude any words listed in the specified stop word file. A *stop word* file is an ASCII list, that can be created using Windows Notepad or almost any text editor. Notes includes a default stop word file called *default.stp*.

N O T E

If you want to create a custom stop word file, consider making a copy of the default.stp file and editing it as opposed to changing the default.stp file directly. This allows you to preserve the defaults that ship with Notes in case you want to refer to them later.

Using a stop word file can decrease the size of a full-text index considerably. Why? Because it excludes common words such as *the*, *of*, *and*, and so forth from an index. However, the trade-off is that words excluded from the index cannot be searched using the Search Bar. For example, if you include the word *of* in your stop word file, you could not search for the phrase *Society of Mind*. Instead, you'd have to search for *Society AND Mind*, where *AND* is a logical operator.

N O T E

The default.stp file includes a line that looks like this:

[0-9]+

This line prevents numbers from being included in the index. If you want to search on numbers and you want to use a stop word file to reduce the size of your index as well, make a custom stop word file or edit the default.stp file and remove this line.

The radio buttons in the Index Breaks group determine whether you can use proximity operators in your searches. A *proximity operator* is used to look for a group of words in close relationship to each other (that is, in the same sentence, or in the same paragraph). Some examples of a query using a proximity operator follow.

Artificial near Intelligence

This query would return all Documents containing the word *Artificial* and the word *Intelligence.* However, Documents where the words are closer together would be given a higher rank in the search.

Artificial sentence Intelligence

This query would return all Documents where the words *Artificial* and *Intelligence* appear in the same sentence.

Artificial paragraph Intelligence

This query would return all Documents where the words *Artificial* and *Intelligence* appeared in the same paragraph.

Selecting the **Words, Sentence, and Paragraph** radio button means that proximity operators can be used. Selecting the **Word Breaks Only** radio button means (you guessed it) proximity operators cannot be used.

Whew! This is starting to sound like a programming language, isn't it? If it does and you're thinking you're not cut out to use full-text indexing, don't give up yet. We have to go through a little awkwardness to get ready to make our first query in the following exercise, but after we get to the part where you actually search for the information, you'll discover that Lotus had done an exceptional job of making a powerful tool very easy to use.

# Taking What We've Learned Step-by-Step

Before we can move into exercises that use full-text searching, we require a database that is full-text indexed. Because Lotus stores all of the on-line help for Notes in a Notes Database, using it in our exercise accomplishes two things:

1. It shows you how to use full-text searching.
2. It gives you glimpse into a wealth of information about Lotus Notes that is contained in the Notes Help database.

## *Step 1*

Locate the help database icon on your Workspace (Figure 7.6).

**Figure 7.6** *The Notes Help database icon.*

If there is not an icon on your workspace, select **Help, Help Topics** from the main menu. This will add the **Help Database** icon to your Workspace and open it to the Index View, as illustrated in Figure 7.7.

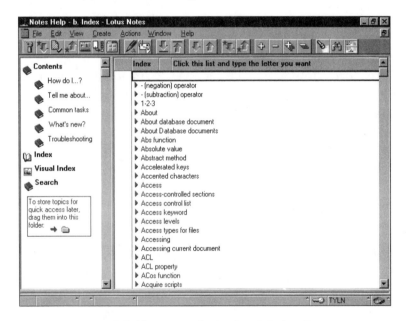

**Figure 7.7** *The Notes Help database's Index View.*

**N O T E** Your copy of Notes may have only the "Lite" version of the Help Database installed. If this is the case, you can still follow along with the exercises, but your screens and results will be slightly different than what I present here.

**N O T E**   As mentioned in Chapter 3, this book was written using beta software. As such, the number of Documents referenced in this exercise and their contents will be different from your results.

## Step 2

Select **File, Database, Properties** from the Notes Client menu (Figure 7.8).

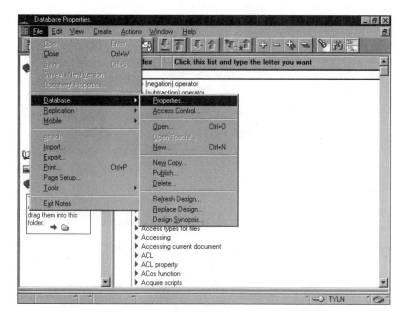

**Figure 7.8** *Creating a full-text index on the Notes Help database.*

## Step 3

Click the **Full Text** tab of the Properties for Database dialog box and click **Create Index...** (Figure 7.9).

Accept the default settings in the Full Text Create Index dialog box by clicking **OK** (Figure 7.10).

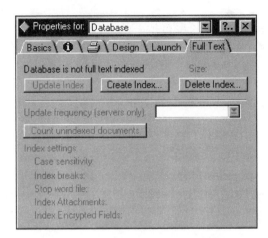

**Figure 7.9** *The Full Text tab of the Properties for Database dialog box.*

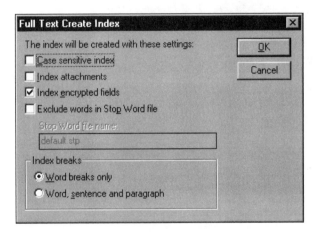

**Figure 7.10** *The Full Text Create Index dialog box.*

If the Notes Help database is on your local hard drive, you will see the message shown in Figure 7.11, to which you should answer **Yes**.

As Notes builds the index, it will display its progress in a window similar to Figure 7.12.

When Notes finishes creating the index, you will see the following dialog box shown in Figure 7.13:

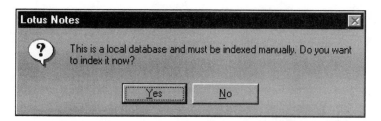

**Figure 7.11** *This dialog box appears when your Notes Help database is on your local drive and you create a full-text index.*

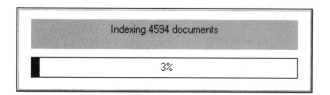

**Figure 7.12** *The progress indicator Notes displays while creating a full-text index.*

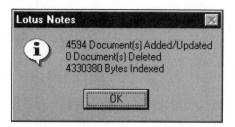

**Figure 7.13** *Notes will provide you with this dialog box after creating a full-text index.*

## Step 4

Once you have indexed the Notes Help database, open it and select the **Search** view from the Navigator or choose **View, c. Search** from the Notes Client menu. Either action will open the Search view.

If the search bar is not visible, click the **Display Search Bar** button at the top of the View, or select **View, Search Bar** from the Notes Client menu to make it active.

***Figure 7.14*** *Opening the c. Search View in the Notes Help database.*

**The Search Bar**

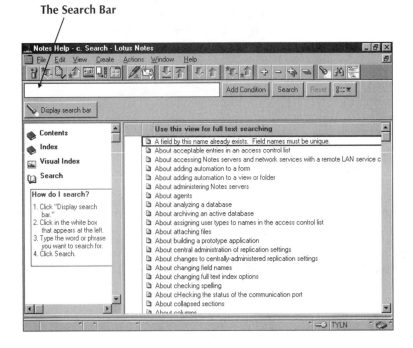

***Figure 7.15*** *The Search view.*

## Step 5

Click **Add Conditions** on the search bar to open the Search Builder dialog box. Make sure the item **Words and Phrases** is selected in the Conditions drop-down list, and the **All** radio button is active. Enter *Full* in text box 1, *Text* in text box 2, *Search* in text box 3, and *Creat\** in text box 4. Click **OK** to close the Search Builder (Figure 7.16).

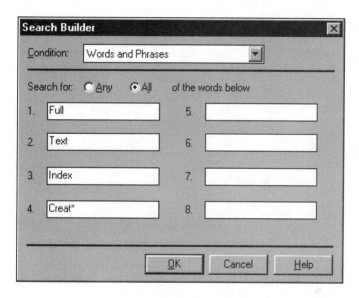

***Figure 7.16*** *The Search Builder dialog box and the values we'll use for this exercise.*

Notice that the values you entered appear in the search bar (Figure 7.17).

***Figure 7.17*** *The values you entered in the Search Builder dialog box are in the search bar.*

To edit the conditions you've entered, select them in the search bar and click the **Edit Conditions** button or double-click them in the search bar.

## Step 6

Click the **Search** button on the search bar, and the documents in the View will display similar to the screen shot in Figure 7.18.

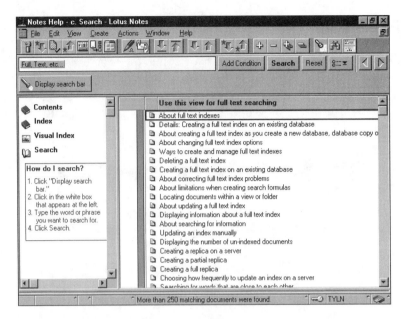

**Figure 7.18** *The results of our query for Documents containing the words Full, Text, Search, and Creat*.*

More than 250 Documents (your number might be different) just like that (sound of snapping fingers).

## Step 7

Double-click the first document in the view and use the **Page up** or **Page down** keys to scroll through the document. Notice that the words you searched for are highlighted in the document by a surrounding box. You can use **Ctrl Grey + (Plus)** to move forward in the Document to each surrounding box in the text, and **Ctrl Grey - (Minus)** to move backward.

## Step 8

To complete the exercise, close the Document and leave the database and the current View open as you read through the next section.

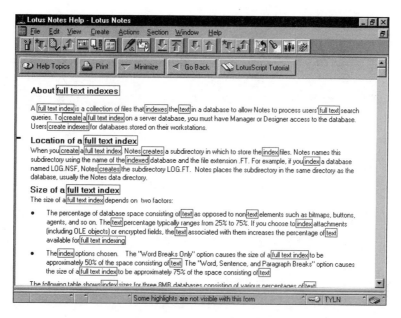

**Figure 7.19** *Words that match the query are highlighted in each document.*

## How the Full-Text Search Results are Displayed

Let's examine the view that Notes created when you executed the full-text search in our step-by-step exercise:

Notice that there's a shaded bar to the left of the Documents in the View. This bar is used by Notes to provide you with a *Relevance Ranking*, which is the result of a formula applied by Notes when you execute a full text search to determine how relevant the document might be to the criteria you've entered for searching.

If you are searching for a single word in Documents that are roughly the same size, ones with more occurrences of the word rank higher than ones with fewer occurrences. Before Notes decides which document is more relevant, however, it considers the length of each Document. A short Document that contains two occurrences of a word you are searching for may rank higher than a much longer Document with three occurrences of a word you are searching for. Once Notes has finished ranking the Documents, it moves the more relevant Documents to the top of the View.

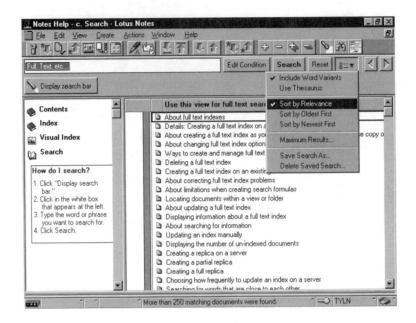

**Figure 7.20** *A view that contains Documents sorted by relevance.*

If you are searching for a group of words, a Document where the words are closer together (in the same sentence, for example) will probably be more relevant than a document where the words are not. In this case, even if the second Document had more occurrences of the words you are looking for, the first Document will have a higher Relevance Ranking.

Since Notes puts the Documents it thinks are most likely to be relevant to your search at the top of the View, you might wonder what the bar to the left of the Documents is for. It is a visual element designed to use shading to help you group Documents.

The Relevance Ranked View is the default View Notes uses when you perform a full-text search. However, there are other ways to View your query results. Using the **Search Options** button on the search bar, you can choose to see the Documents sorted by date in either ascending (oldest first), or descending (newest first) order.

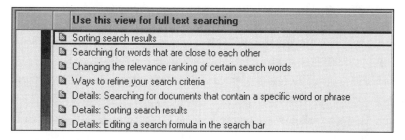

**Figure 7.21** *Notes uses a shaded bar to color-code Documents in a Relevance Ranked View, helping you group them.*

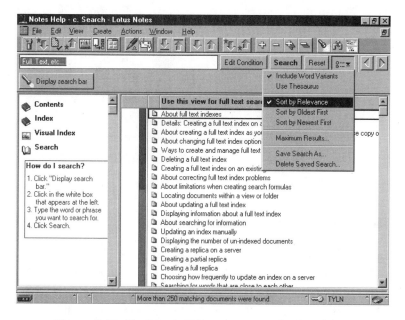

**Figure 7.22** *The Search Options button on the Search bar.*

# Other Search Options

The Search Options button on the search bar also allows you to specify other options Notes should use when executing your query.

When **Include Word Variants** is selected (meaning there is a check mark beside the menu item), your query results will contain not only the exact words you specify but any word variants. This is similar to specifying a wildcard character at the beginning and end of each word or phrase in the query.

When this option is not selected, only the words, phrases, and wildcards you specify will be returned.

When **Use Thesaurus** is selected, your query will return both the words you specified as well as any words with similar meanings. For example, searching on *remove* in the Notes Help database with the Use Thesaurus option active will also return words that contain *delete*, *deleted*, *deleting*, and so on.

Selecting **Maximum Results...** from the Search Options button menu will open a dialog box that allows you to specify the maximum number of Documents you want your query to return to the View. The default value is 250.

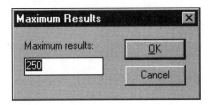

**Figure 7.23** *The Maximum Results dialog box.*

## More Ways to Search

Going back to the Add Conditions button on the search bar for a moment, let's examine a number of other ways Notes gives you to specify the criteria you wish to use for locating Documents.

If you open the Conditions drop-down list on the Search Builder dialog box, you'll notice that **Words and Phrases** is one of many choices you have. These choices include **By Author**, **By Date**, **By Field**, **By Form**, and **By Form Used**.

Selecting **By Author** from the Conditions drop-down list causes the Search Builder dialog box to appear as shown in Figure 7.25.

You can use the drop-down list on this dialog box to specify Contains or Does Not Contain along with one or more Names in the text box below it. Clicking the button to the right of the text box will allow you to enter names using Notes' Name and Address book.

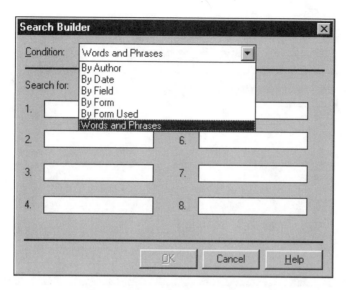

**Figure 7.24** *The Conditions drop-down list on the Search Builder dialog box.*

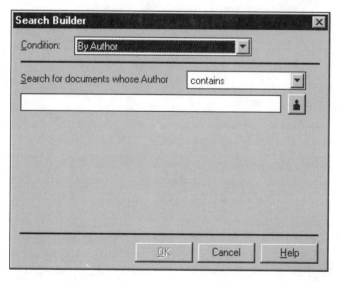

**Figure 7.25** *The Search Builder dialog box using the by Author condition.*

Selecting **By Date** from the Conditions drop-down list causes the Search Builder dialog box to appear as shown in Figure 7.26.

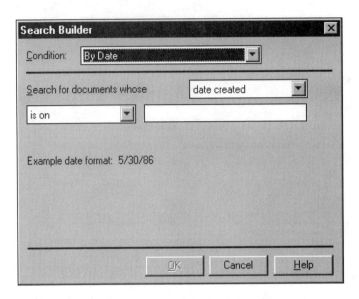

***Figure 7.26*** *The Search Builder dialog box using the By Date condition.*

The first drop-down list in this dialog box allows you to specify whether you are searching based on the date the document was created or the date the document was last modified. The second drop-down list allows you to specify how you want the dates you enter to be compared to the Documents you are seeking (is on, is between, is before, and so on).

Selecting **By Field** from the Conditions drop-down list causes the Search Builder dialog box to appear shown in Figure 7.27.

In this dialog box, the first drop-down list contains all available fields in the database. The second drop-down list allows you to specify what it does or does not contain. The text box lets you enter the value the field should be compared with.

Selecting **By Form** provides you with a drop-down list of Form names that the database's designer has marked for use in queries. Selecting a Form from the drop-down list fills the area below it with a representation of the form. This allows you to perform a query based on a combination of values in different fields (Figure 7.28).

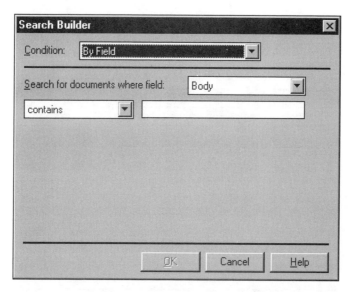

***Figure 7.27*** *The Search Builder dialog box using the By Field condition.*

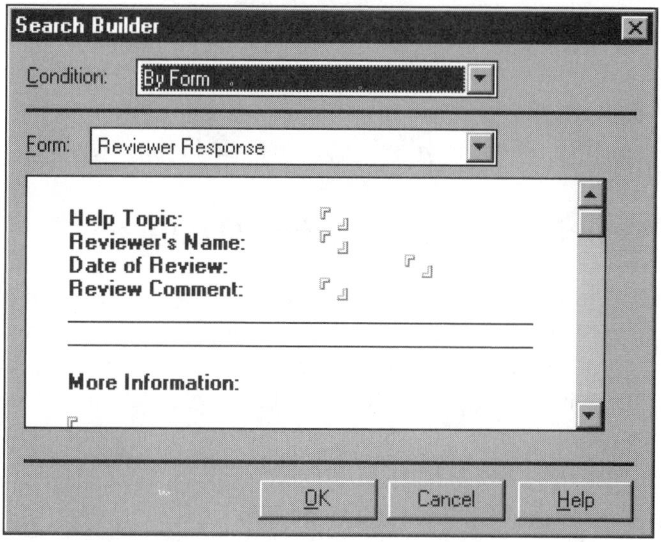

***Figure 7.28*** *The Search Builder dialog box using the By Form condition.*

Selecting **By Form Used** from the Search Builder dialog box causes it to appear as shown in Figure 7.29.

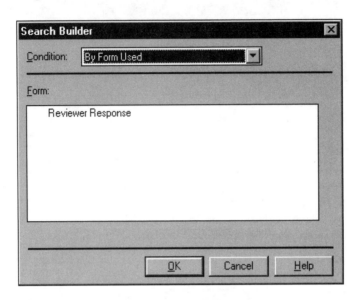

***Figure 7.29*** *The Search Builder dialog box using the By Form Used condition.*

Here, you can restrict your query to Documents that use a specific Form by clicking the name of each Form you want to include in the query.

## Full-Text Searches Across Multiple Databases

You can perform full-text searches in more than one database at a time if all the databases you select are full-text indexed. To begin a full-text search across multiple databases, you must select them by holding down the **Shift** key and clicking on each one with the mouse. After you have selected all of the databases you wish to search, hold down the **Shift** key and double-click one of them.

This will cause the Folders Navigator from each database selected to appear in the Navigator pane, as illustrated in Figure 7.30.

**N O T E**

If you want to follow along on your computer with this section, you will need to create a full-text index for the Teach yourself... Discussion database before continuing. Otherwise, you can use the screen shots to illustrate the concepts for your use later.

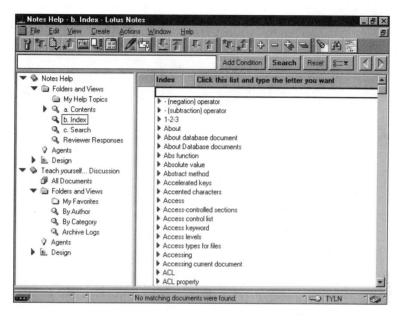

**Figure 7.30** *The Folders Navigator from two databases are combined in the Navigator pane.*

To search the databases, create your query and click **Search**.

**Figure 7.31** *Entering a query by typing directly into the search bar.*

At this point, you might expect to see Grandmother Huebner's rum cake recipe from the Teach yourself... Discussion database appear in the View pane, but if you look at Figure 7.30, you'll notice that we were in the Notes Help Database's Index View when we began the query. So instead, we see the following message in Figure 7.32 in the status bar.

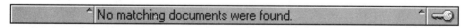

**Figure 7.32** *If you execute a query on a View that does not contain any matching Documents, you will see this message in the status bar of the Notes Client.*

However, if you use the Navigator Pane to change to the Teach yourself... Discussion database's All Documents View, you'll see the results shown in Figure 7.33.

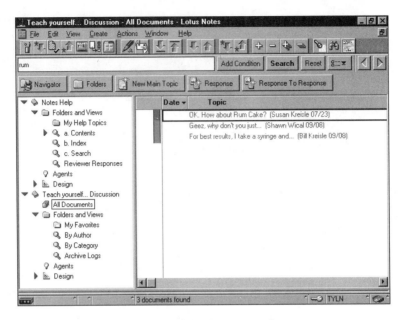

**Figure 7.33** *The results of our query for "rum"*
*against the Teach yourself... Discussion database.*

## Full-Text Search Strategies

As you can see, there are a number of options you can use to locate a specific document in a Notes database. So many, in fact, that Notes has almost made indexing too powerful. To help you get the most out of searching for documents in a database that is full-text indexed, I'd like to offer the following tips:

1.  If you can't think of unique words for a search, string together several common words to help make your search more targeted. If you're look-ing in Notes Help for information about the keys used to delete docu-ments from a view, searching on *deleting* will return more Documents than searching on *deleting AND documents*. You'll narrow the search even more using *deleting AND documents AND (key OR view)*.

2.  Don't be afraid to type your query directly into the text box on the search bar. You can get more powerful results this way. For example, the last query in the tip above couldn't be created using the **Add Condition** button. It combines AND and OR operators and uses paren-theses to group the OR condition. If either condition is met, it is true for

the rest of the search. Also, remember that proximity operators (near, sentence, and paragraph ) are available when you enter queries directly.

3. If you didn't create the index, assume that a stop word file was used when searching for phrases. Break phrases into key words, eliminating words likely to be excluded from the index. For example, if you are looking for *Society of Mind*, search for *Society* or *Mind*, instead.

4. Make a habit of checking to see whether the Word Variants and Thesaurus menu item is checked on the Search Options button before executing a search. If you know exactly what you're looking for, these will return many more documents than you want. If you don't know exactly what you're looking for, these options may make the difference in finding the information you seek.

5. Remember that a full-text search or a plain-text search in a View will query only against the Documents available in the View. If there is a View in the database that will display all Documents, switch to that View before starting your search.

# In Summary

❖ Notes supports two powerful methods for searching a database for specific Documents:

1. Plain-text searching is available in any database and is accessed by opening a View or Document, then selecting the **Edit, Find** command.

2. Full-text searching is only available on databases that have a full-text index created for them, and is executed using the search bar.

❖ A full-text index may be created on any local database, but you must have Designer privileges or higher to create a full-text index on a database that is stored on a Notes Server. Full-text indexes can add 15% to 40% to the overall size of a database.

❖ Full-text indexes support advanced searching operations. You can enter a search request in the current query text box on the search bar, or use the **Add Condition** button to access the Search Builder dialog box.

❖ Plain-text and full-text searching is performed only on the Documents that are available in the current View. It you know of a View in a database that shows all Documents, you should generally switch to that View before executing either type of search.

# Chapter 8

# Replication

## In this Chapter...

Bankers, doctors, lawyers, and even priests are doing it, and nobody who tries it is ever the same again. Are you going to do it, too? I sure hope so. After all, if you don't, you'll miss out on one of the cornerstones on which the foundation of Notes is laid.

What am I talking about? Why, replication, of course. And that's exactly what we'll cover in this chapter.

- ❖ What is replication?
- ❖ What does replication mean to Lotus Notes?
- ❖ Some important replication concepts
- ❖ Creating a new replica
- ❖ Using the Replicator Page on the Workspace
- ❖ More replication concepts

# What is Replication?

Please excuse me while I squirm under extreme pressure. After all, with the build-up I've given replication, it's going to be disappointing if my explanation of what it is misses the mark. OK. Calming breath and here we go: Replication is a process that moves *changes* between files bidirectionally.

Tada! Short, sweet, and completely useless if you don't already know what replication is.

OK, let's try again: Replication consolidates changes made to multiple copies of a file by first comparing them and then merging the most recent actions (such as deletions, edits, or additions) into each copy.

Longer, less sweet, and as cryptic as the instructions printed on the paper sleeve that your chopsticks came in.

One last try: Replication is magic.

You know, I think I like that one. But it can't stand alone—I'll have to give an example to support it. Since I've made reference to a three ring binder and library metaphor about a gazillion times in this book, what should I use as an example this time?

Imagine, if you will, that I have a binder in my library at the company head-quarters that is a collection of executive memos. Across town, at a satellite office building, I have another, smaller library with a copy of the same binder. I add at least one memo to the binder at the headquarters location every day. The librarian at the satellite office adds a memo about once a week. Sometimes I go through the binder at the headquarters library and remove memos older than 90 days. Occasionally, other employees who review the binders at either location add a note with supporting information for a memo or a suggestion regarding a new policy outlined in a memo.

It isn't hard to see that after about a month, the binder I have at the head-quarters location will look nothing like the binder at the satellite office. There are new memos in both binders that aren't at both locations. There are comments made by employees at one office that aren't at the other. Even worse, there are memos that have been removed from one binder that are still con-tained in the binder at the other location. We haven't even talked about the third library in our branch office upstate yet!

Obviously, this isn't what was intended when we decided to create a binder of executive memos—nobody has the same information! How can an employee who comes to the library looking for a memo outlining travel policy be sure he's read everything about travel by just looking at one binder? There might be comments made by the accounting department on the same copy of the memo at another location. Worse yet, maybe there's an outdated memo at one location that's been removed from the others, giving an employee the wrong policies!

The only thing that can fix our problem is to get all three binders together and compare them page by page. If there's a memo in one binder that isn't in the other two, then we need to copy it and put it in the others. If there's a memo that's been removed because it's outdated, we need to make sure it has been removed from all three. If there's a comment about a memo that was made by an employee at one location, that comment should be copied and inserted at the binders at the other two locations.

I call up the other librarians. My binder has about 1,000 pages. The satellite office's binder has about 1,500 (remember, I'm the only location deleting outdated memos). The branch office upstate has about 1,300. After talking on the telephone, we make a time estimate for comparing 3,800 documents and trying to consolidate them so they contain the same information. It will take one full-time employee with a copy machine at least two days. Nobody volunteers. We agree to talk about it more at our weekly meeting the next day.

On the way home, I pass a magic shop. I'm thinking I'll learn a new trick to surprise my three-year old as I walk in. As I'm looking over the list of spells and tricks, I see one called "replication." I read the description. I get really excited, buy the spell, and head home. I leave a message for the other two librarians to be sure to bring their executive memo binders with them to our morning meeting.

The next day, I show the other two librarians the replication spell. They read about it, and become excited, too. We agree to try it and begin reading the directions out loud:

First. Take the two objects that you want to replicate and place them side by side.

Our first snag. We have three objects. What should we do? After some discussion, we decide that we'll just lay the binders out in a straight line, and use the spell on two at a time. We line up the binders as in Figure 8.1.

**Headquarters      Satellite Office      Upstate Office
Binder                  Binder                  Binder**

***Figure 8.1*** *Getting ready to replicate.*

Second.  Place your hand on the first object, and repeat the magic words:

*Of replication, we're desirous,*
*We call upon the help of Iris.*
*To make the replication full,*
*You, little object, must start to pull.*

The satellite office librarian places his hand on the first binder and says the words as instructed.

Third.  Place your hand on the second binder.

Following instructions, he places his hand on the second binder in the row.

Fourth.  Step back.

As he does so, he notices that the headquarters binder and the satellite office binder are shaking slightly.  The headquarters binder bursts open, and the pages start flipping wildly from the first page to the very last.  Next, the satellite office binder bursts open, and it flips from the first page to the last as well.  Suddenly, copies of memos and annotations come flying out of the satellite office binder into the headquarters binder.  Apparently, the spell read both binders, compared what was different between them, and then started pulling copies of the things that were different!

Figure 8.2 illustrates the process.

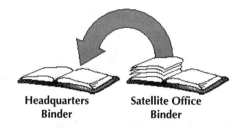

**Headquarters          Satellite Office
Binder                       Binder**

***Figure 8.2***  *The replication process compared both books, then it pulled changes from the Satellite binder into the headquarters binder.*

Next, the spell started pulling things from the headquarters binder into the satellite office binder.  Here's where it got interesting—do you remember how I said that I deleted old memos from the headquarters binder, but the other offices didn't? Well, the replication spell pulled over the deletions I made, too. Pages just started disappearing from the satellite office binder.

As quickly as it started, it was over. Both books slammed shut. The satellite office librarian and I opened our respective binders and compared them...they were exactly the same!

This was powerful magic.

With excitement, we began a replication between the satellite office binder and the upstate office binder. The same thing happened. Both books flew open, the documents were compared, and then changes were pulled from one binder into the other. New documents appeared, deleted documents disappeared, and after the books slammed shut, the satellite office binder and the upstate office binder were exactly the same.

Happily, the satellite office librarian and the upstate office librarian picked up their binders and started for the door. What we thought would take days only took a few minutes! As the other librarians were about to leave, I realized something important and stopped them. They came back, and I compared their binders with mine. They were different. Why?

Because the satellite office binder replicated with the upstate office binder *after* it replicated with the headquarters binder. You see, the satellite binder had all the new information and deletions from the headquarters binder—they replicated first. When the satellite and upstate office binder replicated, the headquarters and satellite office changes were given to the upstate office binder. The upstate office binder passed any additions, deletions, or updates it had back to the satellite office binder. The headquarters binder hasn't replicated with the upstate office binder. It did replicate with the satellite office binder, but that was before the satellite binder's replication with the upstate binder. So, since the headquarters binder hasn't replicated with the upstate binder ever or with the satellite binder since the upstate binders' documents were added, it doesn't know about the changes from the upstate binder.

To solve this problem, the headquarters office binder needs to replicate with either the satellite office binder or the upstate office binder one more time. Once this is done, all three will be the same.

Talk about three happy librarians! All we have to do is bring our binders to the meeting once a week and cast the replication spell and we're set. If only there were some way to get all of our binders to do this automatically without having to remove them from their physical locations...

# What does Replication Mean to Lotus Notes?

Of course, you already know about my leading sentences. The way to have all of those binders replicate automatically is to convert them into Notes databases and to convert the libraries into Notes Servers and Notes Clients. Now, with a modem or network connection, the servers can automatically exchange additions, deletions, edits, and updates.

# Important Replication Concepts

Now that we have a basic idea of how Replication works with Notes, let's refine our understanding by examining some important concepts:

## *Replication IDs*

When the three librarians came together in our story, each had a binder of executive memos that he wanted to synchronize with the others binder. What would have happened if two librarians had brought their executive memo binders and the third one had brought a binder of cookie recipes by mistake? A real (albeit tasty) mess. Recipes would be scattered throughout the two executive memo binders. A user looking for a chocolate chip cookie recipe might wind up with a memo prohibiting the wearing of chicken suits in the office during business hours instead.

Translating that analogy to Notes, what would happen if a user tried to initiate a replication between his mail database and another database containing completely different information? That, too, would be a mess.

Fortunately, Notes has a mechanism that keeps things like this from happening. The mechanism is based on a database's *Replication ID*. A Replication ID is a very long number that is randomly generated whenever a new Notes database is created by a designer. The number is a part of the database that cannot be removed or changed. Whenever a new Replica of a database is created, the Replication ID generated for the first database is stamped on the new Replica as well.

This unique stamping mechanism, combined with the fact that Notes will not allow replication to occur between databases that do not share the same Replica ID, prevents accidents like the ones we described earlier from happening.

To see a Notes database's Replica ID, select it on the Workspace and choose **File**, **Database**, **Properties**... from the Notes Client menu. You can also right click on the database's icon on the Workspace and choose **Properties...** from the pop-up menu that appears. Once the Properties for Database dialog box is opened, click the Information tab (the tab with the lowercase **i** on it).

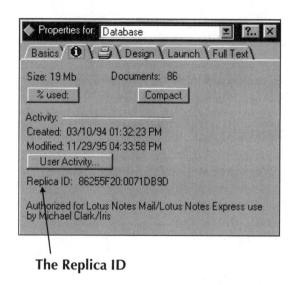

**The Replica ID**

**Figure 8.3** *The Properties for Database dialog box's Information tab will show you a database's Replica ID.*

## Field-Level Replication

A new and important feature in Notes Release 4.0 is called *Field-Level Replication*. Field-level replication allows a Notes Server or Workstation to compare Documents down to the field level, and to move changes only within a field instead of an entire Document. This is useful for a number of reasons, not the least of which is that it allows users who connect by modem to replicate faster.

As an example of how field-level replication works, imagine that I download a piece of shareware from the Internet, and after evaluating it, I want to share it with other people at my company. I create a Document in a Notes database and enter a description of the shareware in a text field along with an attachment (the actual shareware program) in a rich text field.

A couple of days pass. During that time, some people with whom I work who happen to be on the road called in and downloaded the new Notes Document containing the shareware program. About this time, I realize that I forgot to include a piece of important information about the shareware. I open the Document in the Notes database and make a change to the text field that contains the description.

With versions of Notes before Release 4.0, that action would have caused the entire Document I changed to rereplicate to the remote users the next time they called in and initiated a replication. Assuming that the shareware files took up a little over a megabyte, that would mean that in addition to the 15 minutes they spent replicating the Document the first time, they'd have to spend an another 15 minutes downloading the Document again. All that time, just to get one sentence that was added to the text field of the Document.

Of course, even with Notes Release 4.0 the user would still spend the first 15 minutes downloading the Document for the first time. However, the second time, only the text field that changed would be replicated to the user, taking about 15 seconds. That saved the remote user over 14 minutes! Imagine, if you replicate a database that has several small changes made to it regularly how much time you'll save.

## Replication Security

Since the databases are stored on Notes Servers, Notes also brings its security to the databases. For example, if two replicas of a database exist on two separate Notes Servers, it's possible to give one of the Notes Servers reader access only. That means the server with reader access will accept anything added to the other server's database, but it cannot send anything that has been added at its home location.

Why would you want to do that? Well, let's say you maintain a database of technical notes that you want to share with your customers. You want customers to get any up-to-date information you add to the database, and you want to encourage them to add to the database themselves.

However, you don't want Documents that Customer A adds to his database to replicate back to your server, because then those changes would be moved to Customers B, C, D, and so on. By giving the customer's server reader access only, you could enforce this restriction.

## *Selective Replication*

Selective replication allows you to tell a Notes Server to only replicate certain Forms, Folders, or Documents with specific values in their fields to the replicating Notes Server.

As an example of how you might use selective replication, imagine we have a Notes database that contains current events. The database is maintained by the research department. Because the research department's specialty is research, they keep every Document they add to the database in case they need to refer to it again. Other departments, however, would like a replica of the database that has only the most recent events. To solve this problem, the other department's server uses a replication formula to replicate only Documents that were added in the last 15 days. This accomplishes two things:

1. It reduces the size of the current events database on all the other servers in the company.

2. It gives the customers a small, easy to navigate database that won't overwhelm anyone dropping into it to catch up on the industry.

# Creating a New Replica

So, with what replication is, how Notes uses replication, and a discussion of some important replication concepts under our belts, it's time for you to decide: are you ready to replicate?

If you said yes, congratulations! Before you begin, however, you'll need the participation of a consenting Notes Server. If you're working remotely, you'll also need to know how to connect from your location to a Notes Server. We'll discuss remote connections in Chapter 10. But, even with Chapter 10's help, you won't be able to connect alone—you'll need your Notes Administrator to get it working completely.

 Remember that I don't know which databases you have on your Notes Server, so I can't present you screen shots that will look exactly like yours.

NOTE

NOTE

If you've been working on a copy of the Notes Client that isn't set up to connect to a Notes Server at all, you'll be able to do some of the things listed here. For other steps, however, you'll just have to read along and live vicariously through the examples.

The first things we need are two databases that share the same Replica ID or two replicas. You can make a replica of any database to which you have Reader Access. If you make a replica of a database that you have only Reader Access to, remember that you won't be able to send any edits, additions, or deletions back to the server. You will just replicate to receive new information from the server's copy of the database. If you want your changes to be sent back to the server, you must choose a database in which you have Author Access or greater. We discussed how to determine your level of access to a database in Chapter 5.

You can create a new replica of a database by selecting File, Replication, New Replica...from the main menu. If no database is currently selected on the Workspace, you will be prompted to select which database to be replicated using the Choose Database dialog.

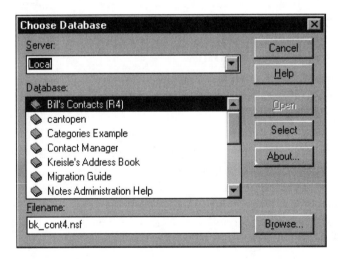

***Figure 8.4*** *The Choose Database dialog box*

You use the Choose Database dialog box in the same way you used the Open Database dialog box in Chapter 3. After you have selected the database to be replaced, you will then see the New Replica dialog box.

**Figure 8.5** *The New Replica dialog box.*

**N O T E**

If you have a database selected on the Workspace when you choose **Replication, New Replica** from the Notes Client menu, you will see this dialog first instead of the Choose Database dialog box in Figure 8.4.

You use the New Replica dialog box to provide Notes with information about the database you are about to create. In the Server drop-down list, you select the name of the Notes Server where you want the new replica you are making to go. If you are making a replica on your local hard drive, enter Local. In the Title text box, you can enter what you want displayed with the database's icon on the Workspace. The Filename text box allows you to select what file name you want the Operating System to use for this database.

Clicking the **Encryption...** button allows you to apply local encryption to the new replica you create (See Figure 8.6). Local encryption uses your *Notes ID* to "scramble" the contents of a database so that only you can open it. This feature is designed to allow you to protect sensitive information on your local drive such as your electronic mail, or a database containing sales figures.

You can choose between no local encryption or encryption using the radio buttons on the Encryption dialog boxes. If you select to enable encryption, you can then choose between Simple, Medium, or Strong encryption levels.

The differences between these encryption levels are explained in the information area at the bottom of the Encryption dialog box, and in Table 8.1.

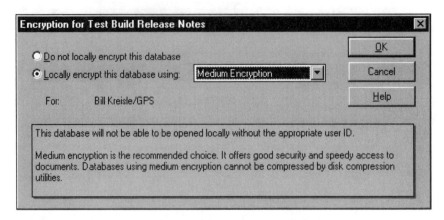

***Figure 8.6*** *The Encryption dialog box.*

***Table 8.1*** *Differences between Local Encryption Methods*

| *Local Encryption Method* | *Description* |
|---|---|
| Simple | Provides limited access from casual snooping. |
| | Offers the fastest access times for encrypted databases. |
| | Can be compressed using your operating system's disk compression utilities. |
| Medium | The choice Lotus recommends. |
| | Good security and Document access times. |
| | Cannot be compressed using disk compression utilities. |
| Strong | Should be used when security is the primary concern. |
| | Documents take longer to open than Medium or Simple Encryption. |
| | Cannot be compressed using disk compression utilities. |

**WARNING**

Once you have encrypted a database, you cannot "decrypt" it, and you can open it only if you have the same Notes ID file you used to encrypt it originally. If your Notes ID becomes corrupt, you will not be able to open a database encrypted by that ID ever again unless you have a backup copy of the ID.

Clicking **OK** or **Cancel** on the Encryption dialog will return you to the New Replica dialog.

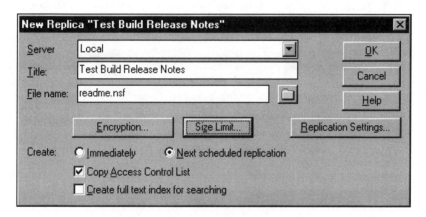

***Figure 8.7*** *The New Replica dialog box.*

Clicking the **Size Limit...** button allows you to set the maximum size you want the new replica to occupy on the disk of the server you specified in the Server text box (Figure 8.8).

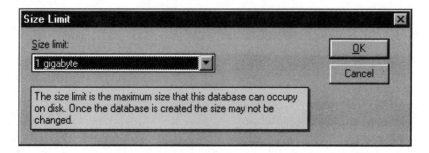

***Figure 8.8*** *The Size Limit dialog box.*

As your choices in the size limit drop-down list are 1, 2, 3, and 4 GB, you will most likely use this option only if you are creating a New Replica on a Notes Server instead of your local drive.

**WARNING**

Once you have selected a size limit for your database, you cannot change it. You will have to create a new Replica.

As with the Encryption dialog box, clicking **OK** or **Cancel** returns you to the New Replica dialog box (Figure 8.9).

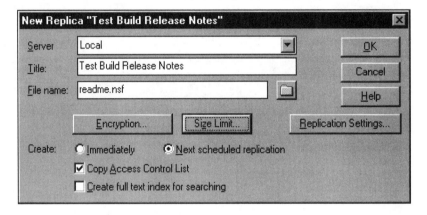

***Figure 8.9*** *The New Replica dialog box.*

The Create radio buttons on this dialog determine whether the new replica will be created as soon as you click the OK button on the Replica dialog box, or if the database will be replicated on the next scheduled replication between the replica's destination and the server you are creating the replica from.

If you choose the **Next scheduled replication** radio button and click **OK**, you will see an Icon on your workspace for the new replica, but if you attempt to open it, you will see the message in Figure 8.10.

What this message is telling you is that the database is currently a *Replica Stub*. A Replica Stub is like a place holder for Notes. It lets it know that at the next scheduled replication event, it should copy the contents of the original replica over to the stub, thereby initializing the new replica.

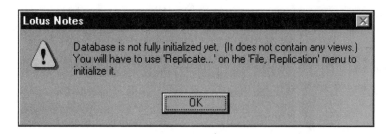

**Figure 8.10** *This message means that the database is a Replica Stub.*

Marking the Copy Access Control List checkbox allows you to use the ACL of the database you are replicating from as the ACL of your new database. Marking the Create Full Text index for searching checkbox will index your new replica after it is created using Notes' default settings.

Finally, clicking the **Replication Settings...** button on the New Replica dialog box allows you to fine tune how replication between your new replica and replicas of the database on any other server act (Figure 8.11).

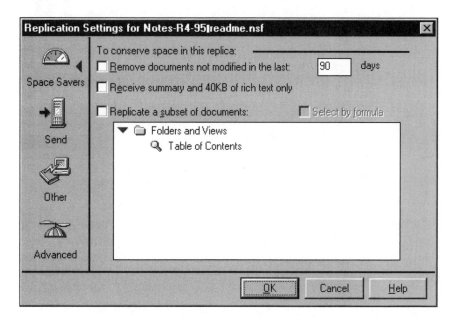

**Figure 8.11** *The Replication Settings dialog box.*

This dialog box is actually several combined into one. Clicking on the icons in the leftmost column of the dialog box will cause new fields to appear in the area to the right.

Selecting the first icon, Space Savers, allows you adjust how Documents replicate to conserve disk space on your local drive (Figure 8.12).

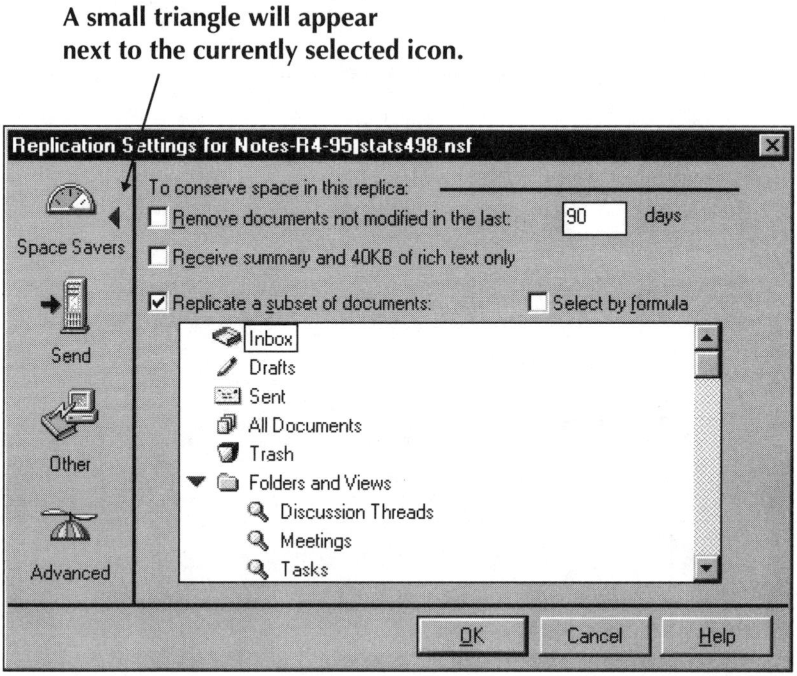

**A small triangle will appear next to the currently selected icon.**

*Figure 8.12 The Space Saver icon and options in the Replication Settings dialog box.*

Checking the Remove Documents not modified in the last ___ days checkbox will only allow Documents that are newer than the value you enter in the days text box to replicate.

If this option is used with Notes databases that incorporate Response Documents, be aware that some Responses may fall within the date range you specify while their parent Documents will not. The result will be "orphaned" Documents, Responses not associated with any parent. These Documents may not be visible in all Views of the database.

Selecting the Receive summary and 40 KB of rich text only check box will keep you from replicating large attachments, or extremely large rich text fields.

**NOTE**

If, after replicating a Document in which a rich text field is truncated by this option, you decide you want to retrieve the full Document, you can do so using the Actions—Retrieve Entire Document command on the Notes Client menu. (This option will be available only with shortened Documents; it does not appear on one that is fully replicated.)

Selecting the Replicate a Subset of Documents checkbox allows you to employ what we referred to earlier as "Selective Replication." As an example, a user who has Notes installed on her computer at home wants to be able to check her mail by dialing into a Notes Server and replicating her mail database. She has a limited amount of space on her home PC, however, so she'd like to replicate only Documents that are in her Inbox.

To do this, she creates a new replica, opens the Replication Settings dialog box, selects the Space Savers icon, marks the Replicate a subset of documents check box, and then clicks only the Inbox folder in the Folders Navigator (Figure 8.13).

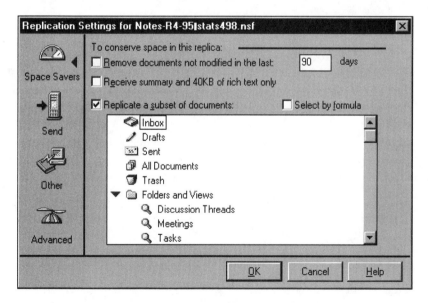

***Figure 8.13*** *Using the Replicate a subset of documents checkbox from the Replication Settings dialog box.*

You can select multiple Folders and Views by clicking on each one you wish to have replicated (Figure 8.14).

**The Views and Folders that are surrounded by a border are the ones that will be replicated.**

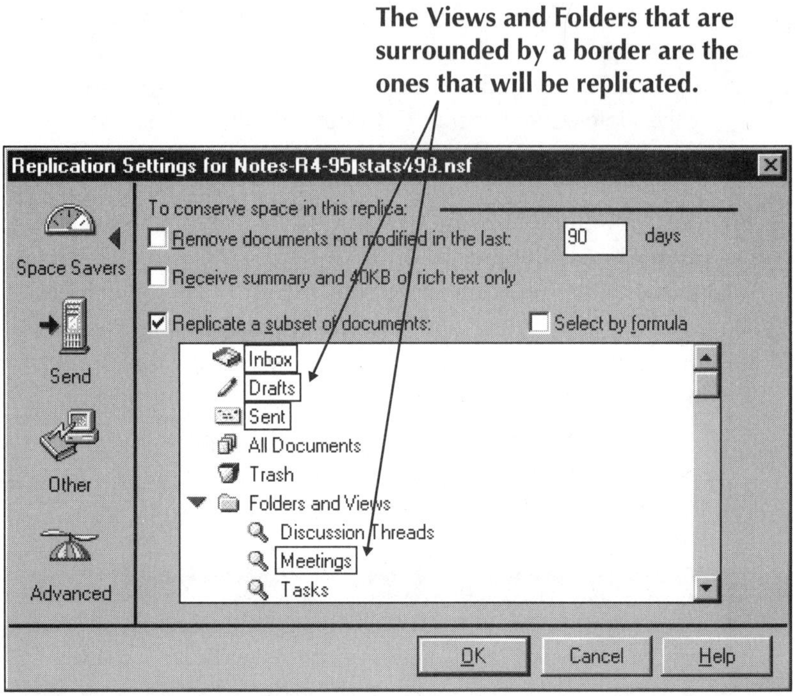

***Figure 8.14*** *You can replicate more than one Folder or View using selective replication.*

If you are experienced with writing Actions in Notes, you can choose to filter Documents that are replicated using the Replicate a Subset of Documents checkbox by activating the Select by Formula checkbox as well. This will cause the area below the check boxes to change to a formula entry window (Figure 8.15).

We aren't going to discuss this option in detail, as it would require another book's worth of information on Lotus' @Function language, which we discussed briefly in Chapter 6.

Selecting the Send icon on the Replication Settings dialog box allows you to control what information is sent to other replicas of your new database once it is created and initialized. (Figure 8.16)

The Do Not Send Deletions Made in this Replica to Other Replicas check box allows you to control whether or not Documents you delete in your new Replica will be removed from any other replicas of the database.

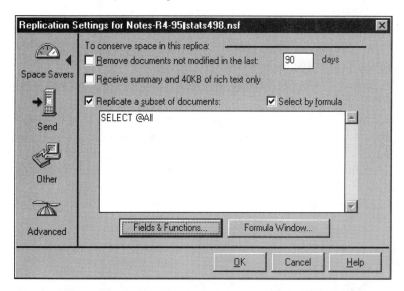

**Figure 8.15** *Using the Select by Formula checkbox.*

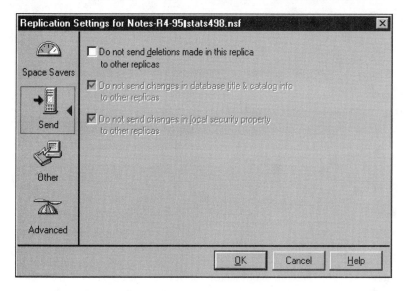

**Figure 8.16** *The Send icon and its options on the Replication Settings dialog box.*

The Do Not Send Changes in Database Title & Catalog Info to Other Replicas check box allows you to change the text that appears on the Workspace for this database without having those changes replicate to other Servers or users.

The Do Not Send Changes in Local Security Property to Other Replicas check box allows you to control whether or not changes made in the Access Control List to enforce local security can be replicated to other Servers. *Local security* means that even on a workstation, the level of access granted to a user is in effect.

**NOTE** Some of these options may be grayed out if you are following along with this section on a Notes workstation. They are set that way in the database which you are replicating from and, therefore, cannot be changed.

Selecting the Other icon from the Replication Settings dialog box allows you to set the replication priority of your databases, disable replication, or use control replication using dates (Figure 8.17).

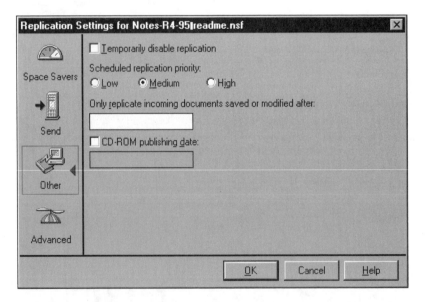

***Figure 8.17*** *The Other icon and its options in the Replication Settings dialog box.*

Marking the Temporarily Disable Replication check box will prevent any user or Notes Server from performing replication with this database. The High,

Medium, and Low Replication priority radio buttons are for use with scheduled replications.

Entering a value in the Only Replicate Incoming Documents Saved or Modified After text box allows you replicate only recent Documents. Checking the CD-ROM Publishing Date checkbox enables the text field below it. This field is for marking the date that a database is moved to CD-ROM for mass distribution. When users copy the database from the CD to replicate, they will replicate only Documents added after the publishing date.

Finally, clicking on the Propeller Head icon in the Replication Settings dialog box allows you to create extremely granular replication guidelines.

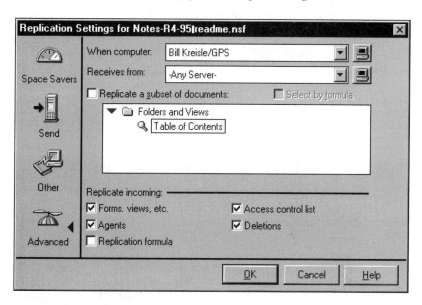

***Figure 8.18*** *The Propeller Head icon and its options in the Replication Settings dialog box.*

In this dialog box, you will see the option to replicate only specific Folders or Views. This is similar to the option we discussed in the section on Space Savers with the exception of the two drop-down lists above it called "When computer", and "Receives from." With these settings, you can control what is replicated between Notes Servers or between Notes Users and Servers.

Here's an example: A user maintains a database of sales leads for a company with five offices worldwide. Each office has a Notes Server. After the user enters a lead, he drags it to one of the Folders in the contact database for each office. In the Propeller Head settings box of the Replication Settings dialog box, he sets it up so that each office only replicates the folder with their leads in it.

Finally, in the Replicate Incoming section of the Propeller Head dialog box, you can control which database design elements are replicated into your database from other replicas.

Checking Forms and Views allows changes made to those design elements or newly created elements to be replicated to your database.

Checking Agents allows changes made to existing Agents or new Agents added in other replicas to be replicated to your database.

Checking Replication Formula allows changes to the Propeller Head settings or new Propeller Head settings to be replicated to your database.

Checking Access Control List allows changes made in the ACL in other replicas of your database to be replicated into yours.

Checking Deletions allows Documents deleted from other replicas of your database to be removed from yours as well.

## Replication Tips

Wow! There are a lot of Replication options to consider! But the good news is that unless you're a database administrator you don't have to worry about a lot of them. The important keys for the casual replicator to remember are:

1. You can replicate only databases that share the same Replica ID.

2. Replication can happen only between a Notes Client and a Notes Server or between two Notes Servers. Two Notes Clients cannot replicate directly with each other.

3. The Access Control List in the database you are replicating with governs whether or not you can send new Documents from your database replica to other replicas. The Access Control List in your database determines what can be sent to you from other replicas.

4. The Space Savers settings are a powerful new addition to Notes as of Release 4. Replicating selected Folders and Views gives you a great deal of flexibility in managing the space on your local hard drive.

5. You can use a lot of different settings when replicating. If a replication doesn't work the way you expect it to, check the settings on *both replicas* involved in the process to see if any of them are the cause for the behavior you are seeing.

# Taking what We've Learned Step-by-Step (Exercise 8.1)

In this example, I'm going to make a local replica of the Teach Yourself... Discussion database that is located on the Notes Server Notes-R4-95/Catalyst/US. To conserve space, I'm going to replicate only the My Favorites folder to my local replica.

## *Step 1*

To begin, I'm going to add an icon to my Workspace for the Teach Yourself... Discussion database on Notes-R4-95 (Figure 8.19).

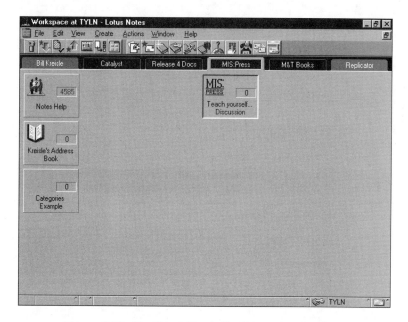

***Figure 8.19*** *The Teach Yourself... Discussion database.*

To be sure that the icon on my Workspace is from the Notes-R4-95 Notes Server, I will select **View, Show Server Names** from the Notes Client menu (Figure 8.20). This will add the name of the server each database is located on to its icon on the Workspace.

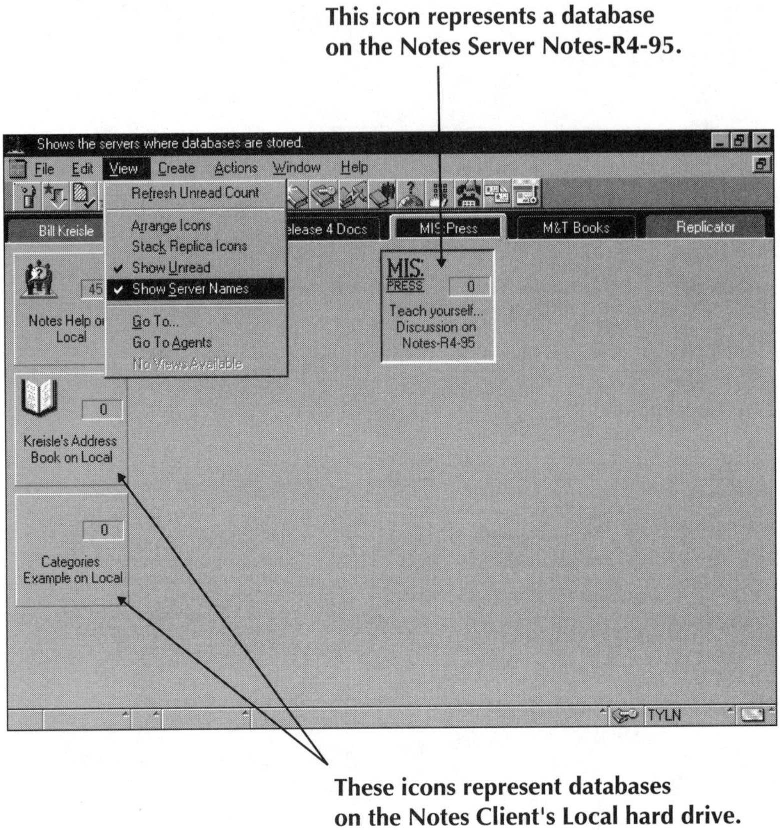

**This icon represents a database
on the Notes Server Notes-R4-95.**

**These icons represent databases
on the Notes Client's Local hard drive.**

***Figure 8.20*** *The **View, Show Server Names** command.*

## Step 2

After selecting the Teach Yourself... Discussion database's icon on the Workspace, I will choose **File, Replication, New Replica** from the Notes Client menu. Since I want the new replica to be on my Notes Client's hard drive, I will choose Local for the Server, and keep the same Title and File name information (Figure 8.21).

Since I only want the Documents in the My Favorites Folder to replicate to my local replica, I must click Replication Settings on the New Replica dialog box, check the Replicate a subset of Documents check box, and select the My Favorites Folder in the area beneath the check box (Figure 8.23).

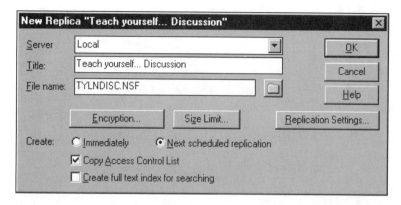

**Figure 8.21** *Creating a New Replica of the Teach Yourself... Discussion database.*

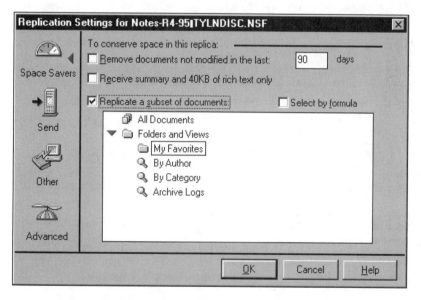

**Figure 8.22** *Using the Replication Settings dialog box to replicate the contents of the My Favorites Folder only.*

## Step 3

After closing the Replication Settings dialog box, I will select the Immediately radio button in the Create group so that my database Replica is created as soon as I click the OK button on the New Replica dialog (Figure 8.23).

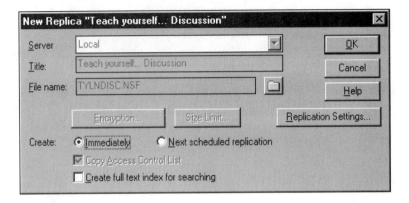

*Figure 8.23* *Selecting* **Create: Immediately** *will cause the new database to be created as soon as the OK button is clicked on the New Replica dialog box.*

## Step 4

The message "Background replication request submitted (check Workspace Replicator Page for status)" appears on the Notes Client status bar (Figure 8.24).

> Background replication request submitted (check Workspace

*Figure 8.24* *The status bar's message.*

Clicking on the Replication Workspace page shows that the replication is in progress (Figure 8.25).

After the new replica is created, there will be two icons for the Teach Yourself... Discussion database on the Workspace page (Figure 8.26).

## Step 5

As a final step, I will verify that the two database icons on the Workspace are replicas using two different methods.

First, I will compare Replica IDs by right-clicking on each database and selecting **Database Properties** from the pop-up menu. Comparing the Replica ID on the Information tab of the Properties for Database dialog box should show them to be the same ID (Figure 8.27).

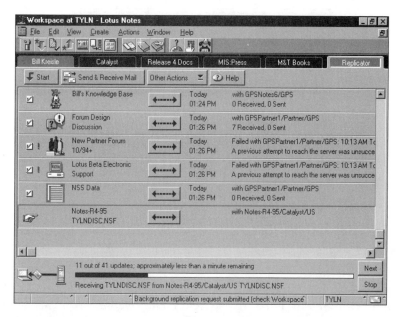

***Figure 8.25*** *The area at the bottom of the Workspace's Replication*
*page will provide information on replications in progress.*

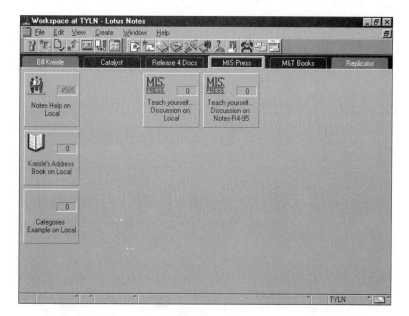

***Figure 8.26*** *An icon for the Teach Yourself... Discussion*
*database on the Local hard drive will be added to the Workspace.*

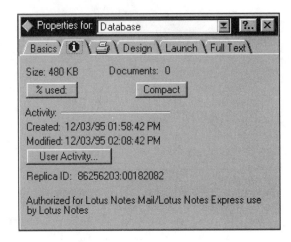

**Figure 8.27** *Examining the Replica IDs of the Teach Yourself... Discussion databases.*

A second way to confirm that the two databases are replicas is to select **View, Stack Replica Icons** from the Notes Client menu (Figure 8.28). This will cause the icons for all databases that share a Replica ID to be "stacked" on top of each other on the Workspace.

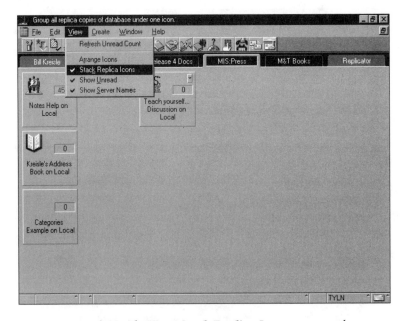

**Figure 8.28** *The **View, Stack Replica Icons** command.*

Any databases that have stacked icons will have a small button in the upper right corner of their icons (Figure 8.29).

***Figure 8.29*** *The small button in the upper right corner of this database's icon indicates that it represents more than one database.*

Clicking this button will open a pop-up menu with a list of all of the locations this database can be opened from. (Figure 8.30)

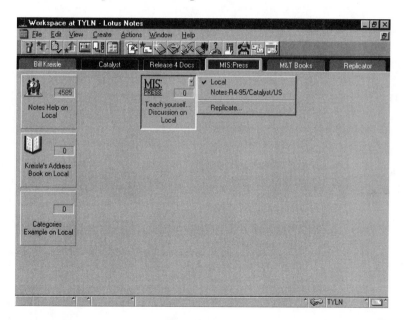

***Figure 8.30*** *To select between different databases using a stacked icon, click the button in the upper right of the icon and select the server from the pop-up menu.*

## Step 6

To complete the exercise, I'm going to open the new Teach Yourself... Discussion database on my local hard drive, and examine the All Documents View and the My Favorites Folder (Figure 8.31)

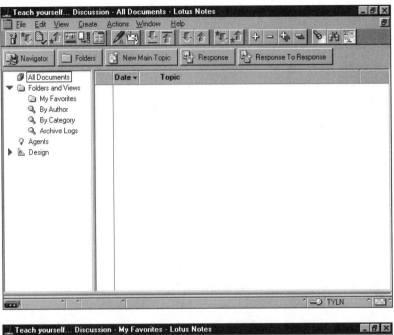

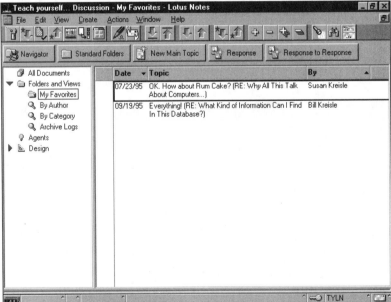

***Figure 8.31*** *The All Documents View and the My Favorites Folder of the new replica.*

As you can see, the contents of the My Favorites Folder was replicated to the local database, but all of the other Documents were not.

## Using the Replicator Page on the Workspace

In Exercise 8.1, we created a new replica of a database on our local drive. That replication gave us all of the information in the database we requested, so for the moment, our replica is up to date. However, over time new items will be added to the database on the Server, and we may want to add new items to our replica. To keep the replicas up-to-date, we'll need to perform regular replications between them in the future. The Replicator Page on the Workspace is a tool specially designed to help us with this task (Figure 8.32).

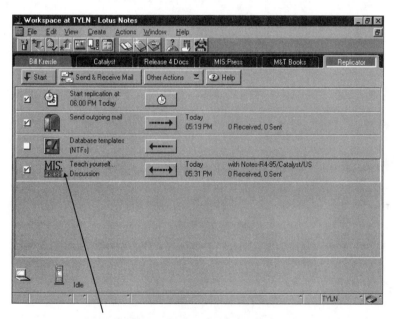

**Instead of representing databases as icons,
the Replicator page represents each database**

***Figure 8.32*** *The Replicator Page of the Workspace.*

As you can see, the Replicator page has a number of features not found on any of the other Workspace Pages. You'll also notice that databases are not represented by icons, but rather panels in the scrolling window at the center of the Replicator Page.

You can add a database panel to the Replicator Page by clicking and dragging it from the page it is currently on to the tab labeled Replicator. You can remove database panels on the Replicator Page by selecting them and pressing the delete key.

**N O T E** When you drag an icon from another Workspace Page to the Replicator Page, Notes will create a new panel for the database in the Replicator Scrolling Window. It will not, however, remove the database icon from the original page as it does when you drag an icon from one Workspace Page to any other Workspace Page.

The main purpose of the Replicator Page is to give you a centralized place to manage common replication tasks such as replicating new mail or telling Notes to deliver your outgoing mail if you are working remotely.

The Start button at the top of the Replicator Page will cause Notes to try to perform replications on all of the currently selected database panels (Figure 8.33). You use the checkbox at the left of each panel to select or deselect them.

**The Start Button**

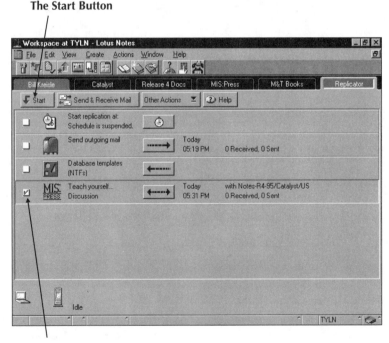

**Panels that are checked will replicate**

***Figure 8.33*** *The Start button and selected panels on the Replicator Page.*

The Send and Receive Mail button on the Replicator Page will replicate your Notes Mail database with your local replica and deliver outgoing messages to the Notes Server specified in your location setup.

The Other Actions button opens a drop down menu.

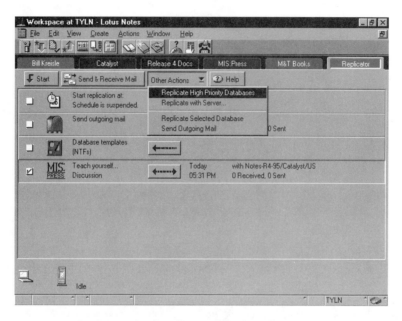

**Figure 8.34** *The Other Actions drop-down menu.*

Selecting **Replicate High Priority** databases will cause Notes to initiate a replication between all databases on the Replicator Page that are marked high priority and their respective Notes Servers. High-priority databases on the Replicator Page have a small exclamation point to the left of the database's panel. (Figure 8.35)

**Figure 8.35** *High Priority databases on the Replicator Page are marked with an exclamation point.*

As you may recall from earlier in this chapter, you can set a database's replication priority by opening the Replication Settings dialog box, selecting the Other icon, and selecting the High, Medium, or Low priority radio button.

You can also make a database a high priority database by right click-ing on the database's panel in the Replicator Page and selecting High Priority from the pop-up menu.

**SHORTCUT**

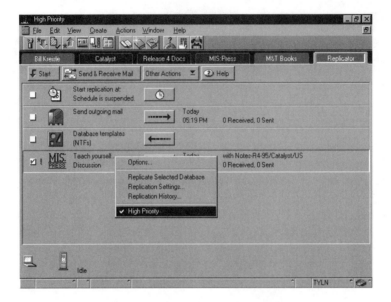

***Figure 8.36*** *Using the right-click pop-up menu to mark a database as high priority*

Selecting **Replicate with Server...** from the Other Actions button on the Replicator Page will cause Notes to initiate a replication between the server you select and all of the databases on the Replicator Page that have a replica on the specified server.

Selecting **Replicate Selected Database** from the Other Actions button on the Replicator Pages causes Notes to attempt to replicate the database currently highlighted with its Notes Server.

You can also use the right-mouse click pop-up menu on a database to initiate the replicate selected database command.

**SHORTCUT**

Clicking the **Send Outgoing Mail...** button on the Replicator Page causes Notes to attempt to deliver any mail it is holding with the server specified in the cur-rent location. We'll discuss locations in greater detail in Chapter 11.

In addition to the buttons at the top of the Replicator Page, there are also buttons on each database panel represented by arrows that point left, right, or in both directions. This button indicates whether or not the currently selected database is set to send Documents to the server, receive Documents from the server, or send and receive Documents whenever it replicates.

You can change these setting by clicking on the button and making changes to the Database dialog box (Figure 8.37).

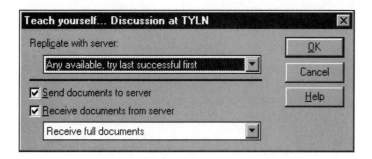

**Figure 8.37** *The Database dialog box.*

You can also use this dialog box to set the selected database to replicate with a specific server using the Replicate with server drop-down list and to replicate only summary information and the first 40 K of rich text using the drop-down list at the bottom of the dialog box.

## Taking What We've Learned Step-by-Step (Exercise 8.2)

In this exercise, I'm going to use the Replicator Page of the Workspace to replicate changes to the Teach Yourself... Discussion database from the Server Notes-R4-95/Catalyst/US to our local replica. You'll notice I didn't say "we're" going to use the Replicator Page. That's because there's no way for me to give you precise step-by-step instructions to replicate the database you used in the previous example. (I don't know what it is, for starters.) For this example, I'd like you to follow through the steps completely before trying to duplicate them on whatever database you've chosen to work with at your location. Obviously, you'll need to make some adjustments.

## *Step 1*

To prepare for this exercise, I added two new Documents to the Teach Yourself... Discussion database on the Notes-R4-95/Catalyst/US Notes Server (Figure 8.38).

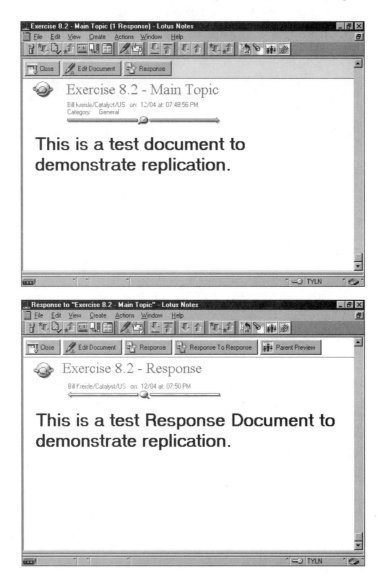

**Figure 8.38** *Adding two new Documents to the Teach Yourself... Database on Notes-R4-95/Catalyst/US.*

After adding the two new Documents, I moved one of the Documents (Exercise 8.2—Main Topic) to the My Favorites folder.

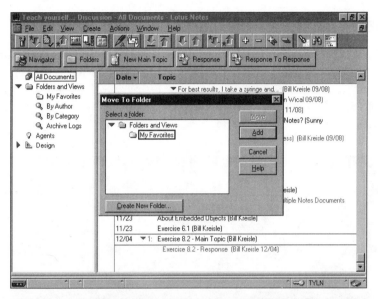

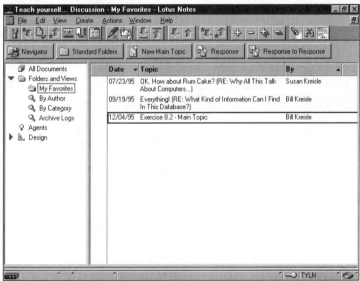

***Figure 8.39*** *Moving one of the new Documents to the My Favorites folder.*

Since the local replica I created is set only to replicate Documents in the My Favorites folder, I'm expecting only one of the two Documents I added to the database on the Notes Server to be added to it.

## Step 2

Next, I will click on the Replicator page and select the Teach Yourself... Discussion database's panel. The panel was added to the Replicator page automatically when I created the new replica in Exercise 8.1. If the database panel were not there, I could add it by clicking on the icon for my local replica on the workspace and dragging it to the Replicator page (Figure 8.40).

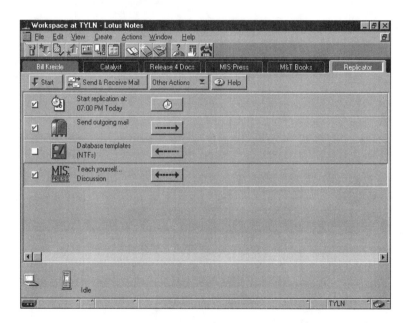

**Figure 8.40** *The Teach Yourself... Discussion panel on the Replicator Page of the Workspace.*

I will click on the Replication Options button (the arrows) to see what the current settings for this database are (Figure 8.41).

After examining the settings, I will close the Database dialog box and right-click on the Teach Yourself... Discussion's database panel and choose **Replicate Selected Database** from the pop-up menu (Figure 8.42).

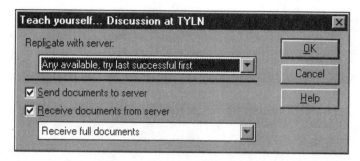

**Figure 8.41** *The Database dialog box.*

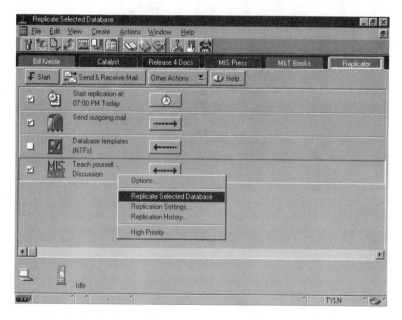

**Figure 8.42** *Using the Replicate Selected Database command.*

If I am connected to the server using a local area network, Notes will establish a network connection between my Notes Client and the needed server. If my replica is of a database on a server I connect with via modem, Notes will examine the location settings and determine how to contact that server. Once a connection is established, replication will begin, and I will see the progress of the replication in the status area at the bottom of the Replicator Page (Figure 8.43).

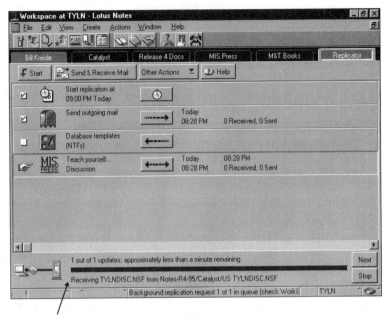

**The Status Area of the Replicator Page.**

***Figure 8.43*** *Ongoing status about a replication is displayed in this area.*

After the replication is complete, you will see information about it in the database panel on the right side of the panel. As you can see, even though we added two Documents to the discussion database, only one Document (the one we moved to the My Favorites folder) was replicated (Figure 8.44).

## Step 3

Just to be sure I have the right Document, I'm going to open my local replica of the Teach Yourself... Discussion database and check the My Favorites folder (Figures 8.45a and 8.45b).And there we have it. Replication in three steps, two of which were added just to demonstrate replication. The last one was extended to cover all of the features. It's really that simple.

**SHORTCUT**

And, if you're using stacked icons, another simple way to initiate a replication between a local database and a Notes Server is to click the button on the stacked icon and select **Replicate...** from the pop-up menu (Figure 8.46).

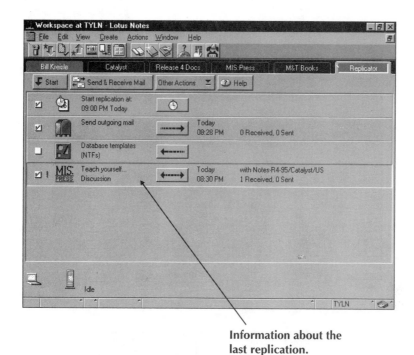

**Information about the last replication.**

***Figure 8.44*** *The right side of the database panel displays information about the last replication.*

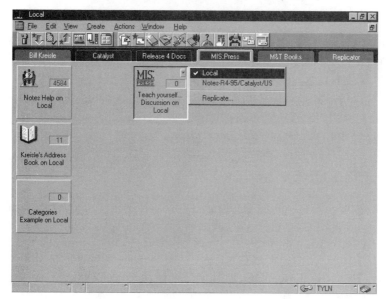

***Figure 8.45a*** *Selecting the local replica.*

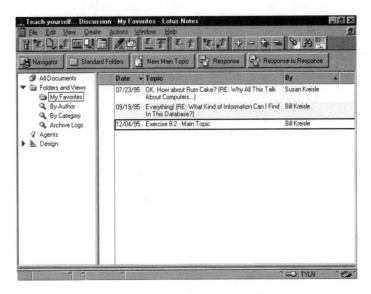

**Figure 8.45b** *The new Document has been added to the database.*

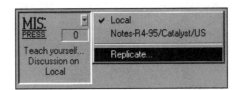

**Figure 8.46** *Using the* **Replicate...** *command on a stacked icon.*

# More Replication Concepts

Congratulations! You have successfully replicated! And just like the story at the beginning of this chapter, it was magic, wasn't it?

## Replication Histories

Just as our original magic spell flipped through every page of both binders, Notes flipped through every Document in each database, building a *replication history*. A replication history is a special index Notes keeps that contains a unique signature for each Document in a database along with the time the Document was added, deleted, or edited. Notes compares Document signatures and the date the last action was performed on a Document to determine whether a change is needed in one of the replicas. In our example, after reading both databases and comparing their replication histories, Notes was able to determine that both of the Documents we added to the database on the Server were new. Then, using the replication settings of the local replica, it decided that of the two new Documents, only one met the selection criteria.

## Replication Conflicts

Occasionally, there will be circumstances that cause Notes to believe that a change should be made to the same Document in both databases (the exact same Document was edited at both locations by someone before a replication occurs, for example). In these cases, Notes decides based on the time stamp in each Document and the number of changes made to the Document which Document is a *winner* and which Document is a *loser*. The winner is displayed as a normal Document in the database. The loser is...

Did you say *deleted?* No, Notes would never do that. The loser is displayed as a Response Document with the winner as its parent. This flags the Document for human intervention (Figure 8.47). These cases are called *replication or save conflicts*. Depending on the size of your Notes database and the number of times Documents are changed, replication or save conflicts may occur frequently or never at all. When replication conflicts occur frequently, it's possible to reduce conflicts through "creative" administration. So if you work with a Notes database that seems to have a large number of conflicts, be sure to let your Notes Administrator know.

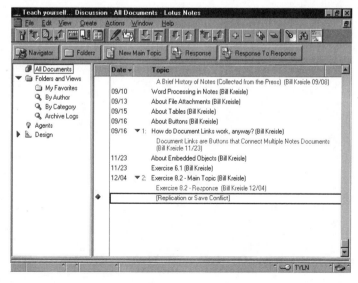

**Figure 8.47** *A Document that is marked as a replication or save conflict Document.*

# In Summary

❖ Replication is a process that moves *changes* (additions, deletions, or edits) between files bidirectionally.

❖ Replication can happen automatically between servers, or it can be initiated by a user between a Notes Client and a Notes Server.

❖ Replication can occur only between Notes databases that share the same replica ID. You can see the replica ID of a Notes database by opening it or selecting it on the Workspace and choosing **File, Database, Properties...** from the main menu, and then clicking the information tab of the Properties for Database dialog box.

❖ The Replicator Page is designed to serve as a central point for managing database replications. You can add a database to the Replicator Page by clicking on its icon on a Workspace Page and dragging it to the Replicator tab.

❖ Notes uses the unique signature of each Document combined with each Document's time and date stamp to determine what Documents should be moved between databases.

❖ If the same Document should be moved to both databases, a replication conflict occurs. Notes resolves replication conflicts by designating one Document as the winner of the conflict and the other as the loser. The loser is not deleted; it is displayed as a Response Document with the winner as its parent.

❖ There are a number of settings you can use to control various aspects of replication.

# Chapter 9

# Lotus Notes Mail

## In This Chapter...

This chapter is important because it covers another cornerstone of Notes—electronic mail. It's also significant because this is where you can tie almost everything you've learned in the other chapters of this book together, including Views, Folders, Navigators, Documents, attachments, objects, and Replication. No matter what concept you name, you'll find it useful here (even plain and Full Text Searching).

In addition, I feel compelled to blurt out here that Lotus Notes Mail is one of the main reasons I am a Notes Evangelist today. I live, work, and think from my mail database, which most likely has you thinking to yourself, "Now there's an insight I could have been spared...how could you 'live' in Lotus Notes Mail?" I'm glad you asked.

Using standard Notes Mail, I tracked to-do items and messages. As I learned Notes development, I worked on creating my own custom mail database. This database not only allowed me to convert incoming messages into to-do items, it allowed me to convert messages into meetings.

I created special fields for my to-dos that allowed me to assign scheduled completion times and track the amount of time I spent on each item. I created views that organized my to-dos in different ways, and showed scheduled meetings. I began relating to-do items with projects by creating a Project Form. Whenever I checked my voice mail, I entered my requests as to-dos in my Notes Mail.

Before long, I had an integrated project, meeting, and action tracking system that incorporated the two mechanisms most often used for delegating and accepting assignments—voice mail and electronic mail. By relating to-dos to projects and tracking time on each to-do, I had a ready-made status report at the end of each week. And because it was all in a Notes database, I could replicate my projects, to-dos, meetings, and mail to my local hard drive and carry my life around with me wherever I went.

Next, I created a contact-tracking database that allowed me to collect information about contacts. Whenever I had a to-do item for one of my contacts or wanted to begin a project for a contact, I designed the contact database to automatically create these items in my mail database. I'd even include a Document Link back to the contact record.

As you can see, Notes is indeed a tool to organize, collect, and share knowledge—and once you get the swing of it, it can also make your teeth whiter, your life brighter, and improve your looks.

But I suppose I should climb down from my soapbox and get to the task at hand, which is explaining Lotus Notes Mail. Here's the plan for this chapter:

❖   What is Notes Mail?

❖   Using Notes Mail

❖   Opening your mail database

❖   Creating a mail message

❖   Addressing mail

❖   Adding content

❖   Delivery options

❖   Special options

❖   Saving and sending messages

❖   Reading messages

❖   Replying to messages

❖   Forwarding documents as messages

❖   Book marks

❖   Phone messages

❖   Serially routed forms

❖   Tasks

❖   Mail Tools

❖   Adding users to your personal name and address book

❖   Archiving Messages

❖   Out of office notification

❖   Letterhead

❖   Stationery

# What is Lotus Notes Mail?

Lotus Notes Mail is a Notes database designed by Lotus to give users a wide range of electronic mail capabilities through an easy-to-use interface. When this database is combined with other Notes features like Replication, rich text fields, and customizable forms, it becomes an extremely useful application for users at all levels of experience.

It's important to understand that from Notes' point of view, Lotus Notes Mail is just another Notes database. This means that all the exercises we've done up to this point can be used with Notes Mail. You create new Documents, delete Documents, and use Views and Folders to sort the documents and categorize them. You can Full Text Index your mail database (if you have sufficient access and space) and then use Plain or Full Text Searching to find messages. You can even Replicate your mail database between your Notes Client and a Notes Server.

The next thing to understand about Notes mail is that, since it is the same as any other Notes database, it can be customized, and your Notes Administrator may have done so. Consequently, if the screen shots you see here are different in your mail database, it may be because you have a different mail database design. In addition, minor differences will appear in quarterly releases of Notes itself, so your screens may appear different even if you're using "standard" Lotus Notes Mail, but a version later than release 4.0.

Finally, before moving on to using Lotus Notes Mail, I'd like to point out one more thing. Just as it is important to know the concepts behind Documents, Responses, Forms, Views, and Replication to use Notes effectively, there are ideas about Notes' mail-enabling process you should understand to help you get the most out of Lotus Notes Mail. This is especially true if you are a remote (Mobile Notes) user.

With that in mind I've included a section on Lotus Notes Mail concepts in Chapter 10 that I would like for you to review. Since it is probably the most technical part of this book, I will make it recommended reading if you are a network Lotus Notes Mail user, to be reviewed after you finish this chapter. It is *strongly* recommended reading if you are a mobile Lotus Notes Mail user.

# Using Lotus Notes Mail

## *Opening your Mail Database*

To begin using Lotus Notes Mail, you need to have an icon for your mail database on the Notes Workspace (Figure 9.1).

**Figure 9.1** *An icon for your mail database must be on the Workspace to use Notes Mail.*

You also need to have your mail database set up correctly in your current Location Document. If you select **Create, Mail** from the Notes Client menu and see None Available on the submenu, you aren't correctly set up, and will need help from your Notes Administrator (Figure 9.2).

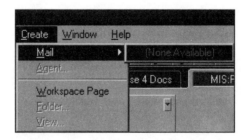

**Figure 9.2** *If you aren't correctly set up for Lotus Notes Mail, you will see this on the **Create, Mail** menu.*

If you aren't correctly set upy, you will see the choices shown in Figure 9.3.

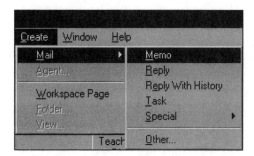

***Figure 9.3*** *The choices on the **Create, Mail** menu if Lotus Notes Mail is set up correctly.*

## Creating a Mail Message

As you saw in the previous section, you can create a mail message in Lotus Notes Mail by selecting **Create, Mail, Memo** from the Notes Client menu (Figure 9.3). You can also create a new message in Notes Mail by selecting your Notes Mail database on the Workspace and choosing **Create, Memo** from the Notes Client menu (Figure 9.4).

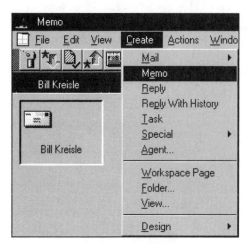

***Figure 9.4*** *Creating a mail message by selecting the Notes Mail database on the Workspace and choosing **Create, Memo** from the Notes Client menu.*

Clicking on the Mail button in the Status Bar of the Notes Client and choosing **Create Memo** will also create a new mail message (Figure 9.5).

SHORTCUT

**The Mail Button
on the Status Bar
of the Notes Client.**

***Figure 9.5*** *Using the Mail Button to create a new Notes Mail message.*

Any of these actions will create a new Document in the Notes Mail database using the Memo Form (Figure 9.6).

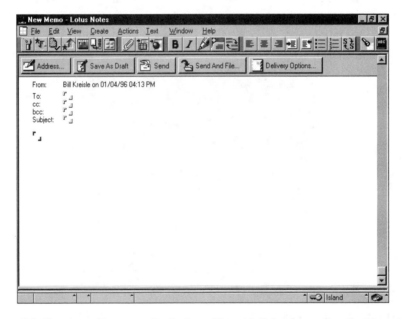

***Figure 9.6*** *Creating a Document in the Lotus Notes Mail database using the Memo Form.*

In the Memo Form, to To:, cc:, and bcc: fields are for entering the names of people who should receive the message.

The **Subject** field is for a short description of the message that will be displayed in the Inbox of the recipients. The field at the bottom of the form is the body—a Rich Text field designed to hold the main body of your message.

## *Addressing Lotus Notes Mail*

As we mentioned in the previous section, the three fields you can use to address a message are the **To:**, **cc:**, and **bcc:** fields. The **To:** field is where you would want to include the primary addressees (e.g., those who should take action on the message or who would be most interested in the message's content.) The **cc:** field is where you would include the names of addressees who might be interested in the message's content, but aren't expected to act on the message. The **bcc:** field is a special field you can use to send a copy of the message to one or more addressees blindly (i.e., recipients in the **To:** and **cc:** fields aren't aware of addressees in the **bcc:** fields).

You do not need to fill in the addresses to save the message as a draft, but to send it, at least one recipient in the **To:** field is required.

N O T E

You can type the names of the people you want to send your message to into these three fields directly, or you can use the **Address...** button on the Action Bar to open the Address Message dialog box (Figures 9.7 and 9.8).

**The Address... button.**

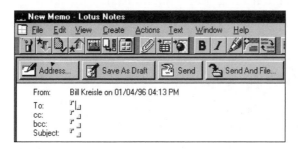

*Figure 9.7 The **Address...** button on the Action Bar of the new mail message.*

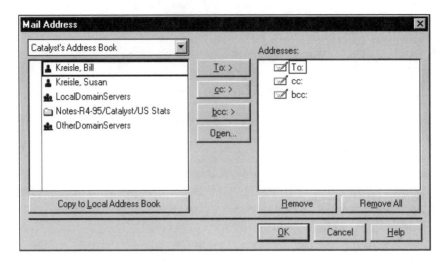

***Figure 9.8*** *The Mail Address dialog box.*

To use the Mail Address dialog box, select the name or group you wish to include in your message, and click **To: >**, **cc: >**, or **bcc: >** to add the selected name to one of the fields. When you are finished addressing your message, click **OK**.

## Adding Message Content

Once you have addressed your new message, you can enter the subject and body of the message. Since the field designed to hold the body of your message is a Rich Text field, you can include any Rich Text feature in your message (attachments, text formatting, paragraph formatting, bullets, etc.).

Figure 9.9 illustrates a message with the address, subject, and body fields filled in.

## Delivery Options

Once have created your message, you can set a number of options that affect how it is delivered and how it will appear in the recipient's Inbox folder.

The first group of options you can set for a mail message are its Delivery Options, accessed by choosing **Actions, Delivery Options...** from the Notes Client menu while you have a memo opened for editing. This will open the Delivery Options dialog box, illustrated in Figure 9.10.

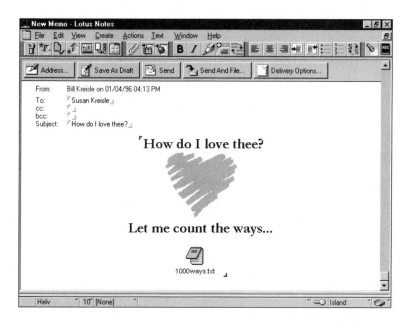

**Figure 9.9** *A mail message with the* **To:**, **Subject**, *and* **body** *fields filled in.*

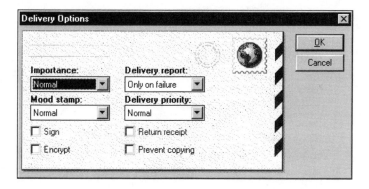

**Figure 9.10** *The Delivery Options dialog box.*

You can use the Importance: drop down list to select whether the message should be regarded by the recipients as of high, normal, or low importance. If you select high importance, the message will appear in the recipient's Inbox Folder with an exclamation point beside it (Figure 9.11).

The Delivery report drop-down list on the Delivery Options dialog box allows you to receive a message when certain delivery criteria are met. Selecting **Only**

**on failure** from the drop down lists instructs Notes to notify you only if the message you are sending cannot be delivered.

| | | Who ▲ | Date ▼ | Subject |
|---|---|---|---|---|
| ❖ | Inbox | ! Bill Clinton | 01/04/96 | Urgent request for your advice! |
| ✏ | Drafts | Lou Gerstner | 01/04/96 | Please look at this if you get time. |
| 📧 | Sent | ★ Madonna | 01/04/96 | OK. This is the last time I'm going to propose (I mean it |
| 🗐 | All Documents | ★ David Letterman | 01/04/96 | Are you sure won't accept our "lucrative" job offer? |
| 📝 | To Do | ★ ! Jeffrey Papows | 01/04/96 | We need your advice, Bill! |
| 🗑 | Trash | | | |

**Figure 9.11** *Identifying a message marked as high importance.*

Selecting **Confirm delivery** instructs Notes to notify you when the message has been successfully delivered to its destination.

Selecting **Trace entire path** instructs Notes to provide you with a message at each step in the delivery process (i.e., a message is generated when you send the message to your mail server, when that mail server hands the message off to another mail server, and so on).

Selecting **None** tells Notes not to inform you about the message once you've sent it under any circumstances.

Choosing an option in the Mood Stamp drop-down list adds a bitmap to your message that helps convey its tone. For example, a humorous message might be sent with the Joke mood stamp attached to it, as illustrated in Figure 9.12.

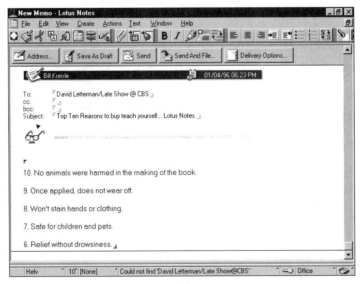

**Figure 9.12** *An example of a Mood Stamp.*

In addition to including the bitmap in the message itself, a smaller version of the image will be displayed in the recipient's Inbox Folder (Figure 9.13). Table 9.1 illustrates some of the Mood Stamps available.

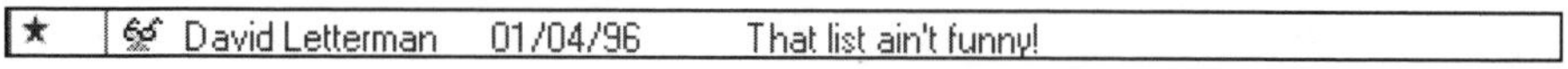

| ★ | 🐌 David Letterman | 01/04/96 | That list ain't funny! |
|---|---|---|---|

**Figure 9.13** *An example of a Mood Stamp displayed from a View.*

**Table 9.1** *Mood Stamps*

| *Stamp Image* | *Stamp Name* |
|:---:|:---|
| ● | Personal |
|  🔵 | Confidential |
|  🕵️ | Private |
|  🙂 | Thank You! |
|  🔥 | Flame |
|  ⭐ | Good Job! |
|  👓 | Joke |
|  📰 | FYI |
|  ❓ | Question |
|  ☝️ | Reminder |

The choices in the Delivery Priority drop-down list on the Delivery Options dialog box allow you to assign values of high, normal, or low. Delivery Priority differs from importance in that the setting you select in this drop-down list may affect the amount of time it takes for your message to be delivered. At some Notes installations, sending a message with a delivery priority of low will cause it to be saved for delivery until late at night when the network's servers aren't as busy.)

Selecting the Sign check box on the Delivery Options dialog box will embed a unique digital signature from your Notes ID into the message you are sending (Figure 9.14). The signature can then be used by the recipient to verify that you are the original sender of the message. Authentication of signed messages depend on the user having access to your *Public Key* (a value most likely stored in your Notes Name and Address Book).

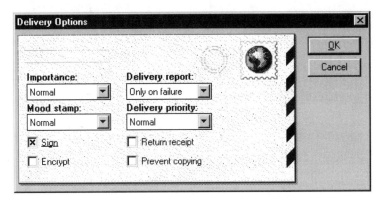

**Figure 9.14** *Selecting the Sign check box on the Delivery Options dialog box.*

When another Notes user opens a signed mail message, he will see a message similar to Figure 9.15 in the status bar of the Notes Client:

**Figure 9.15** *Notes displays name of the user who signed the message along with the date and time of the "signature."*

Selecting **Encrypt** in the Delivery Options check box will scramble the contents of your message so that only the recipients can read it.

Selecting the **Return Receipt** checkbox allows you to receive a message indicating the date and time each addressee opened and read the message you sent to him.

Checking **Prevent copying** on the Delivery Options dialog box will disable the copy and print functions at the Notes Client whenever the recipient has your message open.

## Special Options

The next set of options you can use when creating messages are accessed by choosing **Action, Special Options...** from the Notes Client menu while you are editing a new message. This command will open the Special Options dialog box (Figure 9.16).

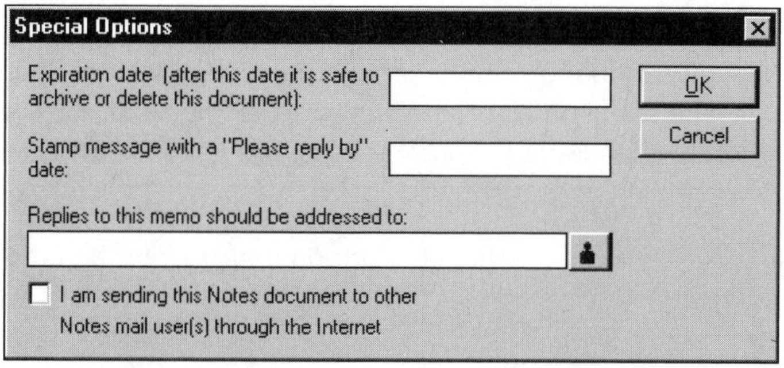

**Figure 9.16** *The Special Options dialog box.*

In this dialog box you can enter an expiration date for your message (so that if its recipient is using automatic archiving it will be deleted at an appropriate time) by entering a date in the first text box in the dialog box.

You can add a "Please reply by" stamp to your messages by entering a date in the second text box in the Special Options dialog box. If you use this option, the text, *Please respond by date* will appear at the top of the message (Figure 9.17).

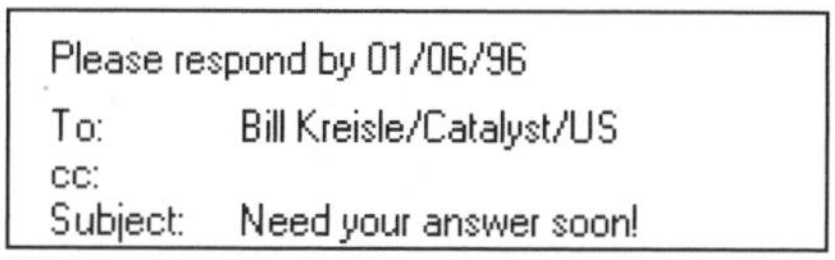

**Figure 9.17** *Using the option to include a suggested response time.*

If you enter one or more names in the **replies to this memo should be addressed to** text box, those people will automatically be addressed when the user chooses to reply to your message.

Clicking the **I am sending this Notes document... Internet** check box will cause Notes to transmit the message in a way that will allow the Notes users who will be receiving your message via the Internet to view it as it was originally formatted.

## Saving and Sending Messages

Now that you have created your message, addressed it, filled it, and set any options you wish to use, you're ready to send it! To send your message, click the **Send** button on the Action Bar, or choose **Actions, Send** from the Notes Client menu. Based on the options you selected in the User Preference dialog box, your sent message may be saved to the Sent Folder after it is delivered.

**SHORTCUT**

If you want to move the sent message to a Folder other than the Sent Folder at the time you are mailing it, click the **Send and File...** button on the Action Bar, or choose **Actions, Send and File...**

If you'd like to save your message and work on it again later before sending it, click **Save as Draft** on the Action Bar (Figure 9.18).

***Figure 9.18*** *The **Save As Draft**, **Send**, and **Send And File...** buttons on the Action Bar.*

You can also save and send a message by pressing the **Esc** key to close the current Document you are editing, and selecting the appropriate radio button on the Close Window dialog box (Figure 9.19).

Choosing **Send and save a copy** and clicking **OK** would be the same as clicking **Send** on the Action Bar. Choosing **Save only** and clicking **OK** would be the same as clicking **Save As Draft** on the Action Bar. Choosing **Send only** and clicking **OK** would allow you override the Send and Save option you may have set in your user preferences. Choosing **Discard changes** and clicking **OK** closes the current window without mailing the Document or saving your changes.

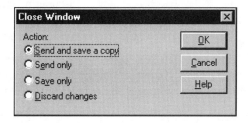

**Figure 9.19** *The Close Window dialog box for Memos.*

## Reading Messages

In addition to creating and sending messages to other electronic mail users, you will want to read and file mail that you receive from others. You can find incoming messages in the Inbox Folder of the mail database. As with any other Document in Notes, you can open it from the Inbox View by selecting it and pressing **Enter**, or by double-clicking the selected document. Once you have read a message, you can move it to another Folder if you wish to save it, or to the Trash Folder if you wish to mark it for deletion.

## Replying to Messages

When you want to reply to a message that you have received, you can do so by clicking the **Reply** or **Reply with History** button on the Action Bar of the message you are currently reading. Choosing **Reply** creates a new message with the original sender of the message in the To: field of the new message, and the same subject as the original message except the text Re: is prepended to it.

Choosing **Reply with History** creates a new message with the same options as **Reply**, but it adds the original body of the message to the body of the new message.

## Forwarding Documents as Messages

In addition to being able to create messages using the Memo Form, Notes can send any Document using any Form. Sometimes Notes accomplishes this by creating special Forms with fields that the mail system needs. Other times, Notes simply takes advantage of the fact that a rich text field can hold anything. The second option is one you can use to forward documents to other Notes users.

Let's say I'm looking at the Teach yourself... Discussion database and I decide that I want to send Grandmother Huebner's Rumcake Recipe to a friend of mine at another company that uses Notes. I could create a Document Link and send it, but since my friend at the other company doesn't have the Teach yourself... Discussion database available, it wouldn't work as expected. I could edit the Document and copy out the body and paste it into a new message, as well, but that's time consuming.

Instead, I'm going to open the Document and choose **Actions, Forward** from the Notes Client menu. This will create a new message for me and fill the body of the message with the Document that contained Grandmother Huebner's Recipe, as illustrated in Figure 9.20.

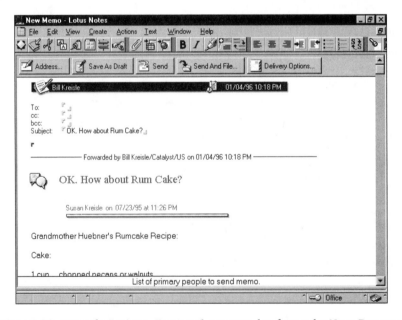

**Figure 9.20** *Using the **Actions, Forward** command to forward a Notes Document.*

## Book Marks

As I mentioned earlier, if I wanted to let a user know about a Document in a Notes database that the user also has access to, an alternative to forwarding the entire Document would be to send him a Document Link. As you recall from Chapter 6, creating a Document Link means selecting a Document or having it open on the Workspace and choosing **Edit, Copy As Link, Document Link** from the Notes Client menu. This copies the Document Link to the Clipboard so that I can paste it into a mail message. Since this is a common procedure for Notes users, Lotus has added a special mail form to Notes Mail to make sending a Document Link quick and easy.

The special Form is called a Book Mark, and you can create one by selecting **Create, Mail, Special, Book Mark** from the Notes Client menu while you have a Document open or selected in a View.

Going back to our example of wanting to forward Grandmother Huebner's Rumcake Recipe to a friend of mine, assuming that my friend has access to the Teach yourself... Discussion database, I can send it to him using the Book Mark form, as illustrated in Figures 9.21 and 9.22.

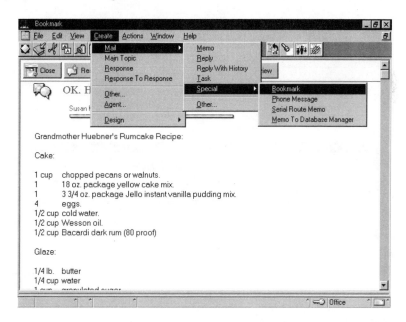

**Figure 9.21** *Using the Create, Mail, Special, Book Mark command.*

When my friend receives this message, he can activate the Document Link to the open Document containing the recipe.

## Phone Messages

Another option in the **Create, Mail, Special** command menu is the Phone Message Form. To create a phone message, select your mail database on the Workspace or open it, and choose **Create, Special, Phone Message** from the Notes client menu. This will open a form similar to Figure 9.23.

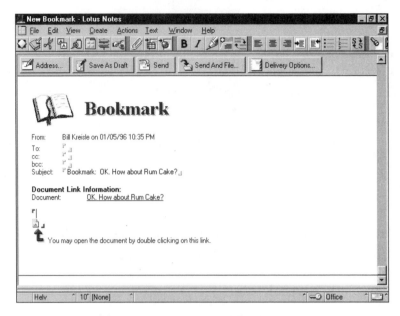

**Figure 9.22** *A Book Mark message.*

**Figure 9.23** *The Phone Message Form.*

## *Serially Routed Forms*

A good example of a process that Notes can supplement with Workflow is one where information flows from user to user in a linear path, with the information being tracked at each point where it stops. A tool to support this type of Workflow in Notes is the Serial Route Memo. You compose a Serial Route Memo in Notes by selecting **Create, Mail, Special, Serial Route Memo** from the Notes Client menu. This opens a new Form, similar to the one illustrated in Figure 9.24.

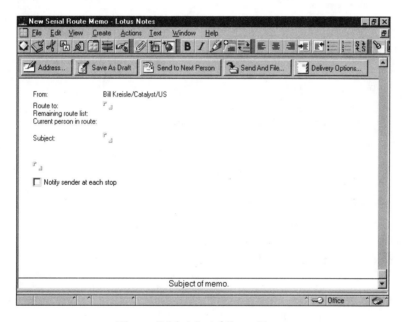

***Figure 9.24*** *A Serial Route Memo.*

Enter a list of people whom you wish to route the Memo in the **Route to:** field, with each name separated by commas. Use the **Subject:** field and the rich text field at the bottom of the Memo the same way you would use them in a standard mail message. If you want to be notified as the memo travels to each person on your list, check the **Notify sender at each stop** check box on the form before clicking the **Send to next Person** button on the Action Bar.

Figure 9.25 shows a Serial Route Memo with the fields filled in.

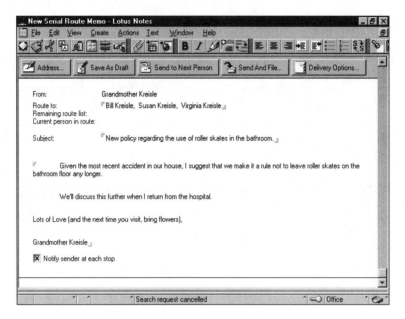

**Figure 9.25** *An example of a completed Serial Route Memo.*

## Tasks

Another type of Workflow you can use Standard Notes Mail for is the delegation of tasks to others by using the Tasks form. You can create a new task by choosing **Create, Mail, Task** from the Notes Client menu. This opens the Task Form, illustrated in Figure 9.26.

In this form, you can enter a description of the task, a priority, as well as a due date and an expected start date for the task. To assign the task to yourself, choose **Close** and save it. To assign the task to others, click **Assign To Others…** in the Action Bar. This will cause **Assign to:** and **cc:** fields to appear on the Task Form and adds an Address and Send button to the Action Bar, as illustrated in Figure 9.27.

To view tasks that you have created or that others have assigned to you, use the To Do View in the Folders Navigator or choose **View, Go To…, To Do** from the Notes Client menu while your Mail database is open or selected.

In addition to being able to create Tasks using the **Create, Mail, Tasks** option, you can also convert incoming messages into Tasks by using the **Actions, Convert to Task** command while you are reading a message.

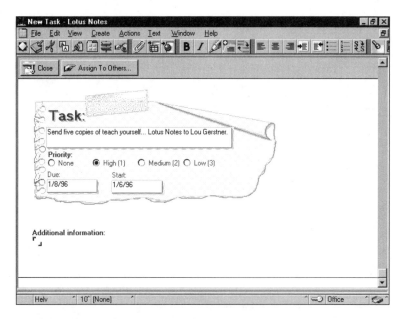

***Figure 9.26*** *The Task Form.*

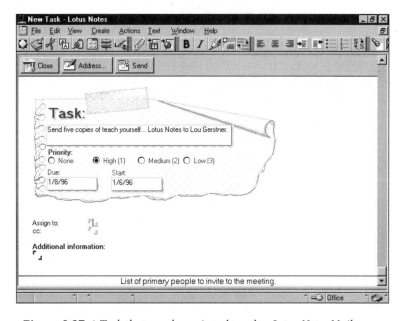

***Figure 9.27*** *A Task that can be assigned to other Lotus Notes Mail users.*

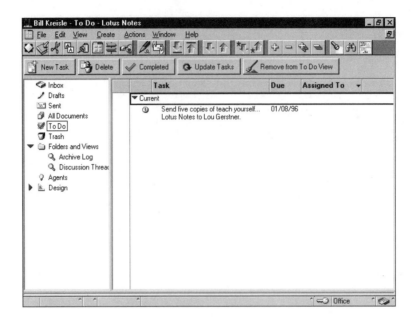

**Figure 9.28** *The Tasks View.*

**Figure 9.29** *The Convert-to-Task Agent on the Actions menu.*

# Mail Tools

In addition to giving you a number of Forms to create and send information, Lotus Notes Mail also provides you with a wide variety of tools to customize and control the information you work with in your Mail database. These are accessed by selecting or opening your Mail Database and choosing **Actions, Mail Tools** on the Notes Client menu. This will provide you with a list of Agents designed by Lotus.

## *Adding Users to your Personal Name and Address Book*

The first Agent in the list is titled Add Sender to Address Book. If you receive a mail message from someone and would like to remember his electronic mail address for future reference, this is a handy command. It will create a new Person entry in your Personal Name and Address Book for you, and fill in the Forwarding Address field with the address used in your message. Once you have added a person to your Personal Name and Address Book, you can use the Address button on new memos to refer to him later.

## *Archiving Messages*

The next Agent in the list, Archive Selected Documents, uses your Archive Profile to manually move the message that is currently open or the messages that are selected in a Notes View to the specified archive database.

To create an Archive Profile, select the Archiving View in the Folders Navigator or select **View, Go To...** Archive Profile from the Notes Client menu while your Mail database is open or selected.

If the View is empty, click the **Setup Archive...** button on the Action Bar to create an Archive Profile. If an Archive Profile already exists in the View, select it and open it for editing to change its settings (Figure 9.31).

If you want to archive expired documents automatically, click **Archive Expired documents** and fill in the number of days after expiration that the Notes Client should wait before performing an archive operation.

If you want to archive documents that you haven't opened for a specific period of time, click **Archive documents which have no activity**. and then type a number to indicate how many days of inactivity the Notes Client should wait before archiving a document.

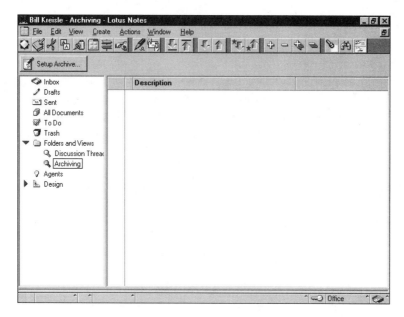

**Figure 9.30** *The Archiving View.*

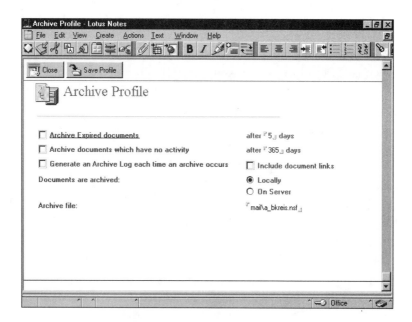

**Figure 9.31** *A new Archive Profile Document.*

Clicking **Generate an Archive Log each time an archive occurs** causes the Notes Client to create a special Document called an *Archive Log* each time it performs an archiving operation. You can have a Document Link to every document that Notes archives, by clicking **Include Document Links.**

NOTE

This option will not appear unless you click **An archive log will be generated each time an archive occurs**.

In the Documents are archived radio buttons select **Locally** or **On Server** to choose where archived Documents are saved. Enter the path and filename you wish to use for your mail archive in the Archive File field. If the file does not exist when you save the Document, Notes will automatically create it for you. Notes will suggest a default name and path for your mail archive.

NOTE

If you select **Documents are archived... On Server**, you must have permission to create databases on the server you specify. If you aren't sure if you have permission, check with your Notes Administrator.

# Taking What We've Learned Step-by-Step (Exercise 9.1)

In this exercise, we'll create an Archive Profile for a Notes Mail user and use the Archive Selected Documents Agent to move Documents to an archive database. The intent of this exercise is to provide you with a series of steps that you can duplicate to achieve the illustrated results using your own mail database. Since the servers, names, and locations cannot be the same, it is obvious you will not be able to follow this exercise to the letter. However, you should be able to follow along making reasonable substitutions.

## *Step 1*

To move Documents to an archive database, we need to create an Archive Profile. To do this, open your Mail database to the Archiving View and click **Setup Archive...** on the Action Bar (Figure 9.32).

**The Setup Archive button.**

**The Archiving View
in the Folders Navigator.**

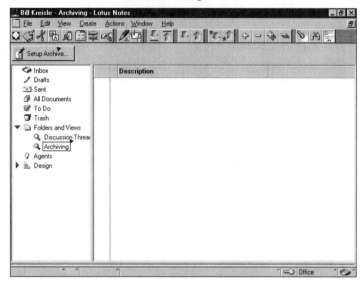

***Figure 9.32*** *The Setup Archive button on the Action Bar.*

In the Archive Profile Form that is opened, check **Generate an Archive Log each time an archive occurs**, and **Include Document Links**.

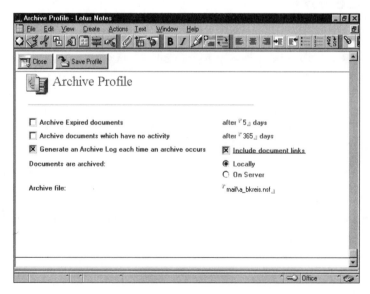

***Figure 9.33*** *Selecting options in the Archive Profile Form.*

## *Step 2*

Click the **Save Profile** button on the Action Bar of the newly created Archive Profile Form, accepting the defaults specified by Notes and saving your changes. Click **Close** on the Action Bar. An Archive Profile Document will appear in the Archiving View (Figure 9.34).

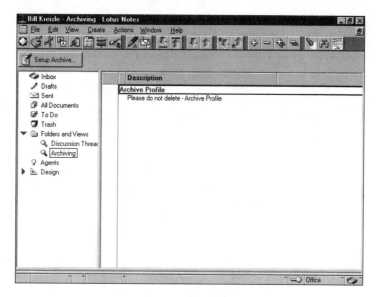

**Figure 9.34**  *The Archive Profile will appear in the Archiving View.*

**N O T E**

You may have to refresh the View by pressing **F9** or clicking on the arrow in the upper left corner of the View (Figure 9.35) to see the new Document.

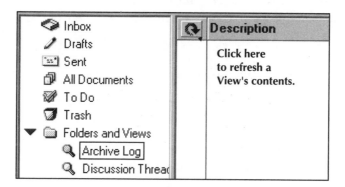

**Figure 9.35**  *Refreshing a View by clicking on the circling arrow in the upper left corner.*

## Step 3

Open a Folder in the Notes Mail database that contains messages you wish to Archive. In this example, I'm going to use the Inbox Folder (Figure 9.36).

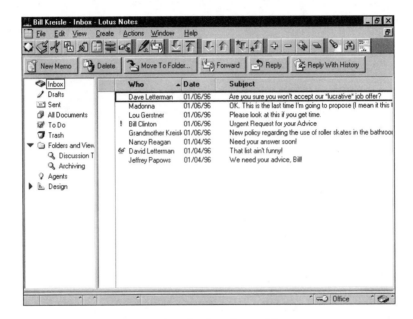

**Figure 9.36** *The Inbox Folder.*

## Step 4

Select one or more messages to move to the archive file and choose **Actions, Mail Tools, Archive Selected Documents** from the Notes Client menu.

After answering yes to the confirmation prompt (Figure 9.38), information about the archiving process will appear in the Status Bar of the Notes Client (Figure 9.39).

Upon completion of the archiving process, Notes will display a prompt informing you how many messages were moved to archives (Figure 9.40).

## Step 5

Returning to the Archiving View, a new Archive Log has been added (Figure 9.41). Open the Archive Log and examine its contents (Figure 9.42).

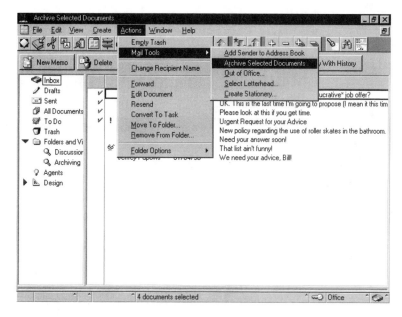

**Figure 9.37** *Selecting multiple documents and choosing **Actions, Mail Tools, Archive Selected Documents** from the Notes Client menu.*

**Figure 9.38** *Notes will ask you to confirm that you are moving messages to an archive file.*

**Figure 9.39** *Status Bar messages.*

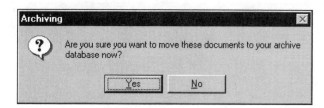

**Figure 9.40** *Notes prompts you at the completion of the archiving process.*

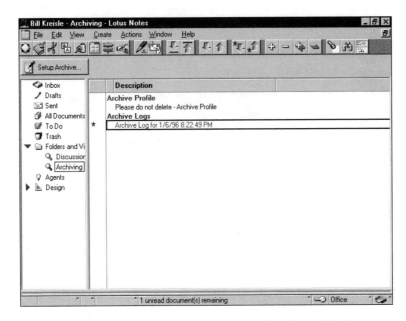

**Figure 9.41** *An Archive Log Document has been added.*

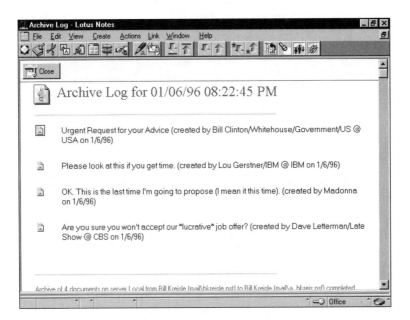

**Figure 9.42** *The entry includes Document Links to the archived Documents.*

Close the mail database to complete the exercise.

## *Out of Office Notification*

The next Agent on the Mail Tools menu allows you to set up an Out-of-the-Office profile by selecting **Actions, Mail Tools, Out of Office...** from the Notes Client menu while the mail database is open or selected on the Workspace.

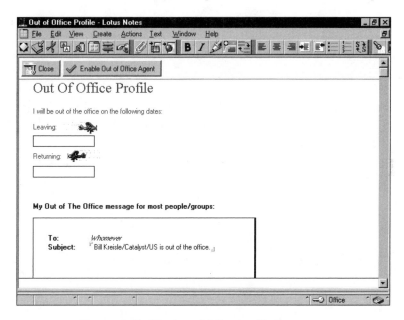

***Figure 9.43*** *The Out of Office Profile Document.*

The purpose of the Out-of-Office Profile is to allow incoming mail to be answered while you are (you guessed it) out of the office. In addition to being able to send others information about your being out of the office, Lotus has added some features to make the system more easily customized to suit your needs.

To use the out-of-office features, enter the dates you will be leaving and returning in the Out-of-Office Profile document. If you want, you can customize the subject of the message that will be sent to users who send you mail by changing it in the boxes that follow the departure and return date.

The first group box, labeled My Out of the Office message for most people/groups is designed to be your default message that anyone will receive when he sends you a message (Figure 9.44).

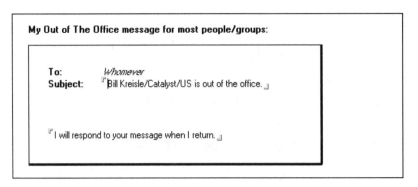

**Figure 9.44** *The first group in the Out of Office Profile Document.*

The second group, My Out of The Office message for special people/groups: is designed to act as a filter, sending a different message to certain individuals or groups (Figure 9.45).

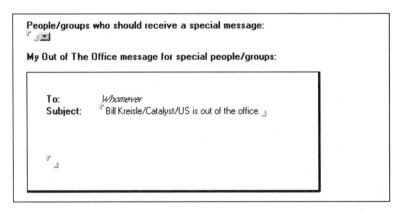

**Figure 9.45** *The second group in the Out of Office Profile Document.*

The final field is to enter the names of people or groups who should not receive any messages (Figure 9.46). This field is useful for entering the names of servers that send you messages automatically or the names of Internet List Servers if you subscribe to an Internet mailing list.

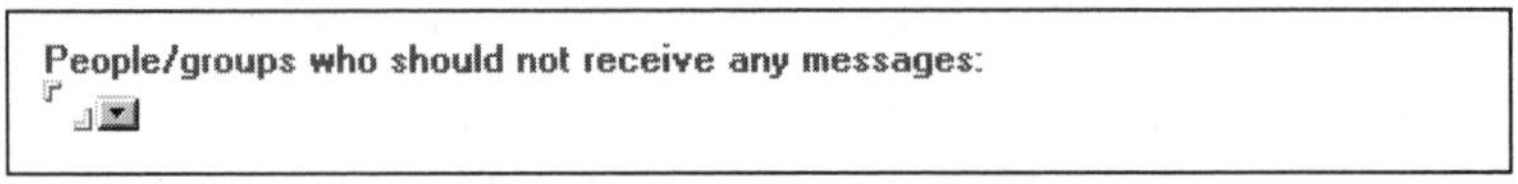

**Figure 9.46** *Specifying people or groups who should not receive any out of office notification.*

Once you have filled in the fields of the Out of Office Profile Document with the values you wish to use, click the **Enable Out of Office Agent** button on the Action Bar to close the document and enable the Out of Office Profile you just entered (Figure 9.47).

**The Enable Out of Office Agent button.**

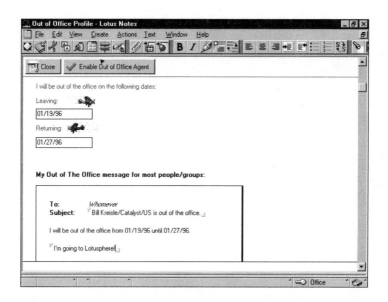

*Figure 9.47* *The Enable Out of Office Agent button on the Action Bar.*

Here are some special things to understand about the Out of Office Agent and Profile:

❖ While the Out of Office Agent is enabled, users will not receive more than one message, even if they sent several messages to you while you were out.

❖ On the date you specified as your return date, Notes will create a "Welcome back" message in your inbox that includes a list of all the people it sent messages to. Until you open the "Welcome back" message, Notes will assume you are still out of the office. (Which is extremely handy if you stay away longer than you expected).

❖ If you return earlier than you expected, select **Actions, Mail Tools, Out of Office** and click **Disable Agent**. Notes then sends you a "Welcome back" message that includes a list of all the people it sent messages to.

## Letterhead

The **Actions, Mail Tools, Letterhead Agent** allows you to customize your mail messages by including a graphic letterhead at the top of each message. Choosing the command from the Notes Client menu opens the Select a Letterhead dialog box (figure 9.48).

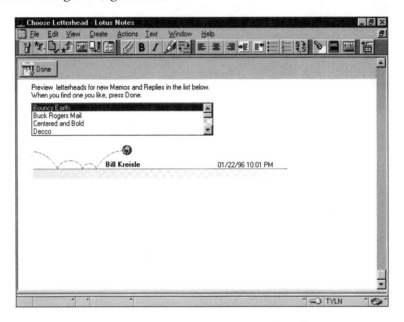

***Figure 9.48*** *The Select a Letterhead dialog box.*

## Stationery

The final Agent in the Mail Tools menu is **Create Stationery....**This Agent allows you to create special mail messages that can be used as templates. For example, if you submit a weekly status report that always follows the same format, you can create a template of the format and save it as stationery to use over and over.

To create your own stationery, select **Actions, Mail Tools, Create Stationery...** from the Notes Client menu. You will be prompted to select whether you want to base the stationery you're about to create on the standard Mail Memo or on the Personal Stationery Form. Since we've already seen the standard Memo Form, the remaining examples in this section will use the Personal Stationery Form (Figure 9.49).

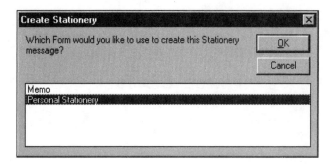

**Figure 9.49** *Basing the stationery we're about to create on the Personal Stationery Form.*

This will open a new Document in your Notes mail titled Personal Stationery—Lotus Notes (Figure 9.50). The new Document will have a rich text field at the top and bottom of the Form, as well as fields for any common addresses, the subject, and the body of the new Stationery you want to create. The two additional rich text fields are there to allow you to add images or formatted text to the Stationery .

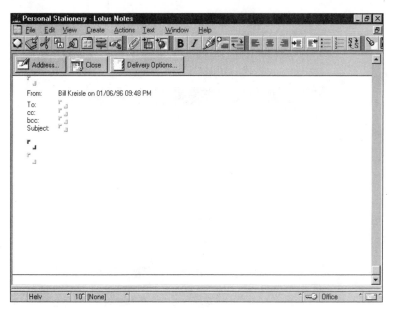

**Figure 9.50** *Creating new Stationery based on the Personal Stationery Form.*

For example, if you sent information that you wanted the recipients to treat as trade secret, you might create a Personal Stationery that looked similar to Figure 9.51.

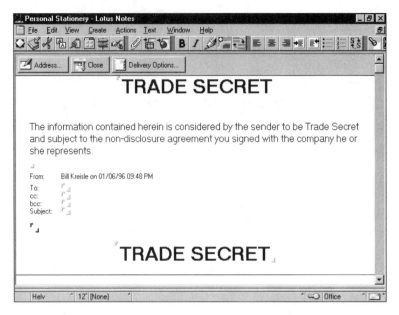

**Figure 9.51** *An example of Personal Stationery.*

When you save this new Document, Notes will ask you to name your new Stationery (Figure 9.52).

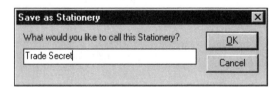

**Figure 9.52** *Naming your new Stationery.*

After you have named it and clicked **OK**, Notes will display the message shown in Figure 9.53.

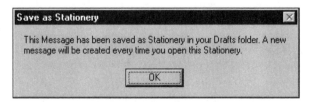

**Figure 9.53** *Instruction on how to use your new Stationery will appear after you have named it.*

To use the new Stationery, go to the Drafts Folder in your mail database and double-click on the **Trade Secret** entry to open it (Figure 9.54).

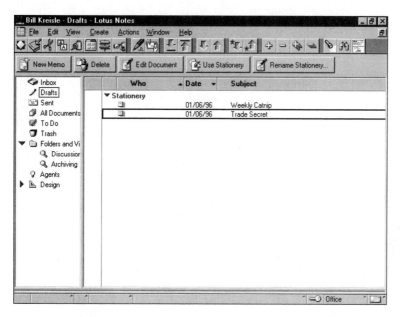

**Figure 9.54** *The new Stationery is saved in the Drafts Folder.*

# Summary

❖ Lotus Notes Mail is a Notes database designed by Lotus to provide users with a robust electronic mail system. It combines the ideas behind electronic mail systems with the features of Notes to create a product that can be useful to customers at all levels of experience.

❖ Composing a message in Lotus Notes Mail is accomplished by creating a Memo Form in your Mail Database. In the Memo Form, you fill in the addressees, the subject, and the body of your message.

❖ A number of options exist in Lotus Notes Mail to help users control the Memo's appearance and method of delivery:

1. Messages can be sent with low, normal, or high importance. Messages that are high importance are indicated by an exclamation point icon in the Inbox of the recipients.

2. Messages can be sent with low, normal, or high delivery priority. Depending on how your Notes Administrator has set up your Lotus

Notes Mail system, these settings may affect the speed at which your message is delivered.

3. Options to trace the delivery path of your messages can be used to determine when the recipient's mail server receives the Memo, or when every server in the delivery chain receives and processes the Memo.

4. Mood Stamps allow you to add an image to the Memo Form to help convey the tone of your message.

5. Options to sign, encrypt, and request return receipts for your messages can be used.

❖ After you have finished composing your message, you can send it to other electronic mail users immediately or save it as a draft and edit it again before sending it.

❖ Messages sent to you from other electronic mail users are stored in the Inbox Folder of your mail database. From the Inbox Folder, you can read your messages, move them to other Folders for later review, convert them into Tasks, or delete/archive them.

❖ A special option in Notes Mail called Forwarding allows you to send any Document in any Notes database to other Notes users by copying the Document into the body of a new Memo.

❖ If you don't want to send an entire Document from a Notes database to other Notes Mail users, you can use a special form called a Book Mark to send a Document Link instead.

❖ Notes Mail also includes Forms for creating Phone Messages, Serial Route Memos, and Tasks:

1. Phone Messages can be created and sent to other Notes Mail users.

2. Serial Route Memos can be created and sent to a chain of Notes Mail users, with each person in the list receiving the message and passing it to the next person in the chain.

3. Tasks can be created for yourself or created and assigned to others by mailing the Task Form to them.

❖ In addition to Forms, Lotus Notes Mail also provides a number of Agents that you can use to manage Documents in your mail database. These Agents are accessible from the **Actions, Mail Tools** menu on the Notes Client:

1. **Add Sender to Address Book** copies the sender's address out of messages that you have received, and and uses it to begin a Person Document in your Personal Name and Address Book.

2. **Archive Selected Documents** moves one or more Documents from your mail database to the archive database you specified in your archive profile.

3. **Out of Office...** opens the Out of Office Profile Document, where you can set up electronic mail responses for people who send you mail while you are away from the office.

4. **Letterhead** allows you to add different images to the top of your Memos and Replies.

5. **Create Stationery...** allows you to make Memos that follow a specific format. You can use these Memos over and over again to send special messages, such as status reports, time cards, etc.

# Chapter 10

# Mobile Notes

## In this Chapter...

You wake up and head downstairs to the coffee pot. While the coffee is brewing, you check your electronic mail, get a summary of the morning news, and see what the latest entries are in the new product naming contest you're sponsoring at the company. You answer some mail, forward an article about a competitor to a coworker, and add a couple of comments to a newly added suggestion to call your latest product "Good Software (Really)."

At your morning visit to a client's site, someone asks you a question about one of the newer product lines that you aren't as familiar with as you'd like to be. During a break, you check an exhaustive collection of technical notes and design documents about the product back at the home office, and have an answer (and a purchase order) by the end of the meeting. You fill out the purchase order on your laptop and during your next phone call to the office, you move the order into the accounting system and have a confirmation for your client before you leave the building.

When you get to the office, a project database that you're working on has several new items added to it. You'd like to look at them but won't have time until tonight, so you don't worry about them for the moment. By the end of the day, you've forgotten about them. But it's okay, because when you get home, the updated documents are waiting for you.

Welcome to the world of Mobile Notes, which we'll discuss in this chapter using the following outline:

❖  Mobile Notes concepts

❖  Setting up a modem

❖  Setting up a server connection document

❖  Setting up a location document

❖  Calling a Notes Server

❖  Configuring a passthru server

❖  Lotus Notes mail concepts

❖  Mobile Lotus Notes mail concepts

 Because of the extensive differences that could exist between your installation of Notes and the system that was used during the writing of this book, this chapter does not include any step-by-step examples.

**N O T E**

## Mobile Notes Concepts

Notes Release 4 offers a wide variety of features that allow you to connect your home computer and/or laptop to the corporate network easily and automatically using telephone lines. One of the key features, of course, is Replication, which we discuss in Chapter 8. Other features, which we'll discuss here, include:

1.  Support for hundreds of modems.

2.  Location documents (which give you the ability to quickly change your setup to use a modem instead of a network connection).

3.  Tools to connect your Notes Client to multiple Notes Servers in a single telephone call.

4.  A special Notes Database designed to hold electronic mail addresses and server telephone numbers while working off-line called a Personal Name and Address book.

Figure 10.1 will help illustrate how these concepts comprise what Lotus calls *Mobile Notes.*

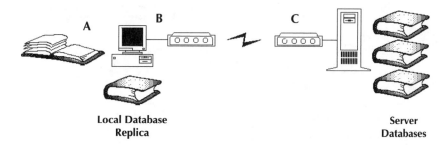

**Local Database
Replica**

**Server
Databases**

***Figure 10.1*** *Mobile Notes concepts.*

Referring to Figure 10.1, the Notes Client looks at the current Location Document (A) in the user's Personal Name and Address book to see if a modem connection is enabled. If a connection is enabled, Notes uses a modem driver to instruct the attached modem (B) to call the Notes Server listed in the Location Document (A). To get the telephone number it is supposed to call, Notes uses another Document in the Personal Name and Address Book called a Server Connection Document (A). Once connected (C), the Notes Client can transfer data between any Local Replicas with the Notes Server's databases.

## Setting up a Modem

As you can see from Figure 10.1, a central requirement of Mobile Notes is the presence of a modem. Typically, Notes asks you a number of questions about a modem during installation and uses your answers to configure itself. However, if you buy a new modem, or decide to attach the modem to another COM port, it is possible to set up Notes to use a modem manually. To do so, you need to know what type of modem you have and which COM port it is connected to.

Modems are connected to a computer using the computer's communications (COM) port. Since most computers have more than one communications port, these ports are generally referred to as COM1, COM2, and so on.

Once you have this information, select **File, Tools, User Preferences** from the Notes Client menu to open the User Preferences dialog box (Figure 10.2).

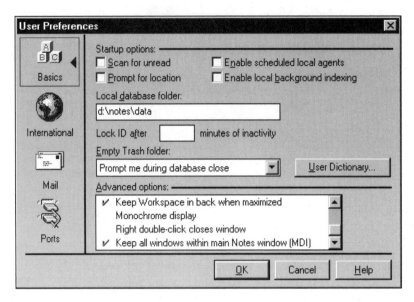

***Figure 10.2*** *The User Preferences dialog box.*

From this dialog box, click the **Ports** icon to examine your current port settings and add new ports (Figure 10.3).

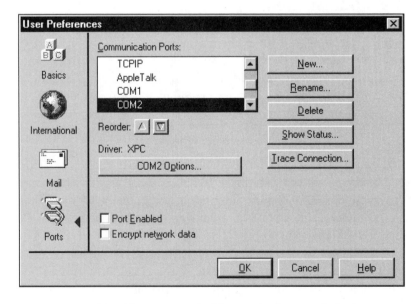

***Figure 10.3*** *The Ports panel of the User Preferences dialog box.*

Here, select the COM port number your modem is connected to in the Communication Ports list box, and click the **Options** button beneath the list to open the Additional Setup dialog box (Figure 10.4).

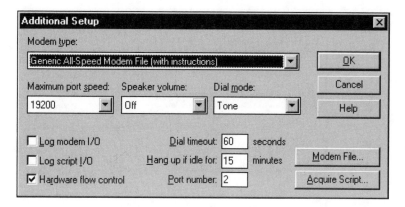

**Figure 10.4** *The Additional Setup dialog box.*

In the Additional Setup dialog box, specify what type of modem you have from the Modem type drop-down list (Figure 10.5).

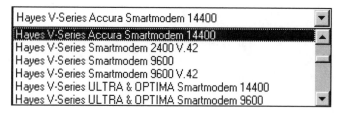

**Figure 10.5** *The Modem type drop-down list.*

**NOTE**

If you don't see your modem in this list, select **Generic All-Speed Modem File (with Instructions)**.

Once you have selected a modem from the list, the rest of the Additional Setup dialog box will be filled in with the values Notes recommends for that modem. If you are familiar with how modems work, you can adjust these settings if you wish to fine-tune your modem's performance. Click **OK** when finished to close the Additional Setup dialog box and return to the User Preferences dialog box.

Now that you've selected a COM port and specified what type of modem is connected to it, the last step is to enable the port for use by Notes. To do this, click the **Port Enabled** check box on the User Preferences dialog box (Figure 10.6).

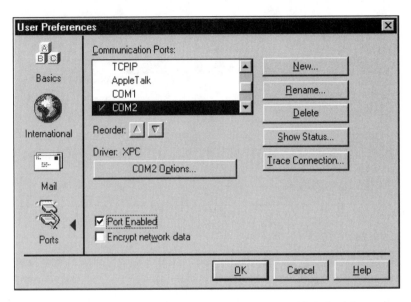

**Figure 10.6** *Enabling the port using the Port Enabled check box.*

A Notes Client can support multiple modems, so if you have modems connected to other COM ports, repeat the process to set them up for use by Notes. When you have added your modem(s), click **Done** in the User Preferences dialog box.

# Setting Up a Server Connection

Now that we have information about our modem associated with a COM port, the next step is to provide Notes with a list of Notes Server names and Telephone Numbers it can call.

This is done by creating a Server Connection Document in your Notes Client's Personal Name and Address Book (PNAB). To create one of these documents, choose **File, Mobile, Server Phone Numbers...** from the Notes Client menu. This will open the PNAB to the Server/Connections view, as illustrated in Figure 10.7.

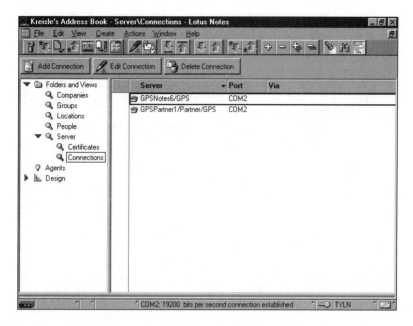

**Figure 10.7** *The Server/Connections View in the Personal Name and Address Book.*

In this view, you will see entries for any servers that may have been configured during the Notes Client install. You can edit these entries the same way you edit any Notes Document. To add a new Server Connection Document, you can click the **Add Connection** button on the action bar or choose **Create, Server Connection** from the Notes Client menu while the View is the active window (Figure 10.8).

In the new Server Connection Document, use the Connection Type field to specify what type of server connection you want to establish. Your choices are **Network**, **Dialup Modem**, **Passthru Server**, and **Remote LAN Service**. The **Network** option would apply to Notes Servers you want to be able to have included in the Open Database dialog box that normally don't appear when you're connected to the network. The **Dialup Modem** choice would apply to any instance where you want your Notes Client to connect to a Notes Server directly by modem. **Passthru Server** would apply when you want to use one Notes Server to reach other Notes Servers connected to the network (which we'll discuss later in this chapter), and **Remote LAN Server** would be used if you have a point-to-point protocol (PPP) server at your office that you can use to connect to the network.

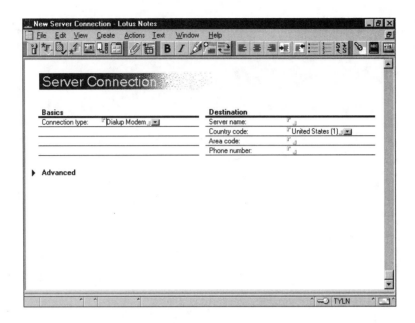

***Figure 10.8*** *A New Server Connection Document.*

Since you would require a special account on the PPP server and additional software on the Notes Client to use the **Remote LAN Server** option, we won't discuss it here. We're also going to skip the Network connection record, focusing our attention on the Dialup Modem type for now and examining the Passthru Server type a little later (Figure 10.9).

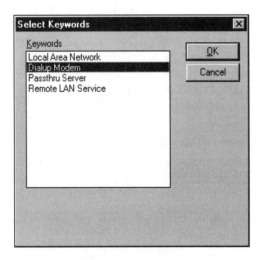

***Figure 10.9*** *Selecting **Dialup Modem** as the connection type.*

Once you have selected **Dialup Modem** as the connection type in the Basics Section, the fields in the Destination section of the Server Connection Document (see Figure 10.8) can be used to specify the name of the Notes Server you wish to call, what country code to use when dialing, and the area code and telephone number.

# Setting Up a Location Document

Now we've told Notes about what type of modem we have, which COM port it's connected to, and what telephone numbers it should call. The next step is to pull all of this information together into a Location Document.

When Notes was first installed on your computer, it is likely that the setup program created one or more Location Documents based on your responses during the installation. If your computer is always connected to the network or is always remote, this probably won't mean much to you. If your computer is a laptop or alternates between being connected to a network and being remote, you'll appreciate the flexibility Location Documents provide.

To examine an existing Location Document or configure one of the standard Documents for your use, select it on the Notes Client using the lower-right corner of the status bar or by using the **File, Mobile, Select Location...** command on the Notes Client menu (Figure 10.10).

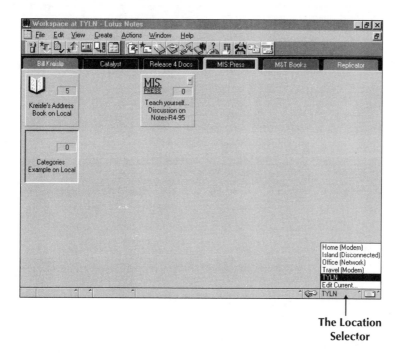

**The Location Selector**

***Figure 10.10*** *The Location selector on the Notes Client status bar.*

Once the desired location is selected, choose **Edit Current...** from the Location selector menu or **File, Mobile, Edit Current Location...** from the Notes Client menu (Figure 10.11).

*Figure 10.11 The **Edit Current...** command.*

This will open the specified Location Document in your Personal Name and Address Book database (Figure 10.12).

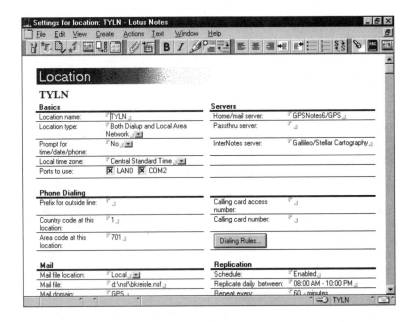

*Figure 10.12 A Location Document in Notes' Personal Name and Address Book database.*

As you can see from Figure 10.12, the location document is broken into several groups of fields. The Basics section provides fields for configuring the Location's Name (what will appear in the Location Selector menu), what type of connection it is, what time zone Notes should use when this Location is active, and which ports the Location document should use to establish connections with Notes Servers..

The Servers section allows you to enter the Notes Server name for three different types of Notes Servers—**Mail**, **Passthru**, and **InterNotes**. Your Home/mail Server is the name of the Server Notes will use to deliver outgoing mail. Also, in many dialog boxes that deal with connecting with Servers, Notes will suggest this Server's name as the first choice because it is your "home" server. If you are working remotely, you can leave this field blank.

A *Passthru Server* is a Notes Server that is willing to serve as an intermediary between a Notes Client connected to it by modem and other Notes Servers on a network. We'll discuss Passthru servers later in this chapter. The *InterNotes Server* is a server that is running Lotus' InterNotes Web Retriever software. We'll discuss InterNotes in Chapter 11.

The Phone Dialing section of the Location Document is for entering information that Notes should use when placing telephone calls, such as what the area code will typically be when this location is active, what needs to be dialed to place a long distance call, and so on.

The Mail section of the Location Document is for specifying the name and exact location of your mail file, as well as information about your mail domain and your preferences for addressing mail. We'll discuss this part of the Location Document again later in this chapter.

The Replication section of the Location Document allows you set up times for the Notes Client to connect with a Notes Server and Replicate automatically.

Once you have entered the settings you want to use for a new Location or edited an existing location, selecting **File, Save** and **File, Close** from the Notes Client will return you to the Workspace.

# Calling a Notes Server

It certainly seems like a lot of work to get set up to connect remotely. When you stop to think about it, however, it's really no different than giving a secretary the information he needs to place a call for you. Who to call, what number to call, under what circumstances to call, and how to place the call. As you saw in the last section, once you have your Location Documents set up, switching between them is very simple using the Notes Status bar.

In addition to the automatic times you may have specified in the Location Document for your Notes Client to contact a Notes Server, there will also be times when you will want to manually initiate a call to a Notes Server. To do this, you have several options.

The first option is to choose **File, Mobile, Call Server...** from the Notes Client menu to open the Call Server dialog box (Figure 10.13).

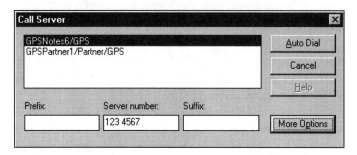

**Figure 10.13** *The Call Server dialog box.*

The names of any Notes Servers that you have created Server Connection Documents for and specified the Dialup Modem connection type for will appear in the dialog box. Selecting a Server from the list and clicking **Auto Dial** places the call.

While Notes is calling, information about the call will be displayed in the Notes Client's status bar.

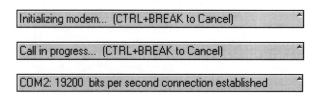

**Figure 10.14** *Following the progress of a call in the Notes Client's status bar.*

Once you are connected, you can use the **File, Database, Open** command to open new databases on that server. You can also initiate replication between a local replica and databases on the Notes Server to which you are connected.

When you have finished working with the Notes Server you have called, choose **File, Mobile, Hang Up...** from the Notes Client menu to open the Hang Up dialog box (Figure 10.15).

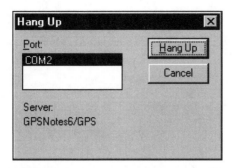

***Figure 10.15*** *The Hang Up dialog box.*

If you are connected to multiple servers on more than one COM port, select the Notes Server you wish to disconnect from, then click **Hang Up** to end your connection. You will see a message similar to that shown in Figure 10.16 in the Notes Client's status bar.

***Figure 10.16*** *The Notes Client using the Status Bar to report that the call is disconnected.*

Another option for calling servers is to use the Replicator Page. By adding panels to call Notes Servers to the Replicator Page, you can have several different calls placed with the click of a single button (Figure 10.17).

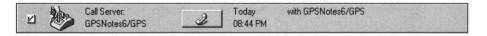

***Figure 10.17*** *Adding a Panel to the Replicator Page to call a Notes Server.*

To add a Panel to the Replicator Page to call a Notes Server, select where on the Replicator page you wish to add the Panel, and select **Create, Call Entry** from the Notes Client. This will add a Pane to the Replicator Page with the name of the server in the Mail/Home Server field of the current Location Document. To change the panel to a different Notes Server, click the **Telephone** button on the panel to open the Call Server dialog box, and choose the name of the Notes Server you want called (Figure 10.18).

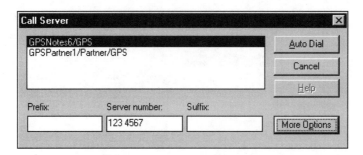

**Figure 10.18** *Using the Call Server dialog box to specify a different Server on the Call Server Panel.*

Now, whenever you click the **Start** button on the Replicator Page, Notes will call the Server specified when it reached that Panel. You can also add a panel to instruct Notes to hang up a connection to a server by selecting the position on the Replicator Page where the panel should appear and selecting **Create, Hangup Entry** from the Notes Client menu.

**Figure 10.19** *A Panel telling the Replicator Page to hang up.*

# Configuring a Passthru Server

A powerful new feature of Notes Release 4 is the option to make one or more Notes Servers in a network a Passthru Server. As you've probably already guessed from other places where the Passthru Server was mentioned in this chapter, its purpose is to allow you to connect to multiple Notes Servers using a single telephone number. Figure 10.20 illustrates a Notes Server that allows passthru services.

Referring to Figure 10.20, note that a Notes Client (A) places a call to a Notes Server (B). Because the Notes Server (B) is connected to a network (C) with other Notes Servers (D) and because the Notes Server being called is also a Passthru Server (B), the Notes Client (A) can open databases on any of the Notes Servers (B,D).

If your network has a Passthru Server, you can set up your Notes Client to use this Server by creating these documents:

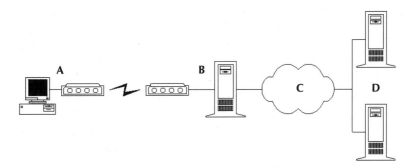

**Figure 10.20** *A Notes Server that also acts as a Passthru Server.*

1. A Server Connection document that is a Dialup Modem connection to the Passthru Server (Figure 10.21). Since a Passthru Server is also a Notes Server, we need a Dialup Modem Connection Record so Notes knows what phone number to call whenever it wants to connect to it or one of the Servers for which it is a gateway.

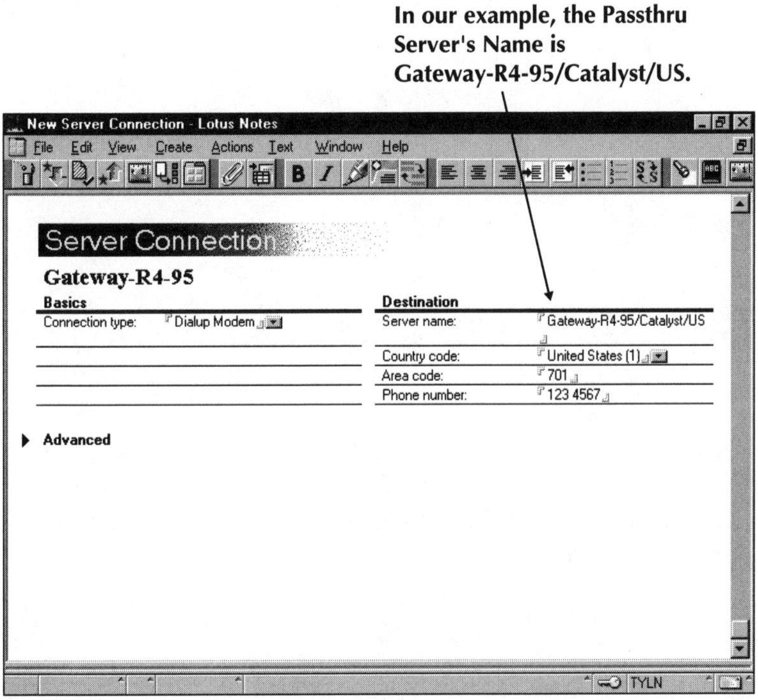

**In our example, the Passthru Server's Name is Gateway-R4-95/Catalyst/US.**

**Figure 10.21** *A Server Connection Document for a Dialup Modem connection to the Passthru Server.*

2. One or more Server Connection Document for the Passthru Server that specify what Server(s) the Passthru Server should be used to connect to (Figure 10.22). Using this Document, Notes will know that whenever I want to open a database on Notes-R4-95/Catalyst/US, it should call Gateway-R4-95/Catalyst/US using the Server Connection Document we created earlier (number 1 in this list).

**In our example, the Passthru Server's Name is Gateway-R4-95/Catalyst/US.**

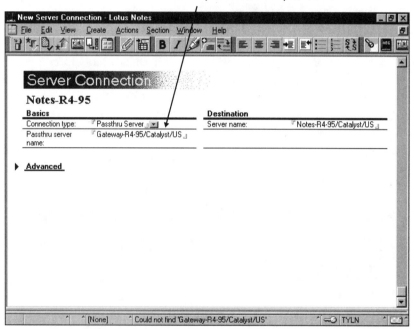

***Figure 10.22*** *A Passthru Server Connection Document.*

3. A Location Document that specifies the name of the Passthru Server (you may want to edit an existing Location Document for this purpose; see Figure 10.23). Adding Gateway-R4-95/Catalyst/US to the Passthru server field of the Location Document makes it "active."

## Lotus Notes Mail Concepts

When we discussed Lotus Notes Mail in Chapter 9, we focused primarily on the features of the mail system itself so the chapter would be useful to both Mobile

Notes users and users who only use Lotus Notes Mail from a network. Because more in-depth coverage is appropriate for Mobile Notes users to get the most out of Lotus Notes Mail, this section talks about the concepts behind its operation.

To begin with, let's talk about Lotus Notes Mail in general, which works by combining several elements:

❖   A network of Notes Clients and Servers

❖   Lotus Notes Mail databases

❖   A Notes Name and Address book

❖   A special Notes database called a *mailbox file*

**In our example, the Passthru
Server's Name is
Gateway-R4-95/Catalyst/US.**

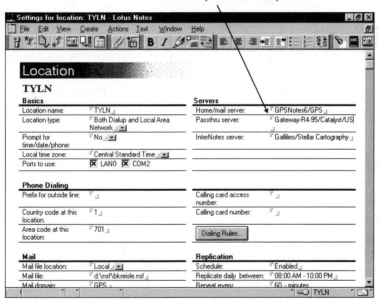

***Figure 10.23***  *Adding the Passthru Server's name to the Location Document.*

As you know from the beginning of this book, a Notes Server is a machine running a Server version of Lotus' Notes software. It is designed to centrally store Notes databases, and to facilitate mail exchange and workflow using a network. This network can be dedicated (meaning a physical connection that is always present) or demand-based (meaning dialing in by modem from a Notes Client to a Notes Server).

Mail databases are simply Notes databases that are designed to collect messages. What makes a mail database different from any other database is that it is listed in the Notes Name and Address Book on one or more servers.

The Notes Name and Address Book is a Notes database called NAMES.NSF. It is a combination user directory, configuration file, mail directory, program scheduler, and groups list. There is a NAMES.NSF on every Notes Server and on every Notes Client. The Name and Address book on a Notes Server is used to route mail and provide users with a means to look up electronic mail addresses and groups. The Name and Address book used by Notes Clients can be used as a personal address list, and, as we saw earlier, a list of Server telephone numbers for remote connections.

The mailbox file is a "holding cell" for Notes messages. It may be located on your local hard drive or on a Notes Server, depending on whether or not you have a dedicated or on-demand network connection.

Now that I've introduced the key players in mail-enabling, I'm going to draw a few pictures of a Notes network of clients and servers, and narrate the life of a Lotus Notes Mail message based on the network in each picture.

In our first illustration (Figure 10.24), we're going to have one Notes Server and two Notes Clients. Each of the Notes Clients has a dedicated connection to the Notes Server, so they will be using *server-based mail*. Server-based mail is automatically routed to a Notes server the moment it is sent. It is given a unique name to differentiate it from *workstation-based mail*, which we will discuss later in this section.

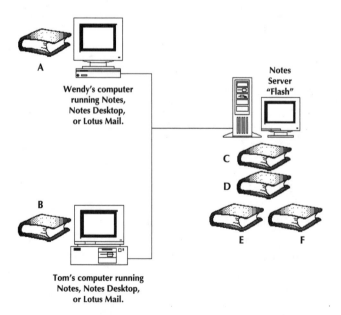

A

Wendy's computer
running Notes,
Notes Desktop,
or Lotus Mail.

Notes
Server
"Flash"

C

D

E        F

B

Tom's computer running
Notes, Notes Desktop,
or Lotus Mail.

**Figure 10.24** *Two Notes Clients and a Notes Server;*
*the Notes Clients are using server-based mail.*

Using Figure 10.24 as our reference, let's examine the steps Tom takes to send a message to Wendy, and the steps Notes Clients and Notes Servers take to deliver the message:

1.  First, Tom needs to create a new Document in his Lotus Notes Mail database (E) using the **Create, Mail, Memo** or **Create, Memo** command on the Notes Client menu (Figure 10.25).

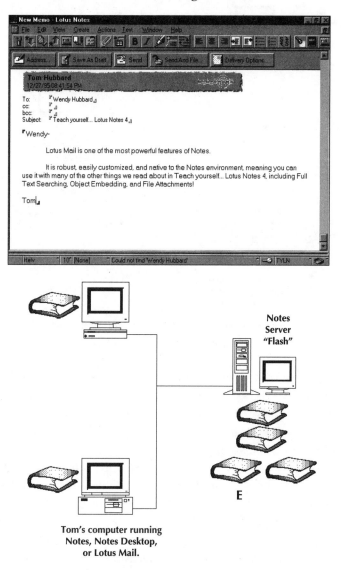

**Figure 10.25** *Creating a new Lotus Notes Mail memo.*

2.  Now that the new Document is created, addressed, and filled with information, Tom sends it to Wendy by clicking the **Send** button on the Action Bar.

3.  Tom's Notes Client looks through its Personal Name and Address Book (B) to see if there is anything special about Wendy's address it needs to act on before passing the message to Notes Server Flash (Figure 10.26).

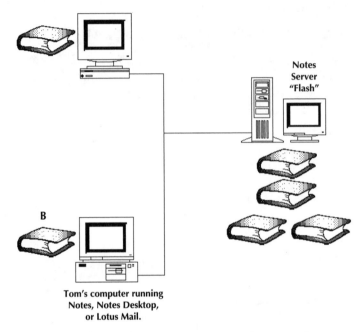

Notes Server "Flash"

B

Tom's computer running Notes, Notes Desktop, or Lotus Mail.

***Figure 10.26*** *Checking the Personal Name and Address Book for Wendy's address.*

4.  There is no entry for Wendy in Tom's local Name and Address book, so the Notes Client contacts Tom's home server Flash over the network, and deposits Tom's message in Flash's temporary mailbox file (C). (See Figure 10.27)

5.  The Notes Server Flash checks the temporary mailbox file (C) and discovers a new message, addressed to Wendy. Flash looks up the address for Wendy by checking the Server's Name and Address Book (D) to see if there is an entry for her (Figure 10.28). Flash finds the entry, and it says that Wendy's mail file is located on the Notes Server Flash (F).

6.  Flash deposits Tom's message into Wendy's mail file (F). The next time Wendy opens her mail file using her Notes Client, she will see Tom's message (Figure 10.29).

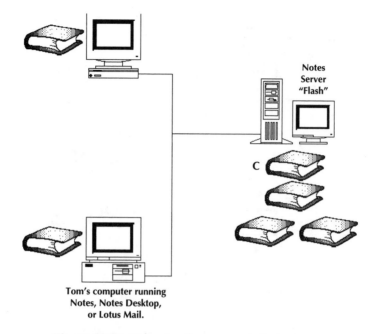

**Notes Server "Flash"**

**C**

**Tom's computer running Notes, Notes Desktop, or Lotus Mail.**

*Figure 10.27* *Delivering the message to the temporary mailbox file on the Notes Server Flash.*

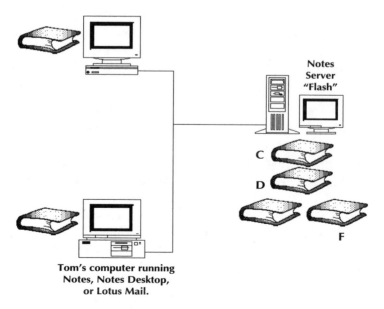

**Notes Server "Flash"**

**C**

**D**

**F**

**Tom's computer running Notes, Notes Desktop, or Lotus Mail.**

*Figure 10.28* *The Notes Server Flash looks up Wendy's address to find out what it should do next.*

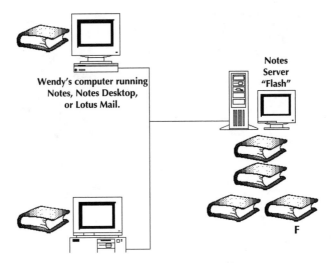

**Figure 10.29** *When Wendy opens her Lotus Notes Mail database, she will see the new message.*

Condensing these six steps:

1.  The user creates and addresses a message.
2.  The user sends the message using the Notes Client.
3.  The Notes Client looks for each addressee in its Personal Name and Address Book, and converts any matches it finds to a forwarding address if one is entered.
4.  The Notes Client deposits message in a Notes Server's mailbox file.
5.  The Notes Server checks the mailbox file and finds a message. It looks up the addressees of the message and compares it to its Name and Address book.
6.  If an addressee has a mail database on the Server processing the message, the Server deposits a copy of the message in his or her mail file.

What happens if there is more than one Notes Server in your network? The same principle. If the addressee has a mail database on another Notes Server, the server processing the message contacts the next server and deposits a copy of the message in its temporary mailbox file.

# Mobile Lotus Notes Mail Concepts

In cases where a user has an on-demand (modem) connection to the Notes network, mail is routed a little differently. Let's add another user, Ted, to the network we created in Figure 10.24, and make Ted a Mobile Notes user who connects to the Notes Server Flash using a modem. Figure 10.30 illustrates our new addition.

Using Figure 10.30 as our reference, we're going to trace mail in two directions this time—from Wendy to Ted and from Ted to Tom. Before we start tracing steps, however, let's compare Figures 10.24 and 10.30. The modems and a PC for the new Notes Client are obvious enough, but why do you suppose Ted's machine has more databases locally than Tom or Wendy's (H, I, J), and one more database is added to Flash's drive (G)?

The answer is because Ted's connection to the network is intermittent. He doesn't stay connected constantly, and dials in only when he needs to exchange information or he wants to check for new mail. That means that in addition to his Personal Name and Address Book (I), he needs to duplicate the resources that the Notes Server has to work off line, including a mailbox file (H), and a Replica of the Server's mail database for Ted on his local hard drive (J).

So what's the file that got added to the Notes Server, Flash (G)? It is also a replica of Ted's Lotus Notes Mail database.

Why does he need to have two mail files? Because Ted is only occasionally connected to the Notes network that Tom and Wendy are connected to constantly. When a mail message is sent by Tom or Wendy to Ted, Flash doesn't want to have to wait for Ted to call in to clear the message out of his temporary mailbox, he wants to put it away and get busy looking for the next incoming message. To do this, Flash uses a replica of Ted's Lotus Notes Mail file to deposit messages in whenever one is addressed to Ted (Figure 10.31).

How these new files affect mail routing is displayed as we trace the steps for Wendy to send a message to Ted, and then for Ted to send a message to Tom:

1.  Wendy composes, addresses, and then mails her message to Ted.
2.  Wendy's Notes Client checks its Personal Name and Address Book (A) for an entry for Ted. It doesn't find one, so it delivers the message with

the address "as is" to Wendy's mail server, Flash. (It places the message in Flash's temporary mailbox file (C).) (See Figure 10.32.)

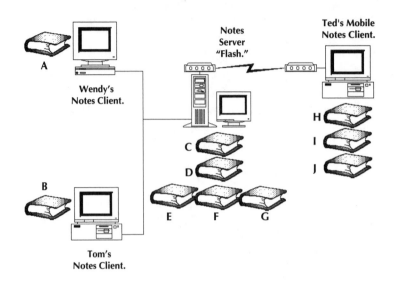

***Figure 10.30*** *The Network in Figure 10.24 with the addition of a remote user.*

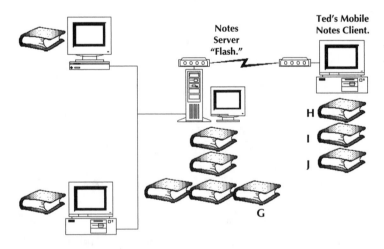

***Figure 10.31*** *The additional files needed to add a Mobile Lotus Notes Mail user.*

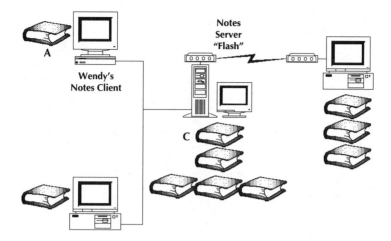

**Figure 10.32** *Wendy's message to Ted begins its journey.*

3. Flash checks the temporary mailbox file, and finds a message addressed to Ted. After searching through the Server's Name and Address Book (D), Flash discovers that it has a replica of Ted's mail file (G). (See Figure 10.33.)

4. Flash deposits the message into Ted's mail file (G).

5. Ted establishes a connection with Flash via modem. Once connected, Ted initiates a replication event between his local mail database (J) and his mail database on Flash. Ted's Notes Client pulls the message that Flash delivered (Figure 10.34).

6. Ted disconnects his Notes Client from Flash and reads his mail.

7. As Ted reads Wendy's message, it makes him think of a question he wants to ask Tom. So Ted composes a message for Tom by selecting his local mail database on his workspace (J) and choosing Create, Memo from the main menu. After he addresses the memo to Tom, and asks his question, he sends it.

8. The Notes-Client Checks Ted's Personal Name and Address Book (I) to see if it has an address for Tom. There's no information about Tom in Ted's Personal Name and Address Book, so the Notes Client deposits the message in Ted's temporary mailbox file "as is" (H). (See Figure 10.35.)

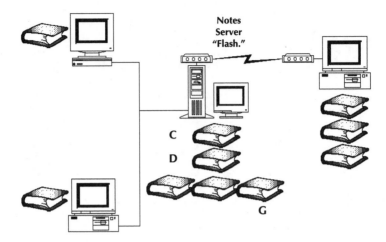

**Figure 10.33** *Flash looks for Ted's address to decide what to do next.*

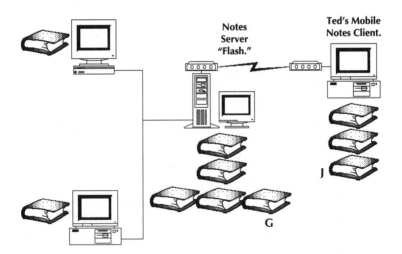

**Figure 10.34** *Ted connects to Flash and replicates his Lotus Notes Mail database.*

9.  A few minutes later, Ted finishes answering his mail, and he calls the Server Flash again. He initiates a replication between Flash and his Notes Client again, and this time, he also transfers outgoing mail using the Replicator Page. The message to Tom, along with any other messages Ted composed or replied to, are moved from the temporary mailbox on Ted's Notes Client to the temporary mailbox on the Notes Server Flash (C). (See Figure 10.36.)

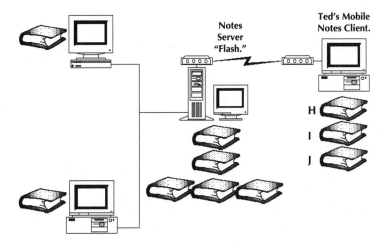

**Figure 10.35** *Ted's Notes Client prepares a message for delivery.*

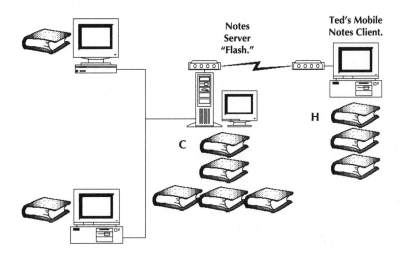

**Figure 10.36** *Ted's Notes Client uses the modem connection to move mail from its temporary mailbox file to Flash's temporary mailbox file.*

10. The Notes Server Flash checks the temporary mailbox (C) and discovers a message addressed to Tom. Flash checks the Server's Name and Address Book and determines that Tom has a mail file on Flash (E), so it deposits the mail message in Tom's mail database.

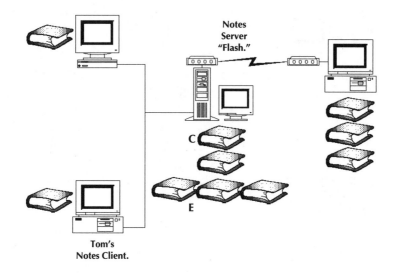

**Figure 10.37** *Flash delivers Ted's message to Tom's mail database.*

## Whew!

As you can see, how Notes delivers mail isn't rocket science, but it isn't exactly simple, either. Of course, if you were to break any electronic mail system down and follow a message from one point to another, you'd find it was a little more complex than you would have guessed.

But the bottom line is that Notes delivers mail based on two modes of operation—server-based mail and workstation-based mail (or, as Lotus calls it with Release 4, *Mobile Mail*). The primary difference between server-based and workstation-based mail is that workstation-based mail clients have their own temporary mail boxes and maintain replicas of their mail databases so they can work with them while they are not connected to a Notes Server.

Which version of mail you are using is set up using two sections of the active Location Document (Figure 10.38).

In the Servers section of the Location Document, Notes uses the value in the Mail/Home server field as well as the Passthru Server field (if enabled) to determine what Server it should try to connect to when asked to deliver mail.

**Servers**

| | |
|---|---|
| Home/mail server: | ⌐ GPSNotes6/GPS ⌐ |
| Passthru server: | ⌐ ⌐ |
| InterNotes server: | ⌐ Gallileo/Stellar Cartography ⌐ |

**Mail**

| | |
|---|---|
| Mail file location: | ⌐ Local ⌐ ▼ |
| Mail file: | ⌐ d:\nsf\bkreisle.nsf ⌐ |
| Mail domain: | ⌐ GPS ⌐ |
| Recipient name type-ahead: | ⌐ Personal Address Book Only ⌐ ▼ |
| Recipient name lookup: | ⌐ Stop after first match ⌐ ▼ |
| Transfer outgoing mail if: | ⌐ 5 ⌐ messages pending |

***Figure 10.38*** *Settings that affect mail in the Location Document.*

In the Mail section of the Location Document:

❖ The Mail file location field is used to specify whether Notes should use a mail file on your local hard drive or on the Server specified in the Servers section when you create new memos.

❖ The Mail file field is where you enter the path and name of your mail file.

❖ The Mail domain field is where you enter the name of your Notes Domain (your Notes Administrator should be able to supply you with this information).

❖ The two Recipient name... fields allow you to control whether or not Notes tries to match names you type into the mail address fields (To:, cc:, and bcc: ) as you type, and what Notes should do if it finds multiple matches.

❖ The Transfer outgoing mail if field allows to set a value that Notes should use as a trigger to automatically call your Mail Server and transfer mail.

If you wish to transfer Mail before the number of messages specified in your Location Document are stored in your mailbox file, you can do so two ways:

1.  Select **Send Outgoing Mail** from the menu that pops up when you click the **Mail** icon on the Notes Client status bar (Figure 10.39).

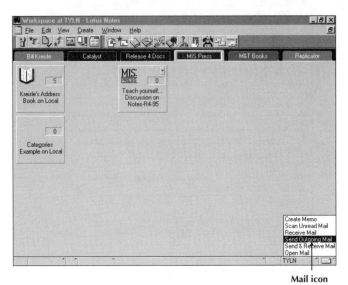

**Mail icon**

***Figure 10.39*** *The menu choices for the Mail icon on the Notes Client status bar.*

2.  You can enable the Send outgoing mail panel on the Replicator Page before clicking the **Start** button.

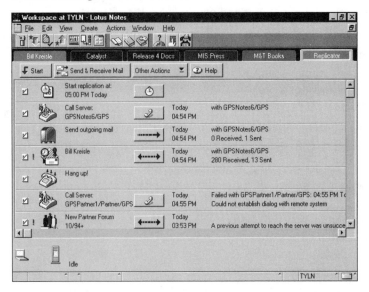

***Figure 10.40*** *The Send outgoing mail panel on the Replicator Page.*

# Summary

Mobile Notes combines replication with a wide array of tools to manage modems, communications ports, Notes Server telephone numbers, and electronic mail to create a powerful tool for keeping your information up-to-date.

With that power, however, comes responsibility. To configure Mobile Notes, you need to set up:

1.  A modem
2.  A Server Connection Document
3.  A Location Document

Once you have these items set up, you can use the **File, Mobile...** menu commands on the Notes Client menu to call and hang up with servers, or you can use the Replicator page.

- ❖ Passthru Servers are Notes Servers that will allow you to pass information through them to other Notes Servers connected to the network you have called.

- ❖ Lotus Notes Mail combines Personal Name and Address Books on the Notes Client with a mailbox file, a Server Name and Address Book, and user mail databases on a Server. Whenever a user sends a message, it is placed in his mail server's mailbox file for processing instantly.

- ❖ Mobile Lotus Notes Mail works by duplicating the resources a Notes Server has for delivering mail, including a mailbox file and a replica of a user's mail database on the local drive. Instead of sending mail instantly, messages are stored in the local mailbox file until a connection is made to the user's mail server.

- ❖ You can switch between Mobile Lotus Notes Mail and Lotus Notes Mail easily by having different Location Documents.

- ❖ When you are working with Mobile Lotus Notes Mail, you can send mail using the Replicator Page or the Mail menu that appears when you click the mail icon on the Notes Client status bar.

# Chapter 11

# Working Faster and Smarter

## In this Chapter

Our final chapter is a departure from the orderly progression we've been following. It is designed to introduce features that enhance some of the things we've already covered as well as discuss new features that aren't absolutely necessary to use Notes but may interest you.

In other words, this chapter is where a lot of cool "power user" stuff is that I couldn't fit into the rest of the book. Some of the things we'll cover in this chapter:

- ❖ SmartIcons
- ❖ Word processing in Notes
- ❖ Building simple Agents
- ❖ The InterNotes web navigator
- ❖ File and database maintenance

# SmartIcons

SmartIcons are shortcuts for common Notes tasks (such as adding a new database to your Workspace or deleting a Document from a View) that you can display as a group of buttons on the Notes Client.

**SmartIcons**

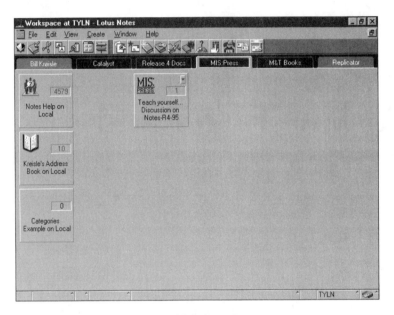

***Figure 11.1*** *SmartIcons.*

SmartIcons can be grouped and located to suit your needs using the **File, Tools, SmartIcons...** command on the Notes Client menu. This will open the SmartIcons dialog box (Figure 11.2).

As of Release 4, Notes has two types of SmartIcons. Standard SmartIcons are icons you group together on the icon bar for your own use into what Notes calls SmartIcon sets. Context SmartIcon, are icon groups that Notes can present on the icon bar at a specific time, such as while you have a View open or while the current window is the Workspace. In other words, they are icons that appear based on the context of what you are currently doing.

You use the SmartIcons dialog box to control whether one, both, or neither of these icon types are displayed on the Notes Client by using the Icon Bar and Context Icons check boxes in the Show group.

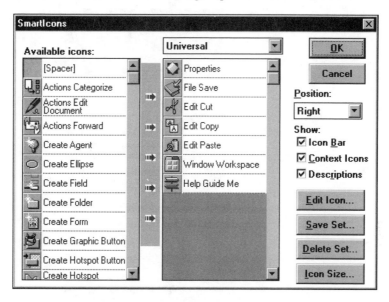

***Figure 11.2*** *The SmartIcons dialog box.*

If you select the **Icon Bar** check box, whatever SmartIcon set specified in the drop-down list at the top of the SmartIcons dialog box will be displayed (in Figure 11.2, the **Universal SmartIcon** set is selected). The scrolling window beneath the SmartIcon set drop-down lists shows the SmartIcons that will be added to the icon bar.

If you have the **Icon Bar** or **Context Icons** check box selected, the Positions drop-down list allows you to control where the SmartIcons will be displayed on the Notes Client. Table 11.1 illustrates the different locations.

You can use the **Descriptions** check box in the Show group of the SmartIcons dialog box to control whether or not SmartIcons will display balloon help. When this box is checked, holding the mouse over an icon on the Workspace for about a second will cause its description to appear in a small pop-up balloon.

**Table 11.1** *The Positions for SmartIcons on the Notes Client*

| Position | Icon |
| --- | --- |
| Top |  |
| Bottom |  |
| Left |  |
| Right |  |
| Floating |  |

**Figure 11.3** *Previewing a SmartIcon's name without running it.*

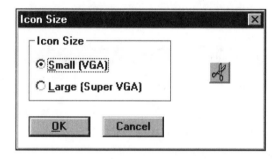

**Figure 11.4** *The Icon Size dialog box.*

**Large SmartIcons**

**Small SmartIcons**

**Figure 11.5** *Large and Small SmartIcons on the Workspace.*

**N O T E**

Even if Descriptions is turned off, you can still preview a SmartIcon without running it by right-clicking on it.

You can use the **Icon Size** button on the SmartIcons dialog box to make the SmartIcons appear on the Workspace as either Large or Small using the Icon Size dialog box.

You can create your own SmartIcon sets using the SmartIcons dialog by clicking and dragging icons between the Available Icons scrolling box and the currently selected set. After you have finished customizing a SmartIcon set, clicking on the **Save Set** button will open the Save Set of SmartIcons dialog box.

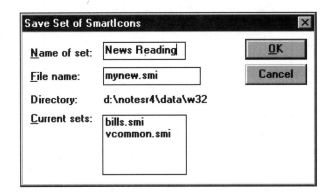

***Figure 11.6*** *The Save Set of SmartIcons dialog box.*

In this dialog box, the Name of Set value is what will be displayed on the SmartIcons dialog box, and the File Name is the name your operating system will use to identify the set whenever Notes starts.

As you can see from the Available Icons list in the SmartIcons dialog box, there are a wide variety of icons you can include in your personal sets. I have created several tables to help you decide which icons might be useful to you. I've also identified which SmartIcons are context sensitive, so that you can know whether or not you need to include them in your custom sets (they might appear automatically whenever you're doing a given task).

**Table 11.2** *SmartIcons for the Workspace*

| SmartIcon | Context | Description |
|---|---|---|
| Edit Mark All Read | | Marks all documents in the selected database as read |
| Edit Mark All Unread | | Marks all documents in the selected database as unread |
| Edit Copy As Link | | Copies a link for the selected database to the Clipboard |
| Edit Scan Choose | | Allows you to add databases to your "preferred list" for quick unread Document scanning |
| Edit Scan Unread Choose Preferred | | Allows you to add database to your "preferred list" for quick unread Document scanning |
| File Database Access Control | Workspace; replicator page | Opens the Access Control List for the selected database |
| File Database New Copy | | Makes a new copy of the selected database or prompts you for a database name to copy from if no database is selected on the Workspace |
| File Database Properties | | Opens the Properties for Database dialog box |
| File Exit Notes | | Closes the Notes Client |
| File Open Database | Replicator page | Opens the Open Database dialog box to allow you to select a database from your local hard drive or any connected Notes Servers |

| SmartIcon | Context | Description |
|---|---|---|
| File New Database | Workspace | Creates a new database replicator page |
| File Replication New Replica | | Creates a new replica of the selected database or prompts you for a database to make a replica if no database is selected on the Workspace |
| View Show Server Names | | Adds information about the Notes Server a database is located on to its icon on the Workspace |
| Window Workspace | | Brings the Workspace Window to the front of the Notes Client |
| Window Cascade | | Cascades all active Windows (including the Workspace) in the Notes Client |
| Window Tile | | Tiles all active Windows (including the Workspace) in the Notes Client |

**Table 11.3** *SmartIcons for the Database Window*

| SmartIcon | Context | Description |
|---|---|---|
| Actions Edit Document | Database window; reading documents | Opens the selected Document in a View/Folder for editing; will also open a document you are reading for editing |
| Edit Clear | | Deletes the selected Document(s) in a View/Folder from the database |
| Edit Copy | | Copies the selected Document(s) in a View/Folder |
| Edit Paste | | Pastes the contents of the Clipboard into the currently selected View/Folder; will only paste Documents that have been cut/copied from another View/Folder |
| Edit Copy As Link | | Copies the selected document as a Document Link; at the time of this book's writing, this icon did not work for Database Links and View Links |
| Edit Cut | | Deletes the selected Document(s) from a View/Folder and leaves a copy of the selected Document(s) on the Clipboard |
| Actions Categorize | | If the current View/Folder is categorized using a special Categories Field (up to the database designer), then this button allows you to move Documents to different categories from the Database Window |
| Edit Find Next | | Finds the next Document in the View that matches your search criteria |

| SmartIcon | Context | Description |
|---|---|---|
| Edit Mark Selected Read | | Marks the selected Document(s) in the Database Window as read |
| Edit Mark Selected Unread | | Marks the selected Document(s) in the Database Window as unread |
| Edit Select All | | Selects all Documents in the current View/Folder |
| File Document Properties | | Opens the Properties for Document dialog box for the currently selected Document in a View/Folder |
| File Export | | Exports the currently selected Documents in the View/Folder to a user specified format. |
| File Import | | Imports records from a user specified format into the current View/Folder as new Documents |
| Navigate Next | Database window; reading documents | Takes you to the next Document in the current View/Folder; useful when reading Documents |
| Navigate Previous | Database window; reading documents | Takes you to the previous Document in the current View/Folder. Useful when reading Documents |
| Navigate Next Main | Database window; reading documents | Takes you to the next main Document in the current View/Folder (skipping Responses); useful when reading Documents |
| Navigate Previous Main | Database window; reading documents | Takes you to the previous main Document in the current View/Folder (skipping Responses). Useful when reading Documents |

| SmartIcon | Context | Description |
|---|---|---|
| Navigate Next Selected | | Takes you to the next selected document in the current View/Folder |
| Navigate Previous Selected | | Takes you to the prior selected document in the current View/Folder |
| Navigate Next Unread | Database window; reading documents | Takes you to the next unread document in the current View/Folder. |
| Navigate Previous Unread | Database window; reading documents | Takes you to the prior unread document in the current View/Folder |
| View Expand | Database window | Expands the selected Document in a View/Folder (if it is a Main Topic, for example, it expands any Responses to it). Also will expand a selected category |
| View Expand All | Database window | Expands all categories/Documents in a View/Folder |
| View Collapse | Database window | Collapses the selected Document in a View/Folder (if it is a Main Topic, for example, it collapses any Responses to it). Also will collapse a selected category |
| View Collapse All | Database window | Collapses all categories/Documents in a View/Folder |
| View Go Up Level | Reading documents | Takes you up one level from the current window (i.e. if you are reading a document, moves up to the last view). |

| SmartIcon | Context | Description |
|---|---|---|
| View Refresh | | Causes the currently selected View/Folder to check the Notes database for any documents that may have been added/deleted during the current session. Updates the View/Folder with the most current snapshot of the database |
| View Show/Hide Preview Pane | Database window | Toggles the Document Preview Pane on or off if you are in a View/Folder. Toggles the Document Link Preview Pane on or off if you are reading a Document |
| View Show/Hide Preview Parent | Reading documents | Toggles the Parent Preview Pane on or off if you are reading a Response Document |
| View Show/Hide Preview Document Links | Reading documents | Toggles the Document Link Preview Pane on or off if you are reading a Document |

*Table 11.4* *SmartIcons for Notes Mail Users*

| SmartIcon | Context | Description |
|---|---|---|
| Create Mail Memo | Workspace | Opens a Mail Document in the mail database specified by the current location |
| Edit Scan Unread Mail | Workspace | Opens the default View/Folder for Mail and shows the first unread Document (Mail Memo) in the database |
| File Preferences Mail | | Opens the File, Preferences dialog box and selects the Mail Settings icon on the dialog |
| Mail Address | | Opens the Name and Address Book(s) specified in the current location, and allows you to select names or groups from it for your Memo |

| SmartIcon | Context | Description |
|---|---|---|
| Mail Open | | Opens the mail database specified in the current location |
| Mail Send Document | | Sends the currently selected/open Document as a Mail Memo |
| Actions Forward | Database window; reading documents | Forwards the currently selected Document as a Mail Memo |
| Text Permanent Pen | Editing documents | Allows you to add comments to a message in a different color |

*Table 11.5* *SmartIcons for Mobile Users*

| SmartIcon | Context | Description |
|---|---|---|
| File Mobile Call Server | Workspace; replicator page | Allows you to select from all Notes Servers specified by the current location to establish a modem connection |
| File Mobile Hang Up | Workspace; replicator page | Closes a modem connection between the specified communications port and Notes Server |
| File Mobile Locations | Workspace; replicator page | Allows you to view or edit your current location Documents in your local Name and Address book |
| File Replication Replicate | Workspace | Initiates a replication between the currently selected database(s) and the associated Notes Server(s) |
| File Replication Settings | | Opens the Replication Setting dialog box for the currently selected database |

**Table 11.6** *Miscellaneous SmartIcons*

| SmartIcon | Context | Description |
|---|---|---|
| [Spacer] | | Adds a space between SmartIcons on the Icon Bar |
| Create Agent | | Opens the Agent View of the currently selected database, and allows you to create an Agent |
| File Database Full Text Create Index | | Opens the Create Full Text Index dialog box and allows you to specify settings for and create a Full Text Index for the selected database |
| File Database Full Text Info | | Opens the Properties for Database dialog box for the selected database and makes the Full Text Index page of the dialog box active |
| File Database Full Text Update Index | | Causes the Notes Client or Notes Server to update the Full Text Index of the currently selected database |
| View Show/Hide Search Bar | Database window | Toggles the Search Bar on or off in the Database Window |
| Navigate Next Highlight | | Moves to the next match to your query in the currently open Document |
| Navigate Previous Highlight | | Moves to the previous match to your query in the currently open Document |
| File Database Header Footer | | Allows you to create header and footer information that will be printed with every document in the database |
| File Database Publish | Workspace | Adds information about the currently selected database to the specified Library Database |

| SmartIcon | Context | Description |
|---|---|---|
| File Preferences Ports | | Opens the File Preferences dialog box and selects the Ports icon |
| File Print | | Prints the current View/Folder/Document |
| File Print Setup | | Opens the Printer Setup dialog box |
| File Switch User ID | Workspace | Allows you to switch to a different User ID at the Notes Client (i.e., log in as a different user) |
| File Tools Server Administration | | Opens the Server Administration window |
| Help Guide Me | | Opens the Notes Help or Notes Help Lite database to the Guide Me Document |
| Help Topics | | Opens the Notes Help or Notes Help Lite database to the Help Topics View |
| Lock ID | Workspace | Clears the active information about the current ID file in use at the Notes Client (to use the ID, a user will have to re-enter the ID's password) |
| Properties | | Opens the Properties dialog box for the currently selected object in the Notes Client |

***Table 11.7*** *SmartIcon Settings*

| SmartIcon | Context | Description |
|---|---|---|
| File Tools SmartIcons | | Opens the SmartIcons dialog box |
| SmartIcons Floating | | Toggles the SmartIcons between their current location on the Workspace and Floating |
| SmartIcons Next Set | | Displays the next SmartIcon set in the Icon Bar |

***Table 11.8*** *SmartIcons for other Lotus Applications*

Start Lotus 123 for Windows    Start Lotus Word Pro    Start Lotus cc:Mail for Windows

Start Lotus Freelance Graphics for Windows    Start Lotus Improv for Windows    Start Lotus Notes:Document Imaging

Start Lotus Smart Pics    Start Lotus Organizer    Start Lotus SmartText

***Table 11.9*** *SmartIcons for Word Processing or Rich Text Fields*

| SmartIcon | Context | Description |
|---|---|---|
| Edit Check Spelling | Editing documents | Activates the Spell Checker in the current field |
| Edit Clear | | Deletes the currently selected text/objects in a rich text field |
| Edit Copy | | Copies the currently selected text/objects in a field |

| SmartIcon | Context | Description |
|---|---|---|
| Edit Cut | | Removes the currently selected text/object from a field and leaves a copy of what was removed on the Clipboard |
| Edit Paste | | Pastes the contents of the Clipboard into the currently selected field |
| Edit Paste Special | | Pastes the contents of the Clipboard in a special format into a rich text field |
| Edit Find Next | | Finds the next item in the Document that matches the search criteria |
| Edit Find/Replace | Database window; reading or editing documents | Finds the next item in the Document that matches the search criteria and replaces it with the specified string |
| Create Graphic Button | | Inserts a graphic button into the rich text field and opens the Programmer's Pane |
| Create Hotspot Button | | Inserts a button into the rich text field and opens the Programmer's Pane |
| Create Hotspot Text Popup | | Creates a text pop-up on for the currently selected text in the rich text field and opens the Programmer's Pane |
| Create Object | | Creates an object in a rich text field |
| Edit Select All | | Selects the contents of the entire Document if reading, the currently selected field if editing |
| Edit Undo | | Undoes the last action performed in Notes (if it is possible to undo it) |

| SmartIcon | Context | Description |
|-----------|---------|-------------|
| File Attach | Editing documents | Inserts a File Attachment into a Rich Text Field |
| File Document Properties | | Opens the Properties for Document dialog box for the currently open or selected Document |
| File Export | | Exports the current document or view to a number of formats |
| File Import | | Imports the contents of a file into a rich text field |
| File Page Setup | | Allows you to input settings about the size and margins of the pages the Documents will be printed on |
| File Save | | Saves changes made to the current Document |
| Paragraph Properties | Editing documents | Opens the Properties for Paragraph for the currently selected paragraph in a rich text field |
| Create Table | Editing documents | Inserts a table into a rich text field |
| Table Delete Selected Row(s) | | Deletes the selected rows from a table in a rich text field |
| Table Insert Row | | Inserts a row before the current cursor location in a table in a rich text field |
| Table Delete Special | | Allows you to delete multiple rows or columns from a table |
| Table Insert Special | | Allows you to insert multiple rows or columns in a table |

| SmartIcon | Context | Description |
|---|---|---|
| Table Properties | | Opens the Properties for Table dialog box for the currently selected table in a rich text field |
| Text Align Paragraph Center | Editing documents | Center Justifies the currently selected paragraph(s) in a rich text field |
| Text Align Paragraph Full | | Fully justifies (even left and right edges) the currently selected paragraph(s) in a rich text field |
| Text Align Paragraph Left | Editing documents | Left justifies (even left edges) the currently selected paragraph(s) in a rich text field |
| Text Align Paragraph Right | Editing documents | Right justifies (even right edges) the currently selected paragraph(s) in a rich text field |
| Text Bold | Editing documents | Toggles bold text on or off for the currently selected text in a rich text field |
| Text Italic | Editing documents | Toggles italics on or off for the currently selected text in a rich text field |
| Text Underline | | Toggles underlining on or off for the currently selected text in a rich text field |
| Text Normal Text | | Sets the currently selected text in a rich text field to the font defined by the database designer as the field's default |
| Text Numbers | Editing documents | Adds or removes numbering based on the currently selected paragraph(s) in a rich text field |
| Text Bullets | Editing documents | Adds or removes bullets based on the currently selected paragraph(s) in a rich text field |

| SmartIcon | Context | Description |
|---|---|---|
| Text Cycle Paragraph Spacing | Editing documents | Cycles the currently selected paragraphs between single, one and-a-half-line, and double spacing |
| Text Reduce Size | | Reduces the size of the currently selected text in a rich text field to the next setting for that font |
| Text Enlarge Size | | Enlarges the size of the currently selected text in a rich text field to the next setting for that font |
| Text Indent | Editing documents | Indents the currently selected paragraph(s)/text in a rich text field |
| Text Indent First Line | | Indents the first line of the currently selected paragraph(s) in a rich text field |
| Text Outdent | Editing documents | Outdents the currently selected paragraph(s)/text in a rich text field |
| Text Paragraph | | Opens the Properties for Text dialog box |
| Text Properties | | Opens the Properties for Text dialog box for the currently selected text in a rich text field |
| Text Style Cycle Key | Editing documents | Applies the next style in the defined styles list to the currently selected paragraph(s) in a rich text field |
| View Ruler | Editing documents | Toggles the ruler on or off for the currently open Document |
| Create Page Break | | Inserts a page break into a rich text field |
| View Show Page Breaks | | Shows any defined pages breaks in the currently open Document |

**Table 11.10** *SmartIcons for the Internet*

| SmartIcon | Context | Description |
|---|---|---|
|  Goto URL address | | Allows you to type an Internet address in the form of a URL and open the specified address using the InterNotes Web Navigator |

**Table 11.11** *SmartIcons for Database Design*

| | | | | | |
|---|---|---|---|---|---|
|  | Create Ellipse |  | Create Field |  | Create Folder |
|  | Create Hotspot Polygon |  | Create Insert Shared Field |  | Create Shared Field |
|  | Create Hotspot Rectangle |  | Create Insert Subform |  | Create Subform |
|  | Create Polygon |  | Create Layout Region |  | Create Navigator |
|  | Create Polyline |  | Create Textbox |  | Create Insert New Column |
|  | Create Rounded Rectange |  | Design Bring to Front |  | Design Send to Back |
|  | Design Form Properties |  | Design Field Properties |  | Design Column Properties |
|  | Design Icon |  | Design View |  | Design View Properties |
|  | Design View Form Formula |  | Design View Selection Conditions |  | File Database Design Synopsis |

*Table 11.12  User-Defined SmartIcons*

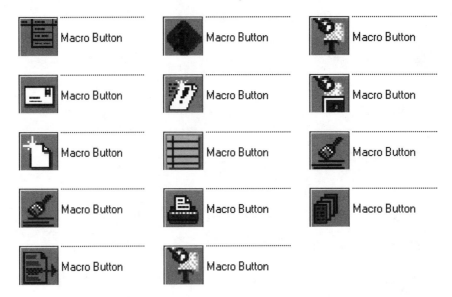

# Taking What We've Learned Step-by-Step (Exercise 11.1)

In this exercise, we're going to create two new SmartIcon sets.

## *Step 1*

Select **File, Tools, SmartIcons** from the Notes Client menu to open the SmartIcons dialog box.

Using whatever set is currently selected in the SmartIcons dialog box, click on the icons in the selected set's scrolling window and drag them toward the

Available Icons scrolling window. This will cause the icons to disappear from the selected set (Figure 11.8).

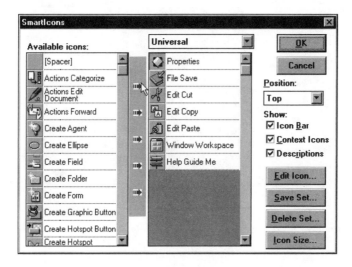

**Figure 11.7** *The SmartIcons dialog box.*

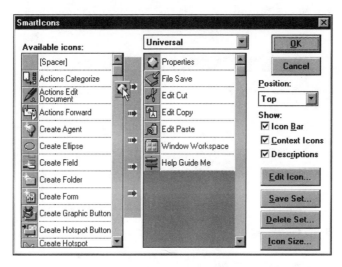

**Figure 11.8** *Dragging SmartIcons off of the selected set to the Available Icons scrolling window.*

Continue to drag off all icons in the selected set until the scrolling window beneath the set's name is empty (Figure 11.9).

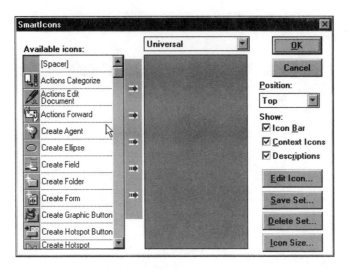

**Figure 11.9** *Removing all SmartIcons from the currently selected set.*

## Step 2

Click the **Save Set...** button to open the Save Set of SmartIcons dialog box (Figure 11.10).

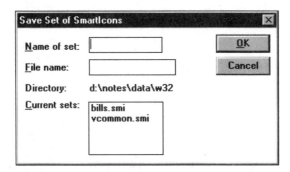

**Figure 11.10** *Getting ready to save a new icon set.*

Enter the phrase *Blank Set* in the Name of Set text box, and the word *blank* in the File Name text box. Click **OK** (Figure 11.11).

The Blank Set SmartIcon set will be the currently selected set in the SmartIcons dialog box (Figure 11.12). This will allow you to create new SmartIcon sets from a blank template.

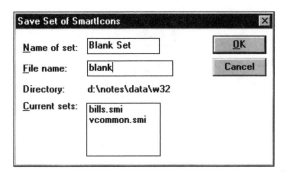

**Figure 11.11** *Saving the Blank Set SmartIcons set.*

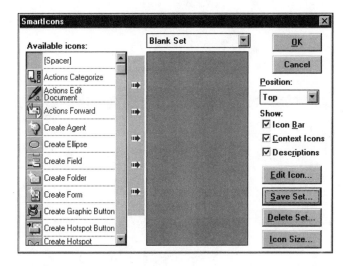

**Figure 11.12** *The Blank Set of SmartIcons in the SmartIcons dialog box.*

# Step 3

Now we're ready to create our own SmartIcon set. Drag the following SmartIcons from the Available SmartIcons list to the Blank Set scrolling window (Figure 11.13).

If you drag a SmartIcon from the Available list to the Blank Set scrolling window and it doesn't land in the right position, you can move the SmartIcon by drag and dropping it up or down the list.

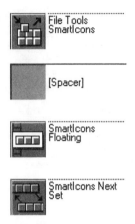

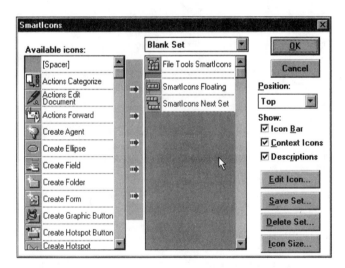

**Figure 11.13** *Creating a new SmartIcons Set.*

The results should appear as shown in Figure 11.14.

**Figure 11.14** *The new SmartIcons.*

Click the **Save Set...** button. Enter the phrase *SmartIcons* in the Name of Set text box, and the word "smart" in the File Name text box. Click **OK** (Figure 11.15).

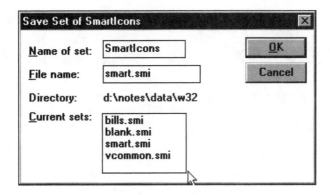

**Figure 11.15** *Saving the New Set.*

Close the SmartIcons dialog box with the SmartIcons set selected in the drop-down list at the top of the dialog box (Figure 11.16).

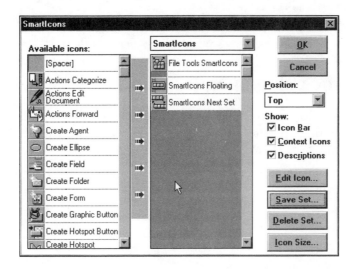

**Figure 11.16** *The new SmartIcons set is the currently selected set.*

The SmartIcons set will appear on the Workspace. Click the different SmartIcons in your new set and examine how each works (Figure 11.17).

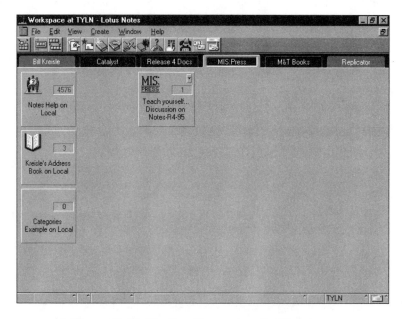

**Figure 11.17** *The SmartIcons set on the Workspace.*

# Word Processing in Notes

While not a full-fledged word processor by today's standards (the kitchen sink is not included), the capabilities Notes gives you for formatting text in a rich text field make working with Notes faster and more effective.

To begin with, let's discuss the elements of a rich text field that Notes gives you control over:

❖ Paragraphs

❖ Paragraph Attributes

❖ Text Attributes

❖ Paragraph Styles

❖ Shortcuts

## *Paragraphs*

Paragraphs in Notes are just the same as paragraphs in this book, a logical group of sentences or text. The only difference between a paragraph in a rich text field and a traditional paragraph is the concept that creates the group.

In a traditional paragraph, sentences are combined to convey a thought or idea. Paragraphs break when the idea changes or the thought being conveyed moves to another logical viewpoint.

In a Notes paragraph, however, sentences are combined by the presence of a *paragraph mark*. A paragraph mark in Notes is produced whenever the **Enter** key is pressed. You can see paragraph marks in Notes by opening a document for editing, and selecting **View, Show, Hidden Characters** from the Notes Client menu.

Looking at Figure 11.18, Notes would consider any group of text between two paragraph marks to be a paragraph. That means that as far as Notes is concerned, the line *1/2 cup Bacardi Dark Rum (80 proof)* is a paragraph, the blank line beneath it is a paragraph, and the block of text beginning with *Grease...* and ending *... is used up*, is a paragraph.

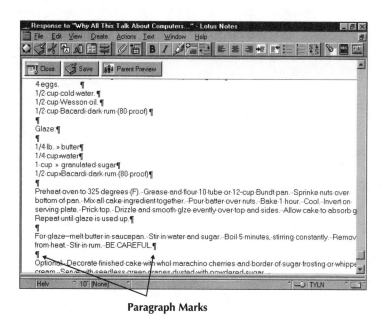

**Paragraph Marks**

***Figure 11.18*** *Paragraph Marks in a Notes Rich Text Field.*

# Paragraph Attributes

Now that we know what a paragraph is by Notes' definition, we can begin to discuss paragraph attributes. A paragraph attribute is a specific bit of formatting that Notes can apply to an entire paragraph. Some examples of paragraph attributes are:

❖ Left-justified text;

❖ Single spacing before the paragraph, double spacing after it;

❖ A bullet or number before the paragraph begins

You apply paragraph attributes by placing your cursor in the paragraph you want to add the attribute to, and then executing a command to apply it. For example, here are the steps needed to change a paragraph from left justified to right justified:

1. Open a Document for editing.
2. Place the text cursor inside the paragraph you wish to right justify.
3. Select **Text, Align Paragraph, Right** from the Notes Client menu.

Let's take a few paragraphs (no pun intended) to discuss several special paragraph attributes in greater detail.

## INDENTS AND OUTDENTS

Indents and outdents are special paragraph attributes that affect the left edge of a paragraph (Figure 11.19). Indents cause the edge of the paragraph to begin further to the right of the remaining text. Outdents cause the edge of the paragraph to begin further to the left than the remaining text. You can create Indents and Outdents in Notes using the **Text, Indent** and **Text, Outdent** commands on the Notes Client menu.

You can also "visually" create indents and outdents in Notes by using the Notes ruler, which is a special bar you can toggle on and off while you are editing a rich text field by choosing the **View, Ruler** command from the Notes Client menu (Figure 11.20).

Examining the ruler for a moment, you can see that two markers appear in the ruler where the paragraph's left edge should be (Figure 11.21).

These markers can be move using the mouse to different positions on the ruler, by clicking and dragging the small rectangle at the bottom of the markers. This will change the left edge of the currently selected paragraph.

The two Paragraph Edge Markers can also be moved individually to create what are known as "hanging" indents and outdents. A hanging indent or outdent is one where the first line of the paragraph is further to the left or right than the remaining lines of the paragraph (Figure 11.22).

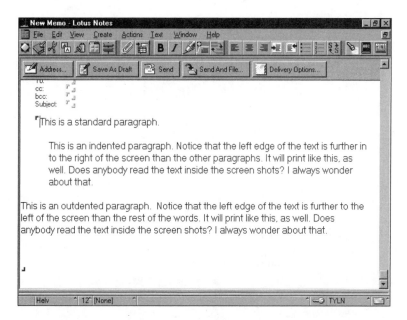

**Figure 11.19**  *Indented and outdented text in a rich text field.*

### The Notes Ruler

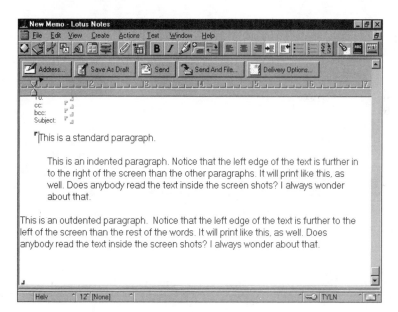

**Figure 11.20**  *The Notes Ruler.*

Paragraph
Edge Markers

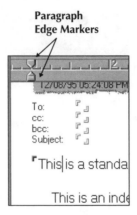

***Figure 11.21*** *The Paragraph Edge markers on the Notes ruler.*

**Paragraph Edge Markers**

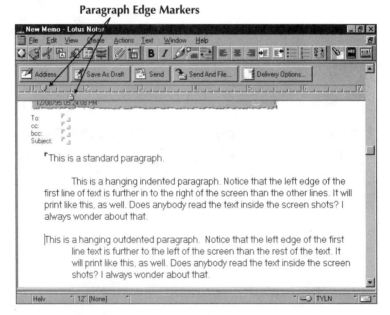

***Figure 11.22*** *Moving the Paragraph Edge Markers*
*independently creates hanging indents and outdents.*

## TABS

Tabs are special characters inside a rich text field that cause the text after them to line up with the next available *tab stops*. Tab stops are set at either a fixed interval (every half inch, for example), or at specific locations in a paragraph.

Tabs are created in paragraphs by placing the cursor in the paragraph you wish to set tabs for and selecting **Text, Properties** from the Notes Client menu, or by right-clicking on a paragraph and selecting **Text Properties...** from the menu that appears. In the Properties for Text dialog box, you then select the  page and choose either **Individually Set** or **Evenly Spaced** from the Tabs drop-down list.

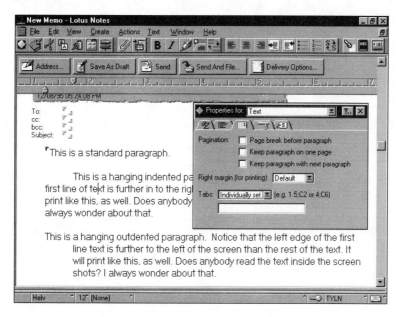

**Figure 11.23** *Using the Properties for Text dialog box to set tab stops.*

If you select **Individually Set**, enter the location for each tab stop separated by a semicolon. If you select **Evenly Spaced**, enter the interval you wish to have between tab stops (such as 0.5," 0.75" or whatever you require).

You can also set tab stops in a paragraph using the Notes ruler. Clicking on the bottom half of the Notes ruler will cause a tab stop to appear, which you can then click and drag to the desired location. You can remove tab stops from the Notes ruler by clicking on them and dragging them off of the ruler toward the bottom (Figure 11.24).

---

It is important to remember that tab stops are an attribute of a paragraph. Different paragraphs in a document can have different tab stops associated with them.

**N O T E**

---

**Tab Stops**

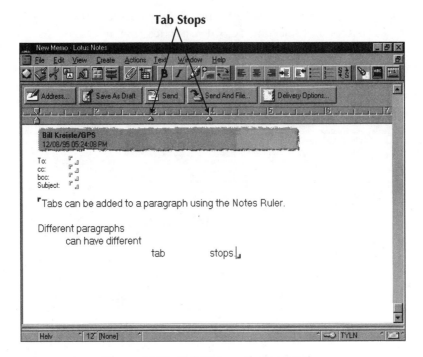

*Figure 11.24* *Tab Stops on the Notes Ruler.*

## Paragraph Spacing

Paragraph spacing is the number of lines that Notes will display between paragraphs. You set paragraph spacing in Notes by placing the cursor in the paragraph you wish to adjust and selecting **Text, Spacing**, and the desired spacing interval from the Notes Client menu.

## Text Attributes

Text attributes are settings that affect the appearance of the words and sentences in a rich text field. Some examples include:

❖   Font

❖   Bold, Italic, Underline.

❖   Color

❖   Size

To change text attributes, you must select the text that is to be affected and then apply the desired commands from Notes.

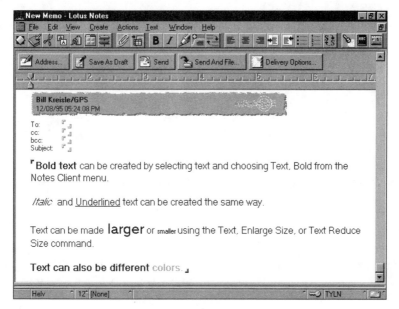

**Figure 11.25** *Examples of different text attributes in Notes.*

 As you can see from Figure 11.25, text attributes can be combined within a paragraph. It's important to note that a single set of text attributes can also be saved as a paragraph attribute.

N O T E

## Paragraph Styles

As you can see, there are a lot of options you can employ to affect the appearance of your text in Notes rich text fields. There's where the paragraph begins (paragraph edge marks), what tab positions are available, what spacing will be used between paragraphs, and the text attributes of the paragraph.

Suppose, over time, that you develop a favorite combination of attributes for your text. Wouldn't it be nice to save those attributes as a set and apply them to a paragraph all at once instead of having to change each one individually?

Notes allows you to do this by creating paragraph styles.

# Taking What We've Learned Step-by-Step (Exercise 11.2)

In this exercise, we're going to pull together all of the different things we've discussed about text and paragraph attributes and paragraph styles by creating our own custom paragraph style.

## *Step 1*

Open the Teach Yourself... Discussion database and compose a Main Topic Document. Enter *Exercise 11.2* in the first field, and position your text cursor in the field at the bottom of the Document (Figure 11.26).

Enter the following text into the field.

NOTE

When you see **Enter** in the following text, don't type the phrase **Enter**. Instead, you should press the **Enter** key to create a new paragraph.

Notes provides a number of tools for working with paragraphs and text.**Enter**

One useful tool is paragraph styles.**Enter**

Paragraph styles combine a set of paragraph and text attributes into a single command.**Enter**

To be sure that each line you entered is a separate paragraph in Notes, select **View, Show, Hidden Characters** from the Notes Client menu and make sure that a paragraph mark is visible at the end of each line (Figure 11.27).

## *Step 2*

Place the text cursor in the second paragraph and select **Text, Align Paragraph, Right** from the Notes Client menu, followed by **Text, Spacing, Double**. The second paragraph should appear similar to Figure 11.28.

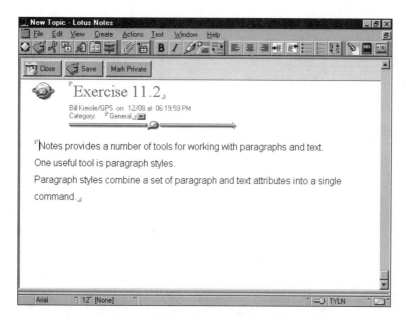

**Figure 11.26** *Getting ready to create a new paragraph style.*

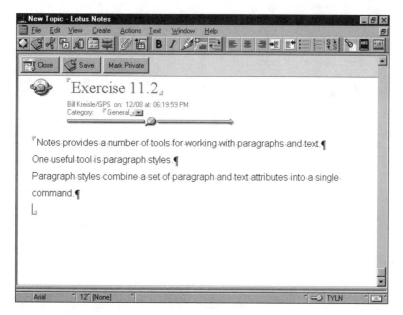

**Figure 11.27** *Looking for paragraph marks at the end of each line.*

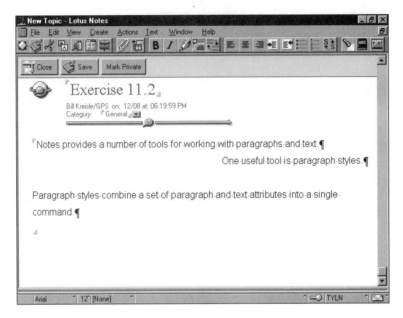

**Figure 11.28** *Applying attributes to the second paragraph.*

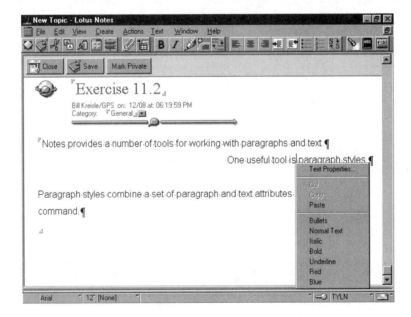

**Figure 11.29** *Opening the Properties for Text dialog box.*

## *Step 3*

Right-click the second paragraph, and choose **Text Properties...** from the pop-up menu.

Click the **Named Styles** tab 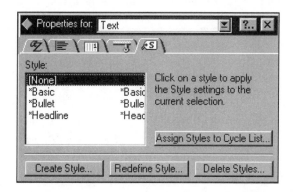 in the Properties for Text dialog box, followed by the **Create Style...** button.

*Figure 11.30   The Properties for Text dialog box, Named styles tab.*

Enter *Right Double* in the style name text box, and select the Include font in named style and make the style available to all documents check boxes (Figure 11.31). Click **OK**.

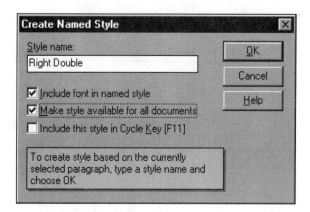

*Figure 11.31   Naming a new style.*

Close the Properties for Text dialog.

## *Step 4*

Notice that while the cursor is in the second paragraph, the style name in the status bar of the Notes Client displays Right Double (Figure 11.32).

***Figure 11.32*** *The named style appears in the status bar.*

---

**N O T E**

Named styles that you create are available only in the database in which the styles were created.

---

## *Step 5*

Finish the exercise by closing the database. You do not need to save your changes unless you wish to refer to them later.

## *Shortcuts*

In this section, I will show you several Notes shortcuts to make your work with Rich Text Fields and formatted text go faster and easier.

***Table 11.12*** *Keyboard Shortcuts*

| *Action* | *Shortcut* |
|---|---|
| Select contents of a document | **Ctrl+A** |
| Bold text | **Ctrl+B** |
| Copy selected text | **Ctrl+C** |
| Edit a document | **Ctrl+E** |
| Find and replace | **Ctrl+F** |
| Find next and replace | **Ctrl+G** |
| Italicize text | **Ctrl+I** |
| Format paragraphs (margins, tabs, line spacing, other) | **Ctrl+J** |
| Format text (font, size, color, other) | **Ctrl+K** |

| *Action* | *Shortcut* |
|---|---|
| Change to normal text | **Ctrl+T** |
| Underline text | **Ctrl+U** |
| Paste | **Ctrl+V** |
| Cut selected text | **Ctrl+X** |
| Undo last action | **Ctrl+Z** |
| Close the current document | **Ctrl+W** |
| Enlarge text to next available point size | **F2** |
| Reduce text to next available point size | **SHIFT+F2** |
| Indent the first line in a paragraph | **F7** |
| Outdent first line in a paragraph (hanging outdent) | **SHIFT+F7** |
| Indent entire paragraph | **F8** |
| Outdent entire paragraph (hanging indent) | **SHIFT+F8** |

## MOUSE SHORTCUTS

While text is selected, right-clicking on the text will open a pop-up menu with several shortcuts (Figure 11.33).

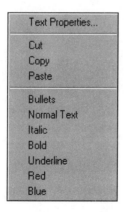

*Figure 11.33* *Right-clicking on selected text provides several shortcuts.*

## STATUS BAR SHORTCUTS

While you are in a rich text field, there are three regions on the status bar you can use to change text and paragraph attributes (Figure 11.34).

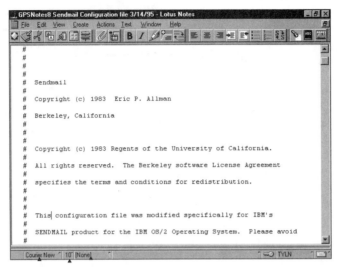

Font Selector          Style Selector

Font Size Selector

***Figure 11.34***  *Areas of the Status Bar that can*
*be used to change text and paragraph attributes.*

Clicking on the **Font Selector** opens a list of available fonts that you can use on the currently selected text (Figure 11.35).

**Selected Text**

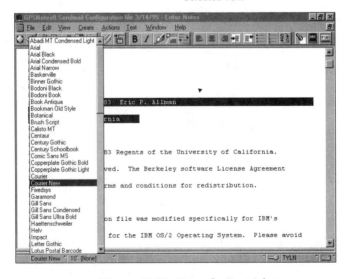

***Figure 11.35***  *Using the Font Selector.*

Clicking the **Font Size Selector** allows you to change the selected font to a different point size. Clicking the **Style Selector** allows you to apply a named style to the currently selected paragraph(s) (Figure 11.36).

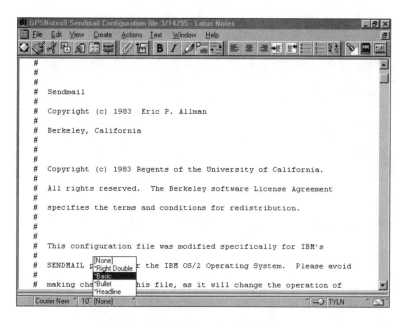

***Figure 11.36*** *Using the Style Selector.*

# Building Simple Agents

Even our brief visit with Notes @Functions in Chapter 6 should have been enough to show you that there is much more beneath the surface of Notes than simply electronic mail and discussion databases. However, it also probably illustrated that learning to write programs in Notes can require a great deal of attention to detail. All those @ signs, brackets, semicolons, and such—when all you want to do is put a value in a field automatically, why should you need to know all of that?

Fortunately for you, with Notes, Release 4, you don't need to know a programming language to do simple tasks. Lotus has a special interface for creating what I call *Simple Agents*, which we're about to discuss here. That other language is still there, and if you're a person who appreciates syntax and want to learn more, I encourage you to explore. However, for the rest of you, I offer this section.

## What are Simple Agents?

Simple Agents represent a collection of *Simple Actions*. Simple Actions are a group of commands that you can group together in the *Design Pane* using the Simple Action(s) radio button. The Design Pane is opened when you choose **Create, Agent...** from the Notes Client menu (Figure 11.37).

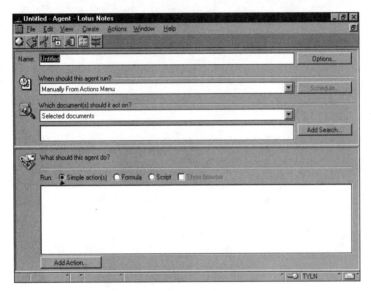

Select this option to build
an Agent using Simple actions(s).

***Figure 11.37*** *The Design Pane is opened by choosing*
***Create, Agent...*** *from the Notes Client menu.*

The top half of the Design Pane allows you to set the name of your new agent, how it should be activated, and what documents it should affect when it is activated.

## Where are Simple Agents Stored?

Agents that you create using the **Create, Agent...** command are stored in the currently selected Notes Database. Depending on some of the options you've selected in the Design Pane, they can be accessed using the Actions menu on the Notes Client, or they will be run automatically by Notes at predefined intervals.

If you have created a Simple Agent in a replica of another database, your Agent may replicate to other databases depending on your level of access control in the database you are replicating with. You must have Designer Access or greater to replicate Agents into another Notes database.

## *Why Should I Use Simple Agents?*

The reason for creating any type of Agent it to automate something that has to do with the Documents that are stored in a Notes database. Sometimes, Agents support a business process that revolves around a certain type of Document. This, as you recall from early chapters in this book, constitutes a workflow.

While Simple Agents can be used to support Workflow, their primary purpose is simply to automate a routine task on a group of Documents in a database. Say you have a database that is sorted by department, and one of the departments that contributes to the database regularly has recently changed its name from Information Systems to Information Services. A simple Agent could go through the database and replace the department field of all forms that currently say "Information Systems" with "Information Services."

Simple Agents can also scan a database and move documents to specific Folders or Views based on their contents.

# Taking What We've Learned Step-by-Step (Exercise 11.3)

In this exercise, we're going to build an Agent in the Teach Yourself… Discussion database that moves any document created by a specific author to a Folder.

## *Step 1*

Open the Teach Yourself… Discussion database.

If it is not already visible, select **View, Show, Folders** to open the Folders Navigator. Choose **Create, Folder** from the Notes Client menu. Enter "Bill's Documents" in the Folder name field. Click the **Shared** check box, followed by **OK** (Figure 11.38).

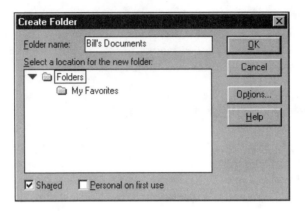

**Figure 11.38** *Creating a new folder called Bill's Documents.*

**Figure 11.39** *The new folder will appear in the Folders Navigator.*

## Step 2

Choose **Create Agent...** from the Notes Client menu.

Enter *Collect Bill's Document* in the Name text box. Select **Manually** from the Actions Menu in the When should this agent run? drop-down list. Select **All documents in database** from the Which document(s) should it act on? drop-down list (Figure 11.40).

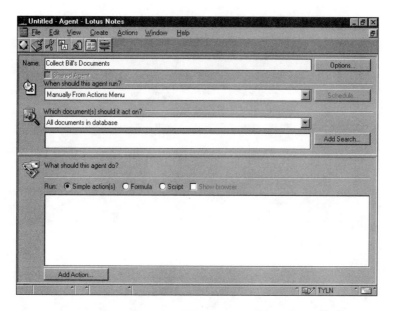

**Figure 11.40** *Creating a new Action.*

Click **Add Search...** button to open the Search Builder dialog box. Click the **By Field** option from the Condition drop-down list. Select **From** from the Search documents using field drop-down list. Select **contains** from the bottom drop-down list, and enter *kreisle* into the text box.

Click **OK**.

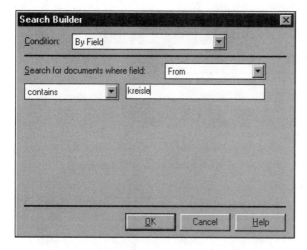

**Figure 11.41** *Using the Search Builder dialog box to filter which documents the action should run on.*

Your search criteria will appear in the Design Pane (Figure 11.42).

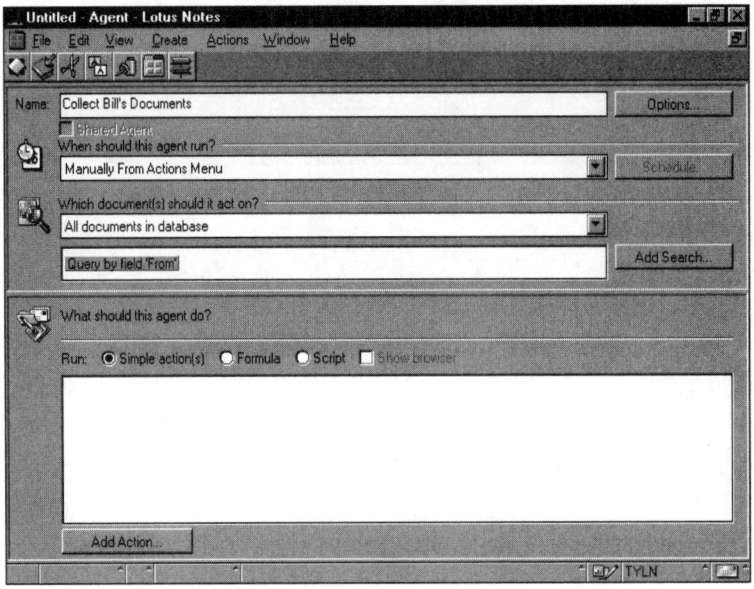

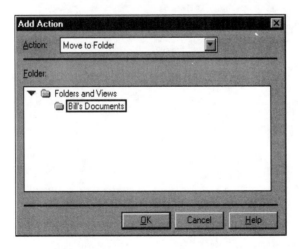

**Figure 11.42** *Looking at what we've done so far.*

## *Step 3*

Click **Add Action...** at the bottom of the Design Pane to open the Add Action dialog box (Figure 11.43). Select **Move to Folder** form the Action drop-down list. Click the Bill's Documents folder in the Folder box. Click **OK**.

**Figure 11.43** *The Add Action dialog box.*

Choose **File, Save** from the Notes Client menu to save the new Action (Figure 11.44).

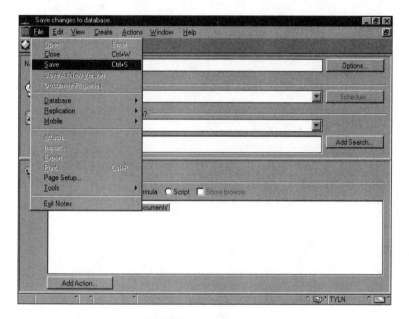

***Figure 11.44*** *Saving the new Action.*

Choose **File, Close** from the Notes Client menu to close the Design Pane.

## Step 4

Open the All Documents View in the Teach Yourself... Discussion database. Choose **Actions, Collect Bill's Documents** from the Notes Client menu (Figure 11.46).

You will see a status window, telling you that the Agent is running (Figure 11.45).

Open the Bill's Documents folder (Figure 11.47).

## Step 5

Uh oh... it looks like there's a flaw in the logic for this Agent. If you look at Figure 11.47, you'll notice that a Document created by Susan Kreisle appears in the Bill's Documents folder as well as the Documents created by Bill Kreisle. To fix this, select the Document created by Susan and choose **Actions, Remove from Folder...** from the Notes Client menu (Figure 11.48).

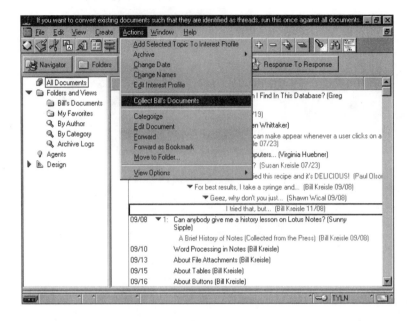

**Figure 11.45** *Activating our newly created Agent.*

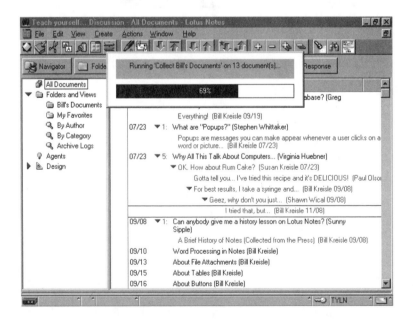

**Figure 11.46** *Notes displays the progress of the Agent as it runs.*

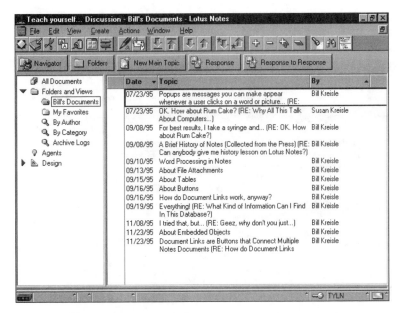

**Figure 11.47** *The Agent moved all Documents where the From field contained kreisle to the Folder named Bill's Documents.*

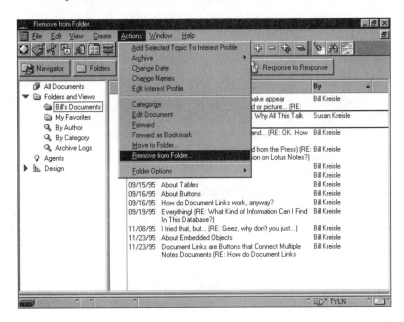

**Figure 11.48** *Removing the Document created by Susan Kreisle from the Folder.*

Now let's go back and edit our Agent so that it only looks for Documents created by Bill Kreisle. Select **View, Go To Agents...** from the Notes Client menu (Figure 11.49).

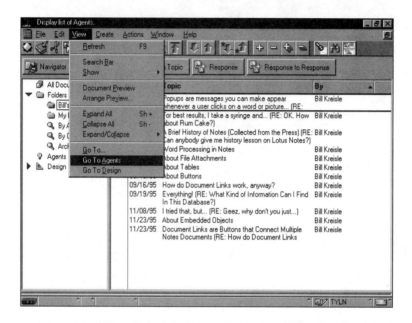

**Figure 11.49** *The View, Go To Agents... command.*

Double-click on the **Collect Bill's Documents Agent** in the Agent List to open the Design Pane (Figures 11.50 and 11.51).

Double-click on the query in the text box near the Add Search... button to open the Search Builder dialog box. Change the string in the text box after contains to *bill kreisle* (Figure 11.52).

Click **OK**. Choose **File, Save** followed by **File, Close** from the Notes Client menu. Select the **All Documents View**. Since the Agent was set to work on all documents in the database each time it is run, let's run it again to make sure that it doesn't move the document created by Susan Kreisle back into the Bill's Documents folder.

Choose **Action, Collect Bill's Documents** from the Notes Client menu. After the Agent completes, open the Bill's Documents folder and check to see if Susan's Document has been added (Figure 11.53).

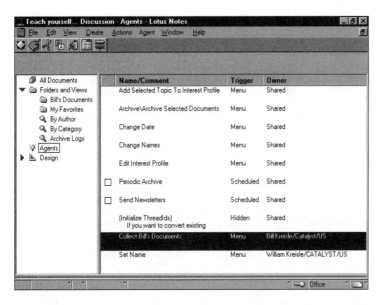

**Figure 11.50**   *The Collect Bill's Documents Agent in the Agent List.*

**The Query created by
the Search Builder dialog.**

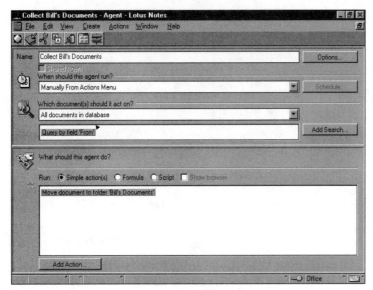

**Figure 11.51**   *The Design Pane.*

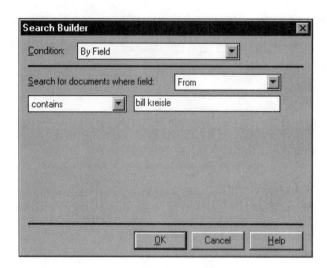

**Figure 11.52** *Modifying the query.*

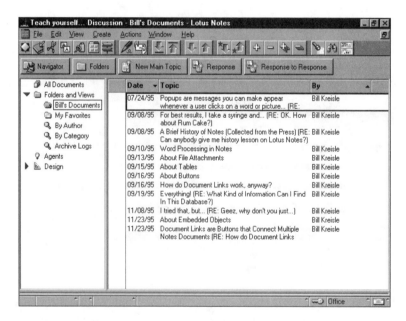

**Figure 11.53** *Our Agent only puts Documents created by Bill Kreisle into the Bill's Documents Folder.*

## *More Questions than Answers*

I expect that the previous exercise did two things:

1. It gave you a glimpse into a powerful way to automate tasks in Notes using Simple Actions.

2. It left you thirsty for more.

What were all of the other options in the dialog boxes we were looking at? What else can you do with Simple Actions? Those are reasonable questions, which I plan to spend the rest of this section discussing.

While I'm not going to go into minute detail, I offer the following tables to help you to begin to explore Simple Actions. To begin with, let's revisit a couple of sections on the Design Pane (Figure 11.54).

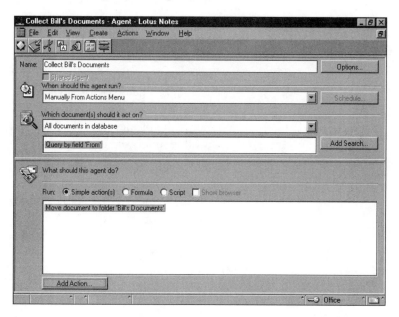

***Figure 11.54*** *The Design Pane.*

The first area to re-examine is the When should this agent run? drop-down list. While we chose **Manually from Action Menu** for our exercise, a number of other options are outlined in Table 11.13.

**Table 11.13** *Options in the When should this agent run? Drop-Down List of the Design Pane*

| Option Name | Description |
|---|---|
| Manually from Action Menu | Action appears in the Actions Menu on the Notes Client. It can be activated by selecting it from the menu. |
| Manually from Agent List | Action only appears in the Agent List (opened by selecting **View, Go To Agents** from the Notes Client or by clicking the Agents area on the Folders Navigator). The user must highlight the Agent in the List and choose **Edit, Run** from the Notes Client menu to activate it. |
| If New Mail has Arrived | Action will run automatically if a Document is mailed into the database. This is useful for creating Agents that support Workflow processes. (For example, a database of travel requests could look at an incoming form and notify the proper travel agent based on a value in it by sending a message.) |
| If Documents have been Created or Modified | Makes an Agent "change activated," meaning it is run whenever a change occurs in the database (a Document is modified or created). The Agent is run at the time the new Document or changes are saved. |
| If Documents have been Pasted | Action will run whenever a Document is pasted into the database. |
| On Schedule Hourly | The default run time is every hour, starting at 12 A.M. and ending at 12 A.M. |
| On Schedule Daily | Action will run once per day. The default run time is 1 A.M. |
| On Schedule Weekly | Action will run once per week. The default run time is Sunday at 2 A.M. |

| Option Name | Description |
| --- | --- |
| On Schedule Monthly | Action will run once per month. The default run time is on 1st day of each month at 2 A.M. |
| On Schedule Never | On Schedule Never is reserved for Release 3 background macros that have the "Never" schedule selected. To run such a macro, select one of the above schedule options in Release 4. |

Next, let's look at the Which document(s) should it act on? drop-down list (Table 11.14).

***Table 11.14*** *Options in the Which document(s) should it act on? Drop-Down List of the Design Pane*

| Option Name | Description |
| --- | --- |
| All documents in database | Agent runs on every Document in the database. |
| All new and modified documents since last run | Agent only runs on new documents or Documents that have been modified since the last time the Agent ran. For example, once an Agent scheduled to run weekly was activated, it would act on all Documents added or modified in the last week whenever it ran again. |
| All unread documents in view | Agent runs on all unread Documents in the current view only. |
| All documents in view | Agent runs on all Documents in the current view only. |
| Selected documents | Agent runs on currently selected Document(s) only. |
| Run once | Agent runs one time (the scope of the Documents the Agent will affect depends on the programming behind the Agent). |

Depending on the option selected in the When should this agent run? drop-down list, all options in Table 11.14 may not be visible.

**N O T E**

Since we've already covered the Search Builder dialog box that appears when you click **Add Search...** on the Design Pane, the next part to examine are the Simple Actions you can employ using the **Add Action...** button (Table 11.15).

*Table 11.15* Simple Actions

| Simple Action Name | Description |
| --- | --- |
| Copy to Database | Allows you to specify a Notes Server and Database that the Agent selected Document(s) should be copied to when the it is run. |
| Copy to Folder | Creates a copy of the Document(s) selected by the Agent in the Folder specified. This is different from the Move to Folder command, which adds a "place holder" for the Document(s) in the selected Folder but does not create another Document. |
| Delete from Database | Deletes the Document(s) selected by the Agent settings from the Database. |
| Mark Document Read | Marks the Document(s) selected by the Agent setting as read. |
| Mark Document Unread | Marks the Document(s) selected by the Agent setting as unread. |
| Modify Field | Replaces the contents of a field with a specified value. |
| Modify Field by Form | Replaces the contents of a field on a specific form with a new value. |
| Move to Folder | See the Copy to Folder action. |
| Remove from Folder | Removes the document(s) selected by the Agent setting from the specified folder. |

| Simple Action Name | Description |
|---|---|
| Reply to Sender | For mail-enabled databases, sends a message back to the sender whenever a Document is received. |
| Run Agent | Runs another Agent in the Database. |
| Send Document | Activates the Mail, Send command for the Document(s) selected by the Agent setting. Documents must already have addressee information for this Agent to work. |
| Send Mail Message | Sends a mail message whenever the Agent is activated. |
| Send Newsletter Summary | Sends a document link along with summary information about the Document(s) selected by the Agent setting whenever it is activated. |
| @Function Formula | Runs a formula created using Lotus' @Function programming language. |

# The InterNotes Web Navigator

Our next stop on the Notes power user circuit covers how Notes, Release 4, can be set up to work with the Internet—a collection of computers that share a common set of networking protocols to exchange files, electronic mail messages, and other information. If you're thinking that sounds a lot like just a plain old network, you're right. In fact, *Internet* is short for *Internetwork*. What makes the Internet distinctive from other networks however, is its size. Over 20 million machines are estimated to be connected to it.

Much of the Internet's recent popularity is owed to the implementation of a protocol for exchanging information called the Hyper Text Transfer Protocol (HTTP). This protocol allows software to use a special language called Hyper Text Markup Language (HTML) to display information that is contained on remote machines to a local computer.

The software that uses HTML and HTTP to read information is referred to as a *World Wide Web* (WWW) *browser.* Software that uses HTML and HTTP to disseminate information is called a World Wide Web (WWW) *server.* Figure 11.55 illustrates what we've just discussed.

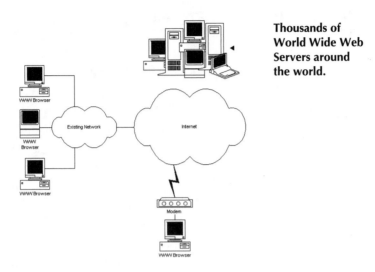

**Thousands of World Wide Web Servers around the world.**

*Figure 11.55  How WWW Browsers connect to WWW Servers.*

Looking at Figure 11.55, you might wonder how the World Wide Web browsers find anything on those thousands of World Wide Web servers? Just as the Notes Client uses information about a Notes Server, a directory, and a database name to locate information, the World Wide Web browser use a similar system. The server name, a directory, and information about which document in the directory to retrieve are converted into what is called a Uniform Resource Locator (URL).

As you can see, the Internet makes a tremendous amount of information available to people. With 20 million some-odd machines in the network (many of them belonging to computer geeks and college kids), a wide variety of topics can be found using a WWW browser. And of course, the Internet is international. In one sitting, you can visit an Irish pub, an English leather shop, and a special site set up by the New York Times to broadcast some of its daily news to Internet users. It is a tool to allow the transfer of knowledge.

So far, this doesn't look or sound very different in concept to our portrayal of a Notes installation way back in the first chapter—specialized clients get their information from specialized servers. That's the first of many similarities between Notes Clients and Notes Servers and World Wide Web browsers and World Wide Web servers.

Another similarity is the presentation of information. HTML documents work a lot like Documents with rich text fields do in Notes—they can contain formatted text, colors, pictures, file attachments, and even run other programs. This allows information to be presented in a knowledge-oriented context, instead of simply as data. And, like Document Links in a Notes Rich Text Field, HTML documents can contain links to other HTML documents located on other World Wide Web Servers on the Internet.

HTML documents designed for World Wide Web browsers and Notes rich text field capabilities are so similar that, with very little effort, the entire Internet can be accessed through the Notes Client and a cooperative Notes Server using what Lotus calls its InterNotes technology. Lotus InterNotes represents an entire suite of applications designed to help Notes integrate the advantages of the Internet's diverse information base into its system without compromising the security or workflow capabilities that are contained within the Notes system. The two InterNotes applications we're going to discuss are the InterNotes Web Navigator and the InterNotes Web Retriever.

The InterNotes Web Navigator is built into every Notes Release 4 Client. The InterNotes Web Retriever is included with every Notes Release 4 Server. The two programs work together to bring information from the World Wide Web to Notes users, as illustrated in Figure 11.56.

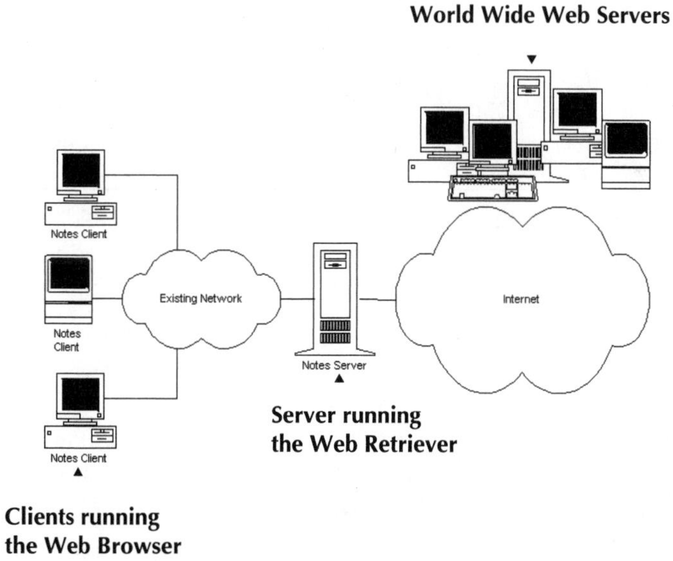

*Figure 11.56* *How the InterNotes Web Navigator and Web Retriever work together to bring Notes users World Wide Web documents.*

What happens is this:

1. A Notes user requests information about a World Wide Web page using a Uniform Resource Locator (URL) as an address.

2. The Notes client asks the InterNotes Web Retriever to use the HTTP protocol to retrieve the HTML document and copy it into a Notes Database on the Server.

3. The Notes Client then opens the Document on the Server from the database where it is stored.

You might notice, after comparing Figure 11.55 and 11.56 and reading the three steps above that the Notes Client never directly connects to the World Wide Web. That is something unique to the InterNotes technology. You can have all of the security of Notes, and you can minimize the interaction with the larger, less secure Internet by having only a single point of access from your internal network.

## Taking What We've Learned Step-by-Step (Exercise 11.4)

In this exercise, we're going to look at the settings in the Notes Client that enable the InterNotes Web Navigator and use it to connect to a World Wide Web site at Lotus Development Corporation in Cambridge, Massachusetts.

You must have the InterNotes Web Retriever installed on a Notes Server that you are authorized to access to complete this exercise.

N O T E

## Step 1

Our first step is to make sure that your Notes Client has the proper settings to use the InterNotes Web Navigator. To do this, we need to look at your current location setup and see if an InterNotes Server is specified.

Click on the **Location Bar** at the bottom of the Notes Client and select **Edit Current...** from the menu.

This will open your local Name and Address book to the Location Document currently in use.

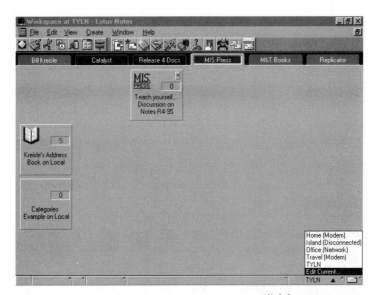

**Click here to open
the Location Bar menu.**

***Figure 11.57*** *Selecting **Edit Current…** from
the Location Bar menu at the bottom of the Notes Client.*

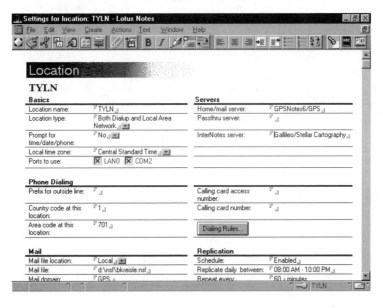

***Figure 11.58*** *A Location Document in your local Name And Address book.*

Ensure that the name of a Notes Server you have access to that is running the Notes Web Retriever is in the field labeled InterNotes Server on this document. Close this document and, if necessary, save changes to return to the Notes Client and the Workspace.

## *Step 2*

Select **File, Tools, User Preferences...** from the Notes Client menu.

On the Basics page of the User Preferences dialog box, ensure that Make Internet URLs (http:/...) into Hotspots is selected in the Advanced options list (Figure 11.59).

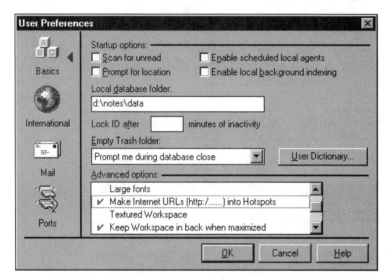

***Figure 11.59*** *Ensuring that the Make Internet URLs (http:/...) into Hotspots setting is selected in the Advanced options list.*

Click **OK**.

## *Step 3*

Open the Teach yourself... Discussion database and select the **by Category View**. Locate the category called Internet, and open the single Document under that category (Figure 11.60).

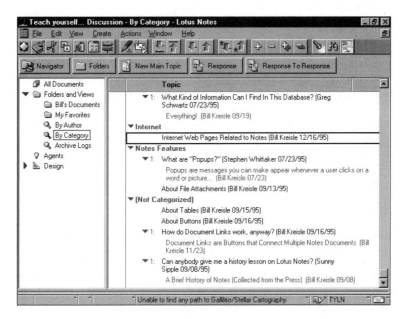

**Figure 11.60** *The Document in the Teach yourself...*
*Discussion database that we want to open.*

## Step 4

Locate the line in the document that reads http://www.lotus.com. When your mouse cursor is over this line, it will change to a pointing finger (Figure 11.61).

Double-click the line http://www.lotus.com. You will notice several messages in the Status Bar indicating activity by the Notes Client (yours will be similar to the ones illustrated, but will have different Server Names).

First your Notes Client will connect to the specified InterNotes Web Retriever. Then, the InterNotes Server will look on the Internet for the specified URL. Finally, the requested page will be cached at the InterNotes Web Retriever (Figure 11.62).

## Step 5

Shortly, a new document will appear. This is the current home page of the Lotus Development Corporation's World Wide Web site.

**Figure 11.61** *Locating an Internet URL... in the Document.*

**First your Notes Client will connect to the specified InterNotes Web Retriever. . .**

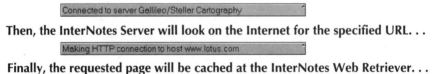

**Then, the InterNotes Server will look on the Internet for the specified URL. . .**

**Finally, the requested page will be cached at the InterNotes Web Retriever. . .**

**Figure 11.62** *Different messages will appear in the Notes Status bar.*

The page will almost certainly look different from Figure 11.63 as Lotus changes the appearance and content of this page frequently.

**N O T E**

Congratulations! You just "surfed the Web." Close the Teach yourself... Discussion database to complete the exercise.

As you can see, the InterNotes Web Navigator integrates the World Wide Web with Notes seamlessly and efficiently.

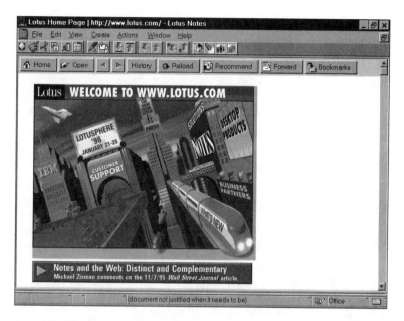

***Figure 11.63*** *Lotus Development Corporation's World Wide Web home page.*

# File and Database Maintenance

For our final section, I want to take a couple of pages to give you some file and database maintenance tips. These suggestions are geared to helping you keep your Notes Client software running as quickly and smoothly as possible.

## *Database Compacting*

If you keep local copies of Notes databases, you need to understand two things about your local database files:

1.  Whenever you add a Document to your local database (either through replication or directly), Notes allocates more space on your local hard disk to store the document.

2.  Whenever you delete a Document from your local database (again, through either replication or manually), Notes marks the document as deleted internally, but it *does not* decrease the size of the file on your hard disk.

This means that there may be wasted space in your local Notes databases because Notes doesn't automatically decrease the size of a database when a document is deleted.

To find out if a Notes database is wasting space, use the Properties for Database dialog box's Information Page (the tab with a lowercase *i* in a circle). As you recall from earlier chapters, this dialog box is opened by selecting a database and choosing **File, Database, Properties...** from the Notes Client menu, or by right-clicking on a database icon and choosing **Database Properties...** from the pop-up menu that appears (Figure 11.64).

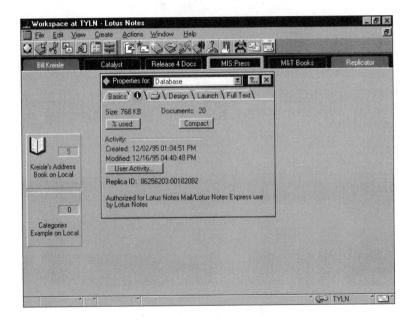

***Figure 11.64*** *The Properties for Database dialog box.*

Click the **% Used** button to display a number to the left of the button. This number indicates the amount of space in the selected database that is in use. For example, if it displays 75%, then 25% is wasted space, which you can reclaim by clicking the **Compact** button.

Clicking **Compact** will open a window displaying the compact command's progress (Figure 11.65).

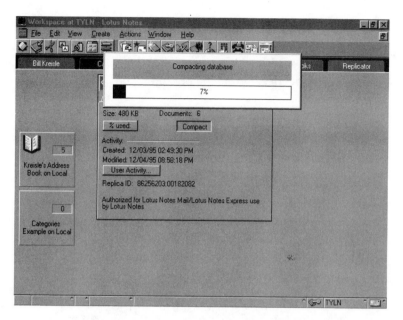

***Figure 11.65*** *Compacting a database locally.*

**WARNING**

If you have recently upgraded to Notes 4 from a previous version of Notes, you should know that compacting a Notes, Release 3 or earlier database using the Compact command in Notes Release 4 will cause Notes to perform a conversion on the database being compacted. That means the structure of the database will change so that new features in Notes Release 4 can be used. This is fine under most circumstances, but if you are upgrading a local database that will, in turn, replicate to a Notes 3 Server, make sure you check with that server's Administrator before you compact it.

## Compacting the Workspace

In addition to performing maintenance on your local databases, there is another important file on the Notes Client that needs occasional attention—the file that stores your Workspace. This file, DESKTOP.DSK, like a Notes Database, will expand when database icons are added, but will not decrease when they are removed.

To compact your Workspace, right mouse click on the Workspace and select **Workspace Properties...** from the pop-up menu.

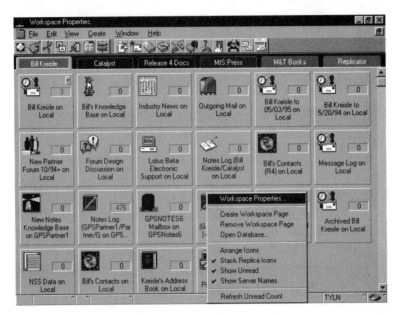

**Figure 11.66** *The* **Workspace Properties...**
*command on the right-click menu of the Workspace.*

Click on the **Information Page of the Properties for Workspace** dialog box.

Just as we did with the Information Page in the Properties for Database dialog box, you can click on the **% Used** button to determine how much space can be reclaimed if the Workspace is compacted and the Compact button to perform the process. You will see a progress indicator after clicking the **Compact** button (Figure 11.68).

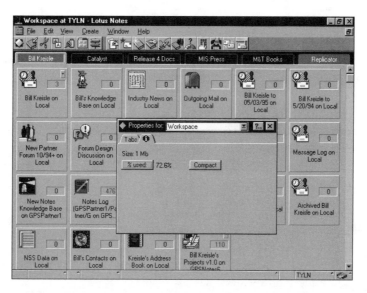

**Figure 11.67**  *The Information page of the Properties for Workspace dialog box.*

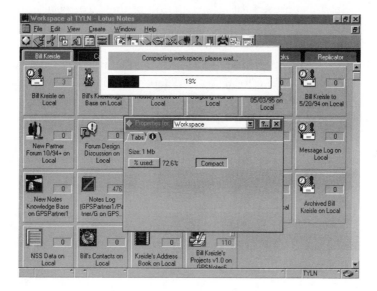

**Figure 11.68**  *Seeing the progress of the Compact Workspace command.*

# Summary

❖ SmartIcons are buttons that allow the user quick access to commonly performed tasks in Notes. They can be grouped together into SmartIcon sets, which can be displayed in a number of places on the Notes Client. All SmartIcon settings are controlled using the **File, Tools, SmartIcons...** command on the Notes Client menu.

❖ When working in a rich text field, there are a number of powerful word processing features available to Notes users, including text formatting, paragraph formatting, and tab settings.

❖ Even if a user isn't familiar with programming in Notes, he can create Agents using Notes' Simple Actions.

❖ The InterNotes Web Navigator works with the InterNotes Web Retriever to allow Notes users access to documents stored on the Internet on World Wide Web servers.

❖ Database files on your local hard drive may contain extra space after they have been used for a long period of time. To reclaim that space, you can use the **Compact** button on the Information page of the Properties for Database dialog box.

❖ Settings for the Notes Workspace are stored in a file called DESKTOP.DSK. Like local Notes databases, this file may contain extra space after extended use which can be reclaimed using the Compact button on the Information page of the Properties for Workspace dialog box.

# Appendix A

# The Appearance of the Notes Client on Different Operating Systems

This appendix is designed to provide you with a means to compare the Notes Client on your operating system to the Notes Client on Windows 95, which was the operating system I used to create the step-by-step examples and illustrations for this book.

Since Lotus works very hard to ensure that the Notes Client is as similar across all of its Client Platforms, the focus of this appendix will be on areas of Notes that rely on the operating system, such as window controls, common dialog boxes, and keyboard commands.

# Windows 95

## *Window Controls*

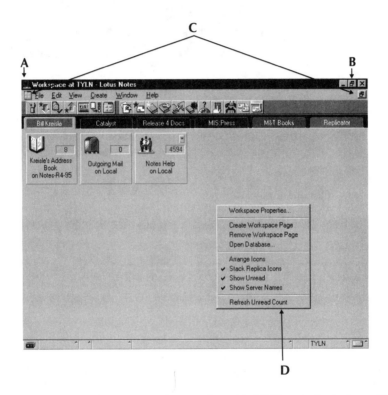

**Figure A.1** *The Notes Client running on Windows 95. (A) The window's Control Box. In Windows 95, this box gives the user the option to restore, move, size, minimize, maximize, and close the parent window. (B) Buttons to minimize, restore/maximize, and close the parent window, respectively. (C) The control box and restore/maximize button for a child window. Notes is an MDI (Multiple Document Interface) compliant application. (D) An example of the appearance of menus in the Notes Client for Windows 95.*

## *Operating System Specifics*

When using the Notes Client on Windows 95 to locate files, drives are designated by letters (C:, D:, etc.), subdirectories are represented as folders, and files are displayed with an icon that reflects their associated file types (see Figure A.2).

Windows 95 supports long names for files and directories.

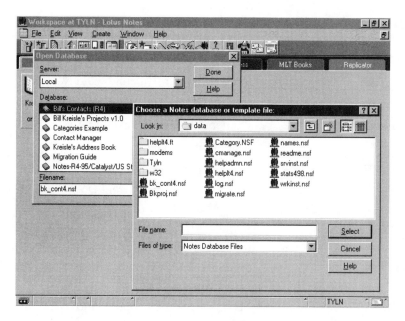

**Figure A.2** *The Notes Client running on Windows 95.*

## Keyboard and Mouse Commands

**Table A.1** *Function Key Shortcuts*

| Key Combination | Action |
| --- | --- |
| **F1** | Get context-sensitive help |
| **F2** | Enlarge text to next available point size |
| **SHIFT+F2** | Reduce text to next available point size |
| **F3** | Go to next selected Document |
| **SHIFT+F3** | Go to previous selected Document |
| **F4** | Go to next unread Document |
| **SHIFT+F4** | Go to previous unread Document |
| **ALT+F4** | Exit Notes |
| **F5** | Lock Notes (revoke password login but leave Notes running) |

*(Continued)*

| Key Combination | Action |
| --- | --- |
| **ALT+F5** | Restore Notes program window to default size |
| **CTRL+F6** | Cycle through open child windows (MDI) |
| **F7** | Indent the first line in a paragraph |
| **SHIFT+F7** | Outdent first line in a paragraph |
| **F8** | Indent entire paragraph |
| **SHIFT+F8** | Outdent entire paragraph |
| **F9** | Update all fields in current Document, View, or Workspace |
| **SHIFT+F9** | Rebuild all views in current Document, View, or Workspace |
| **CTRL+F9** | Minimize active window and cascade other active windows |
| **CTRL+F10** | Maximize all open child windows (MDI) |
| **F10 or ALT** | Access the menu bar so you can use arrow keys to choose commands |

***Table A.2*** *Shortcut Keys for Editing Documents*

| Key Combination | Action |
| --- | --- |
| **CTRL+A** | Select contents of a Document |
| **CTRL+B** | Bold text |
| **CTRL+C** | Copy selected text |
| **CTRL+E** | Edit a Document |
| **CTRL+F** | Find and replace |
| **CTRL+G** | Find next and replace |
| **CTRL+I** | Italicize text |
| **CTRL+J** | Format paragraphs (margins, tabs, line spacing, other) |

*(Continued)*

| Key Combination | Action |
| --- | --- |
| **CTRL+K** | Format text (font, size, color, other) |
| **CTRL+T** | Change to normal text |
| **CTRL+U** | Underline text |
| **CTRL+V** | Paste |
| **CTRL+X** | Cut selected text |
| **CTRL+Z** | Undo last action |
| **CTRL+W** | Close the current Document |
| **F2** | Enlarge text to next available point size |
| **SHIFT+F2** | Reduce text to next available point size |
| **F7** | Indent the first line in a paragraph |
| **SHIFT+F7** | Outdent first line in a paragraph |
| **F8** | Indent entire paragraph |
| **SHIFT+F8** | Outdent entire paragraph |

**Table A.3** *Shortcut Keys for reading Documents*

| Key Combination | Action |
| --- | --- |
| **ENTER** | Move to the next Document |
| **BACKSPACE** | Move to the previous Document |
| **F4** or **TAB** | Move to the next unread Document |
| **SHIFT+F4** or **SHIFT+TAB** | Move to the previous unread Document |
| **CTRL+E** | Edit the current Document |
| **CTRL+P** | Print the current Document |
| **ESC** | Close the Document |
| **DELETE** | Move the current Document to the trash folder |
| **SPACE BAR** | Activate a button or Document/View/Database Link |

***Table A.4*** *Shortcut Keys for Views*

| Key Combination | Action |
| --- | --- |
| **CTRL+A** | Select all Documents |
| **CTRL+C** | Copy selected Documents |
| **CTRL+F** | Find |
| **CTRL+G** | Find next |
| **CTRL+P** | Print view |
| **CTRL+X** or **SHIFT+DELETE** | Cut selected Documents |
| **ENTER** | Open the selected Document |
| **SHIFT+ENTER** | Go to next main Document |
| **SPACE BAR** | Select or deselect |
| **SHIFT+UP ARROW** or **SHIFT+DOWN ARROW** | Select multiple documents |
| **F3** | Go to next selected Document |
| **SHIFT+F3** | Go to previous selected Document |
| **F4** or **TAB** | Go to next unread Document |
| **SHIFT+F4** or **SHIFT+TAB** | Go to previous unread Document |
| **F9** | Update all fields in current Document, View, or Workspace |
| **SHIFT+F9** | Rebuild all views in current Document, View, or Workspace |

***Table A.5*** *Shortcut Keys for the Workspace*

| Key Combination | Action |
| --- | --- |
| **F1** | Get context-sensitive help |
| **ALT+F4** | Exit Notes |
| **F5** | Lock Notes (revoke password login but leave Notes running) |
| **ALT+F5** | Restore Notes program window to default size |
| **CTRL+F6** | Cycle through open child windows (MDI) |
| **F9** | Update all fields in current Document, View, or Workspace |
| **SHIFT+F9** | Rebuild all views in current Document, View, or Workspace |
| **CTRL+F9** | Minimize active window and cascade other active windows |
| **CTRL+F10** | Maximize all open windows |
| **F10** or **ALT** | Access the menu bar so you can use arrow keys to choose commands |
| **CTRL+M** | Create a new memo |
| **CTRL+N** | Create a new database |
| **CTRL+O** | Open a database (add a database to Workspace) |
| **ESC** | Close a Database Window or Document |
| **CTRL+BREAK** | Cancel a server operation |
| **CTRL+SHIFT+UP/DOWN/ LEFT/RIGHT ARROW** | Move a database icon |
| **DELETE** | Delete a database icon, or mark Document for deletion |

**Table A.6** *Shortcut Keys for the Windows Operating Systems.*

| Key Combination | Action |
| --- | --- |
| **CTRL+ESC** | Open the Windows 95 Taskbar or Windows/Workgroups/NT Task List |
| **ALT+TAB** | Cycle through all currently running programs |

**Table A.7** *Mouse Shortcuts*

| Key Combination | Action |
| --- | --- |
| **SHIFT**+Click | Select/deselect multiple Documents in a View |
| | Select/deselect multipledatabases on the Workspace |
| **SHIFT**+Double-Click | Open all currently selected databases on the Workspace |
| Double-Click | Place the Document currently being read in edit mode |
| Right-Click | Opens a pop-up menu with choices specific to the selected object. |
| Right-Double-Click | Close the currently open Document if specified in the **Tools, User Preferences** dialog box Advanced Options list. |

# Windows, Windows for Workgroups, and Windows NT

## *Window Controls*

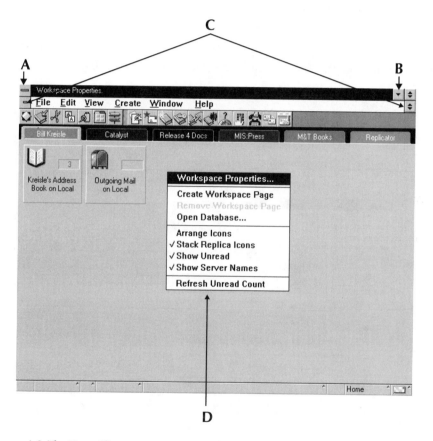

**Figure A.3** *The Notes Client running on Windows for Workgroups 3.11. (A) The window's Control Box. In Windows, Windows for Workgroups, and Windows NT, this box gives the user the option to Restore, Move, Size, Minimize, Maximize, and Close respectively the parent window. (B) Buttons to minimize and restore/maximize the parent window. (C) The control box and restore/maximize button for a child window. Notes is an MDI (Multiple Document Interface) compliant application. (D) An example of the appearance of menus in the Notes Client for Windows, Windows for Workgroups, and Windows NT.*

## Operating System Specifics

When using the Notes Client on the Windows, Windows for Workgroups, and Windows NT operating systems to locate files, drives are designated by letters (C:, D:, etc), subdirectories are represented as folders, and files by name and extension (See Figure A.4).

Windows NT supports long names for files and directories.

Windows and Windows for Workgroups use DOS naming conventions for files (eight characters for the file's name, and three characters for a file extension).

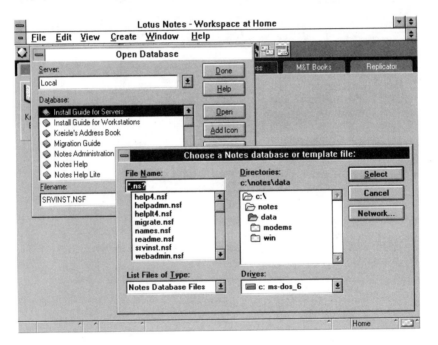

**Figure A.4** *The Notes Client running on Windows for Workgroups 3.11.*

## Keyboard and Mouse Commands

See Tables A.1 through A.7.

# OS/2 Warp

## *Window Controls*

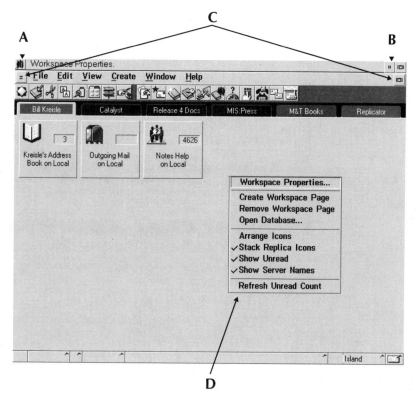

**Figure A.5** *The Notes Client running on OS/2 Warp. (A) The window's Control Box. In OS/2 Warp, this box gives the user the option to restore, move, size, minimize, maximize, hide, and close the parent window, as well as display a list of windows currently active. (B) Buttons to Minimize and Restore/Maximize the parent window, respectively. (C) The Control Box and Restore/Maximize button for a child window. Notes is an MDI (Multiple Document Interface) compliant application. (D) An example of the appearance of menus in the Notes Client for OS/2 Warp.*

## Operating System Specifics

When using the Notes Client on the OS/2 Warp Operating System to locate files, drives are designated by letters (C:, D:, etc), subdirectories are represented as folders, and files by name and extension (see Figure A.6).

OS/2 Warp supports long names for files and directories if the computer's drives are formatted using IBM's High Performance File System (HPFS).

OS/2 Warp uses DOS naming conventions for files (eight characters for the file's name, and three characters for a file extension) if the computer's drives are formatted using IBM's File Allocation Table (FAT) file system.

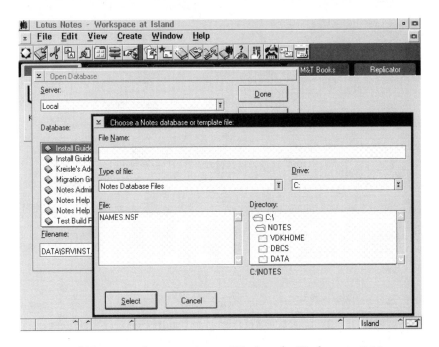

***Figure A.6*** *The Notes Client running on Windows for Workgroups 3.11.*

# Keyboard and Mouse Commands

**Table A.8** *Function Key Shortcuts*

| Key Combination | Action |
| --- | --- |
| **F1** | Get context-sensitive help |
| **F2** | Enlarge text to next available point size |
| **SHIFT+F2** | Reduce text to next available point size |
| **F3** | Go to next selected Document |
| **SHIFT+F3** | Go to previous selected Document |
| **F4** | Go to next unread Document |
| **SHIFT+F4** | Go to previous unread Document |
| **ALT+F4** | Exit Notes |
| **F5** | Lock Notes (revoke password login but leave Notes running) |
| **ALT+F5** | Restore Notes program window to default size |
| **CTRL+F6** | Cycle through open child windows (MDI) |
| **F7** | Indent the first line in a paragraph |
| **SHIFT+F7** | Outdent first line in a paragraph |
| **F8** | Indent entire paragraph |
| **SHIFT+F8** | Outdent entire paragraph |
| **F9** | Update all fields in current Document, View, or Workspace |
| **SHIFT+F9** | Rebuild all views in current Document, View, or Workspace |
| **CTRL+F9** | Minimize active window and cascade other active windows |
| **CTRL+F10** | Maximize all open child windows (MDI) |
| **ALT+F10** | Maximize the Notes program window |
| **F10** or **ALT** | Access the menu bar so you can use arrow keys to choose commands |

***Table A.9*** *Shortcut Keys for Editing Documents*

| Key Combination | Action |
| --- | --- |
| **CTRL+A** | Select contents of a Document |
| **CTRL+B** | Bold text |
| **CTRL+C** | Copy selected text |
| **CTRL+E** | Edit a Document |
| **CTRL+F** | Find and replace |
| **CTRL+G** | Find next and replace |
| **CTRL+I** | Italicize text |
| **CTRL+J** | Format paragraphs (margins, tabs, line spacing, other) |
| **CTRL+K** | Format text (font, size, color, other) |
| **CTRL+T** | Change to normal text |
| **CTRL+U** | Underline text |
| **CTRL+V** | Paste |
| **CTRL+X** | Cut selected text |
| **CTRL+Z** | Undo last action |
| **CTRL+W** | Close the current Document |
| **F2** | Enlarge text to next available point size |
| **SHIFT+F2** | Reduce text to next available point size |
| **F7** | Indent the first line in a paragraph |
| **SHIFT+F7** | Outdent first line in a paragraph |
| **F8** | Indent entire paragraph |
| **SHIFT+F8** | Outdent entire paragraph |

**Table A.10** *Shortcut Keys for Reading Documents*

| Key Combination | Action |
| --- | --- |
| **ENTER** | Move to the next Document |
| **BACKSPACE** | Move to the previous Document |
| **F4** or **TAB** | Move to the next unread Document |
| **SHIFT+F4** or **SHIFT+TAB** | Move to the previous unread Document |
| **CTRL+E** | Edit the current Document |
| **CTRL+P** | Print the current Document |
| **ESC** | Close the Document |
| **DELETE** | Move the current Document to the Trash Folder |
| **SPACE BAR** | Activate a button or Document/View/Database Link |

**Table A.11** *Shortcut Keys for Views*

| Key Combination | Action |
| --- | --- |
| **CTRL+A** | Select all Documents |
| **CTRL+C** | Copy selected Documents |
| **CTRL+F** | Find |
| **CTRL+G** | Find next |
| **CTRL+P** | Print view |
| **CTRL+X** or **SHIFT+DELETE** | Cut selected Documents |
| **ENTER** | Open the selected Document |
| **SHIFT+ENTER** | Go to next main Document |
| **SPACE BAR** | Select or deselect |

*(Continued)*

| Key Combination | Action |
|---|---|
| **SHIFT+UP ARROW** or **SHIFT+DOWN ARROW** | Select multiple documents |
| **F3** | Go to next selected Document |
| **SHIFT+F3** | Go to previous selected Document |
| **F4** or **TAB** | Go to next unread Document |
| **SHIFT+F4** or **SHIFT+TAB** | Go to previous unread Document |
| **F9** | Update all fields in current Document, View, or Workspace |
| **SHIFT+F9** | Rebuild all views in current Document, View, or Workspace |

*Table A.12  Shortcut Keys for the Workspace*

| Key Combination | Action |
|---|---|
| **F1** | Get context-sensitive help |
| **ALT+F4** | Exit Notes |
| **F5** | Lock Notes (revoke password login but leave Notes running) |
| **ALT+F5** | Restore Notes program window to default size |
| **CTRL+F6** | Cycle through open child windows (MDI) |
| **F9** | Update all fields in current Document, View, or Workspace |
| **SHIFT+F9** | Rebuild all views in current Document, View, or Workspace |
| **CTRL+F9** | Minimize active window and cascade other active windows |
| **CTRL+F10** | Maximize all open windows |
| **ALT+F10** | Maximize the Notes program window |
| **F10]** or **ALT** | Access the menu bar so you can use arrow keys to choose commands |

| Key Combination | Action |
| --- | --- |
| **CTRL+M** | Create a new memo |
| **CTRL+N** | Create a new database |
| **CTRL+O** | Open a database (add a database to workspace) |
| **ESC** | Close a database window or document |
| **CTRL+BREAK** | Cancel a server operation |
| **CTRL+SHIFT+UP/DOWN/ LEFT/RIGHT ARROW** | Move a database icon |
| **DELETE** | Delete a database icon, or mark Document for deletion |

**Table A.13** *Shortcut Keys for the OS/2 Warp Operating System*

| Key Combination | Action |
| --- | --- |
| **CTRL+ESC** | Open OS/2 Task List |
| **ALT+TAB** | Cycle through all currently running programs |

**Table A.14** *Mouse Shortcuts*

| Key Combination | Action |
| --- | --- |
| **SHIFT+Click** | Select/deselect multiple Documents in a View |
| | Select/deselect multiple databases on the Workspace |
| **SHIFT+Double-Click** | Open all currently selected databases on the Workspace |
| **Double-Click** | Place the Document currently being read in edit mode |
| **Right Double-Click** | Close the currently open Document if specified in the **Tools, User Preferences** dialog box, Advanced Options list. |

# Mac OS (System 7.1 or higher)

## *Window Controls*

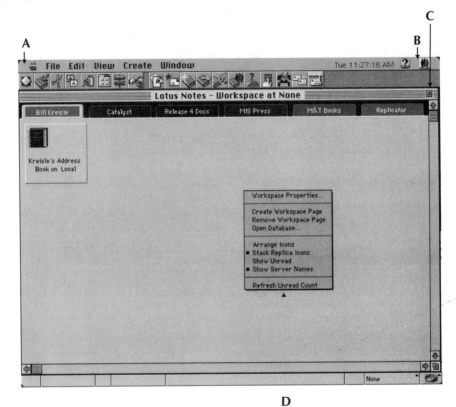

**Figure A.7** *The Notes Client running on the Mac Operating System. (A) The Control menu. In the Mac OS, this box gives the user the option to launch other programs as well as access system settings. (B) Buttons to enable balloon help settings and control the Notes window, respectively. (C) The restore/maximize button for a child window. Notes is an MDI (Multiple Document Interface) compliant application. (D) An example of the appearance of menus in the Notes Client for the Mac OS.*

**SHORTCUT**

**OPTION**-click simulates a right mouse click to open pop-up menus in Notes.

## Operating System Specifics

When using the Notes Client on the Mac operating system to locate files, drives and subdirectories are represented as folders, and files by name. The Mac operating system supports long filenames for directories and files (see Figure A.8).

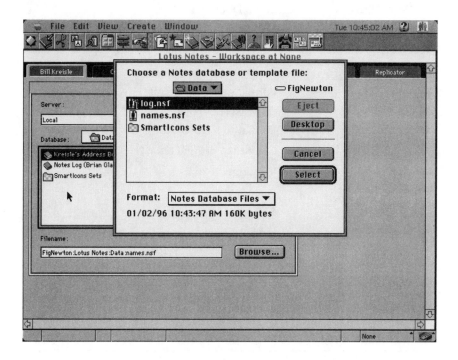

**Figure A.8** *The Notes Client running on the Mac operating system.*

## Keyboard and Mouse Commands

***Table A.15*** *Shortcut Keys for Editing Documents*

| Key Combination | Action |
| --- | --- |
| **COMMAND+A** | Select contents of a Document |
| **COMMAND+B** | Bold text |
| **COMMAND+C** | Copy selected text |
| **COMMAND+E** | Edit a Document |
| **COMMAND+F** | Find and replace |
| **COMMAND+G** | Find next and replace |
| **COMMAND+I** | Italicize text |
| **COMMAND+J** | Format paragraphs (margins, tabs, line spacing, other) |
| **COMMAND+K** | Format text (font, size, color, other) |
| **COMMAND+T** | Change to normal text |
| **COMMAND+U** | Underline text |
| **COMMAND+V** | Paste |
| **COMMAND+X** | Cut selected text |
| **COMMAND+Z** | Undo last action |
| **COMMAND+W** | Close the current Document |

***Table A.16*** *Shortcut Keys for Reading Documents*

| Key Combination | Action |
| --- | --- |
| **ENTER** | Move to the next Document |
| **BACKSPACE** | Move to the previous Document |
| **TAB** | Move to the next unread Document |
| **SHIFT+TAB** | Move to the previous unread Document |
| **CTRL+E** | Edit the current Document |
| **CTRL+P** | Print the current Document |
| **ESC** | Close the Document |

| Key Combination | Action |
| --- | --- |
| **DELETE** | Move the current Document to the Trash Folder |
| **SPACE BAR** | Activate a button or Document/View/Database Link |

**Table A.17** *Shortcut Keys for Views*

| Key Combination | Action |
| --- | --- |
| **COMMAND+A** | Select all Documents |
| **COMMAND+C** | Copy selected Documents |
| **COMMAND+F** | Find |
| **COMMAND+G** | Find next |
| **COMMAND+P** | Print view |
| **COMMAND+X** | Cut selected Documents |
| **ENTER** | Open the selected Document |
| **SHIFT+ENTER** | Go to next main Document |
| **SPACE BAR** | Select or deselect |
| **SHIFT+UP ARROW** or **SHIFT+DOWN ARROW** | Select multiple Documents |

**Table A.18** *Shortcut Keys for the Workspace*

| Key Combination | Action |
| --- | --- |
| **COMMAND+M** | Create a new memo |
| **COMMAND+N** | Create a new database |
| **COMMAND+O** | Open a database (add a database to workspace) |
| **ESC** | Close a Database Window or Document |
| **CTRL+SHIFT+UP/DOWN/ LEFT/RIGHT ARROW** | Move a database icon |
| **DELETE** | Delete a database icon, or mark Document for deletion |

***Table A.19*** *Mouse Shortcuts*

| Key Combination | Action |
| --- | --- |
| **SHIFT+Click** | Select/deselect multiple Documents in a View |
| | Select/deselect multiple Databases on the Workspace |
| **SHIFT+Double-Click** | Open all currently selected databases on the Workspace |
| **Double-Click** | Place the Document currently being read in edit mode |

# Appendix B

# Installing the Sample Applications that Ship with this Book

To help you get the most from the step-by-step exercises included in this book, a single 3.5" floppy diskette with a Notes Database is included. This database contains a number of Documents designed to illustrate many important concepts in Lotus Notes.

It is recommended that you copy the database TYLNDISC.NSF from the diskette to a subdirectory or folder beneath your Notes data directory.

For example: If you are using Windows 95/NT/3.1, it is likely that your Lotus Notes software is installed in a directory called NOTES. Beneath this directory is subdirectory called DATA. I suggest you create a subdirectory beneath DATA called TYLN, and copy the database on the included disk to it. The path for your database would then be NOTES\DATA\TYLN\TYLNDISC.NSF.

*Figure B.1* *The recommended path for the Teach yourself...discussion database.*

If you choose another location for your Notes database, remember to substitute the path you used when working with the step-by-step example in Chapter 3 that involves adding the example database to your workspace.

# Appendix C

# Glossary

The symbol ★**NEW**★ indicates a new feature in Notes Release 4.

Italicized words in the following entries are defined in this glossary.

## *About Document*

The About Document is usually displayed when you open a *database* for the first time. It contains information supplied by the *database's designer* to help you understand more about the database, such as its purpose and tips on its use. While the About Document generally appears the first time you open a database, the designer may have elected to have the About Document appear every time you open the database or whenever the contents of the About Document have changed.

## Access Control List (ACL)

An *Access Control List* is stored internally in every Notes *database* and allows selective access to a database and its contents. It combines *Access Levels* along with *Access Types* to create a wide combination of possible security levels. Some examples of how the Access Levels and Access Types can be combined to create security include:

❖ A person who can create new *Documents* in a database but cannot edit them once they have been created

❖ A person who can create and edit any Document in a database

❖ A *Notes Server* that can add new Documents and edit existing Documents but cannot delete any

## Access Levels

Levels of security in an *Access Control List*. They are combined with *Access Types* and other options in the Access Control List dialog box to create a security model for a database. The seven *Access Levels* are:

1. No Access—A person or *Notes Server* in the *ACL* whose access is set to No Access will not be able to open the *database* containing that *ACL*.

2. Depositor—A person or *Notes Server* in the *ACL* whose access is set to Depositor will be able to open the *database* containing that *ACL*, and create new *Documents* in the database. Once the new Document is created and saved, however, the Document's creator will not be able to see the Document, or any other Document in the database.

3. Reader—A person or *Notes Server* in the *ACL* whose access is set to Reader will be able to open the *database* containing that ACL, and read any *Documents* in the database that are not restricted from the user by security features other than the *ACL*. A person or *Notes Server* with Reader Access in an *ACL* cannot create new Documents in the database containing that *ACL*.

4. Author—A person or *Notes Server* in the *ACL* whose access is set to Author will generally be able to create new *Documents* in the *database* containing the *ACL*, as well as edit the Documents he creates after each

Document is saved. It is possible, however, that security features other than the *ACL* may restrict a person or *Notes Server* with *Author Access* from editing *Documents* once they have been saved. An Author may also have the privilege of creating *Private Agents* and *Private Folders* in a database.

5. Editor—A person or *Notes Server* in the *ACL* whose access is set to Editor has the same privileges as a person or *Notes Server* with *Author Access*. In addition, an Editor has the ability to edit his own *Documents* as well as Documents created by other users. An Editor may have the privilege of creating *Private Agents* and *Private Folders* in a database, as well.

6. Designer—A person or *Notes Server* in the *ACL* whose access is set to Editor has the same privileges as a person or *Notes Server* with *Editor Access*. In addition, a Designer has the privilege to create new database *Forms*, *Views*, *Navigators*, and *Shared* or *Private Folders*, as well as *Shared* or *Private Agents*.

7. Manager—A person or *Notes Server* in the *ACL* with *Manager Access* in a *database* has the same privileges as a user or *Notes Server* with *Designer Access*. In addition, a Manager may make changes to the *Access Control List* of a database or delete the database in its entirety from a *Notes Server*.

## *Access Types* ★*NEW*★

Access Types allow *Database Managers* to group members of an *Access Control List (ACL)* together for security purposes. *Access Types* are combined with *Access Levels* to create granular security.

Examples:

1. A group of persons and a group of servers in the *ACL* may both have *Editor Access*. However, to prevent deletions from replicating to other instances of a database, the group of servers could be restricted from deleting Documents.

2. Before executing, an *Agent* may check to see if the user executing it is a person or a *Notes Server*. If the *Agent's* executor is a person, the *Agent* may display a message saying "This Agent is designed to be run from a Notes Server. Please contact your Database Manager for assistance."

The six *Access Types* are:

1. Person

2. Group of Persons

3. Server

4. Group of Servers

5. Group (Persons and Servers)

6. Unspecified

## Actions (1)   ★*NEW*★

Actions represent a condensed programming language new to Release 4.0. Using Actions, common tasks that a user performs can be represented programmatically. What makes Actions distinctive from other methods of programming in Notes Release 4.0 is the Action Builder dialog box, an interactive window designed to allow users extensive control combined with ease of use. One or more Actions can be combined into an *Agent.*

## Actions (2)   ★*NEW*★

A special type of Notes *Agent.* In this context, an Action is an *Agent* that is specifically designed to be included in an *Action Bar.*

## Action Bar   ★*NEW*★

The *Action Bar* is a bar across the top of a Notes *View* or *Document* that allows you to execute *Agents* by clicking a button.

## Agent

Agents are a combination of *@Functions, @Commands, LotusScript* Commands, and *Actions.* Agents are designed to automate a process or task in Notes. Prior to Notes Release 4, Agents were referred to as Macros. Agents are created using the **Create, Agent** command on the *Notes Client* menu. Agents can be executed using the **Actions** command on the Notes Client menu, an *Action Bar,* or automatically by a Notes Client or *Notes Server.*

# Attachment

Attachments are files that can be included in a *rich text field* on a *Document*. Attachments can be any file type. For example, you could insert a Microsoft Word Document, an image, or even another Notes *database* as an attachment in a *rich text field*. Attachments appear as an icon with a text label underneath them that is the file's name.

They are created by choosing **File, Attach...** from the *Notes Client* menu while the cursor is in a *rich text field* on a Document. Once inserted, attachments are activated by double-clicking them and choosing **Launch**, **Detach**, or **View** from the Attachments dialog box.

**NOTE** When Attachments are added to a Document programmatically (by a program instead of a manual user), they may appear at the bottom of the Document or in an area other than a rich text field.

# Button

Buttons are images that can be inserted into a *rich text field* in a *Document*. When a user clicks it, a small program built specifically for the button, or one or more *Agents* will run. *Document Links*, *View Links*, and *Database Links* are special Notes buttons created using the **Edit, Copy As Link** command from the *Notes Client* menu. Instead of running a program, these buttons open a linked *database*, *View*, or *Document* on the Notes Client where the link was activated from.

Buttons may also be added programmatically by a *Database Designer* to a *Form* (meaning the button is present whenever a user creates a new Document, or reads an existing Document using a specific Form).

# Category

A Category is an element of a Notes *View* or *Folder*. Its purpose is to allow *Views* and *Folders* to group *Documents* based on *Fields* that share a common value. For example, in the By Author View of the Teach Yourself... Discussion database, every *Document* created by a different author is grouped into a different *Category*.

## Database

A Notes *database* is a collection of *Documents*, *Responses*, design elements (*Views*, *Folders*, *Forms*, *Navigators*, *Agents*, and *Fields*), security features (*ACL*), and administrative information (*Replica ID*, *Replication History*, and *Selective Replication* information). It is generally stored with an NSF extension, and opened using a *Notes Client* or *Notes Server*.

## Database Designer

One or more persons with an *Access Level* of *Designer* or greater to a *Notes Database*. Database Designers are responsible for the creation of the design elements of a Notes Database (*Forms*, *Views*, *Navigators*, *Action Bars*, *Agents*, etc.).

## Database Manager

One or more persons with an *Access Level* of *Manager* or greater to a *Notes Database*. Database Managers are responsible for the administration of a *Notes Database* on a *Notes Server* (ensuring that *Replication* is performed successfully, for example). Database Managers also maintain the *Access Control List* of a Notes Database. A database's manager may also be the *Database Designer*.

## Database Link ★NEW★

Database Links are special *buttons* that can be included in a *rich text field* by a user. They are created by selecting a *database* and choosing **Edit, Copy As Link, Database Link** from the *Notes Client* menu. This moves the Database Link to the clipboard, from which it can be pasted into one or more rich text fields by the user. When a user double-clicks a *Database Link*, the database specified in the link is opened at the *Notes Client*.

---

N O T E

Database Links do not override the *Access Control List* settings (if you create a *Database Link* and send it to a person via *Notes Mail* to a user who does not have access to the database, he will not be able to use the link).

---

# Database Window ★*NEW*★

The Database Window combines several subwindows referred to by Lotus as *panes*. It is the primary means of locating and displaying *Documents* in a Notes *Database*, and is opened whenever a user double-clicks an icon on the *Workspace*.

The Panes of the *Database Window* are called

1. The *Navigator Pane*
2. The *View Pane*
3. The *Preview Pane*

At any time, two of the three panes of the Database Window are optional (they can be turned off by the user, or forced off of the screen by the *Database Designer*). The location of the three panes within the Database Window can be controlled by the user via the **View, Arrange Preview** command on the *Notes Client* menu.

# *Document*

A collection of *Fields* and *Labels* arranged for display using a *Form*. Similar in function to a record in a SQL table or DBMS.

A special type of *Document* called a *Response* can be included by a *Database Designer* in a database. *Response Documents* are similar in function to Post-it notes—they contain additional information that is loosely related to a main Document.

# *Document Link*

*Document Links* are special *buttons* that can be included in a *rich text field* by a user. They are created by selecting a *Document* and choosing **Edit, Copy As Link, Document Link** from the *Notes Client* menu. This moves the *Document Link* to the clipboard, from which it can be pasted into one or more *rich text fields* by the user. When a user double-clicks a *Document Link*, the *Document* specified by the link is opened at the Notes Client.

*Document Links* do not override the *Access Control List* or other security settings (if you create a *Document Link* and send it to a person via *Notes Mail* to a user who does not have access to the database that contains the *Document,* he will not be able to use the link).

## Embedded Objects

Data from other applications can be stored in a Notes *Document* as an embedded object. When activated, embedded objects call the original application that created the embedded data and allow you to update the information. When saved, the updated information is stored in the Notes *Document.*

This differs from a file *attachment* in that, when activated, file *attachments* are copies of the data originally stored in the Notes *Document.* The information in the *Document* will not be updated unless extra steps are taken by the user.

## Fields

Fields are elements of a Notes *Document* designed to hold specific information. *Fields* are arranged for the user via *Forms.* A user knows what type of information to enter into a *Field* based on its field type and information contained in the *Field's Label.* The different types of *Fields* that Notes supports are:

1.  Text—Text fields contain letters, punctuation, space, and numbers that are not used mathematically.

2.  Rich Text—Rich text fields allow users to insert pictures, *buttons, attachments,* or *embedded objects* as well as use text styles (bold, italics, underlining, different fonts, or color).

3.  Keywords—Keyword fields offer predefined text choices that make data entry more convenient and lend consistency to documents. You can generate keywords in several different ways and choose from a variety of display styles.

4.  Number—Number fields are used for information that can be used mathematically and can include the characters 0 1 2 3 4 5 6 7 8 9 - + . E e.

5.  Time—Time fields contain time and date information and are made up of letters and numbers separated by punctuation.

6. Authors—Authors fields generate a text list of names (user names, group names, and access roles) and are useful for giving people with an *Access Level* of *Author* in the *Access Control List* the right to edit documents they didn't create without expanding their database *Access Level* to *Editor.*

7. Readers—Readers fields allow you to restrict who can read documents created with a form, even if users have *Reader* (or higher) access in the access control list.

8. Names—Names fields display user or server names as they appear on Notes' IDs and are useful for displaying names when you don't need to assign any type of access rights to documents.

## Folders ★NEW★

Folders let you store and manage related documents without putting them into a *Category*, which requires a Categories *Field* in the *Form* used to create the *Document*. *Folders* are also convenient because you can drag *Documents* to them.

You can create *Private Folders* or *Shared Folders*. No one else can read or delete your *Private Folders*, while *Shared Folders* can be accessed by everyone with the ability to read *Documents* in the *database*.

To create *Private Folders* in a *database*, you must have an *Access Level* of *Reader* in the *Access Control List* of the database. To create *Shared Folders* in a database, you must have an *Access Level* of *Designer.*

## Form

Forms allow users to create *Documents* that store the *database*'s data. A form contains one or more *Fields*. It may also contain *Labels* and graphics to make the form attractive and easy-to-use and *buttons* that automate tasks or give users extra information. Most *databases* have several *forms*, each serving a particular purpose.

## Function Language

See *@Functions.*

## InterNotes Web Browser ★NEW★

A component built into every *Notes Client*, the *InterNotes Web Browser* recognizes *Uniform Resource Locators* in *rich text fields* and uses them to request information from the Internet via a *Notes Server* running the *InterNotes Web Retriever*.

## InterNotes Web Retriever ★NEW★

A program that can be run on any Release 4 *Notes Server*, the *InterNotes Web Retriever* requests information from the Internet and stores it in a Notes *Database*. Retrieval can happen on demand (when requested by a *Notes Client* running the *InterNotes Web Browser*), or automatically by the *Notes Server*.

## Location Document

A Location Document is a *Document* in your *Notes Client's Personal Name and Address Book*, which contains communication settings you use when you work with Notes in a particular place. For example, you might use a network port at the office to connect to Notes servers on a local area network and use a remote port at home to connect to Notes servers over a modem.

Each of these configurations could be represented by a Location Document that you could make active on the Notes Client when you were at those places.

## LotusScript ★NEW★

LotusScript is Lotus' object-oriented basic language. It is designed to allow Database Designers access to the greatest possible set of Notes' features programmatically.

## Mail Enabling

A feature of a Notes Server that allows any *database* to transfer *Documents* to any other database, similar to the way a person would send information to another person via *Notes Mail*.

## Mobile Notes

*Mobile Notes* is a collection of features in a *Notes Client* designed to allow you to access a *Notes Server* or a network or *Notes Servers* via a telephone line.

## Name and Address Book

This is a file called NAMES.NSF that is stored on every *Notes Client* and *Notes Server*. The purpose of the *Name and Address Book* is to allow users and *Notes Servers* access to the information they need to deliver *Notes Mail* and to make connections to each other for *Replication* or database access.

At the *Notes Client*, the *Name and Address Book* may be referred to as the *Personal Name and Address Book*. On the *Notes Server*, the *Name and Address Book* may be referred to as the *Server Name and Address Book*.

## Navigator ★NEW★

Navigators provide a graphical way for users to find documents or take actions without having to maneuver through views or find menu commands. Notes provides standard navigators called *Folders* that appear in the *Navigator Pane* when you open a *database*. A *Database Designer* can create additional *Navigators* for an application to perform specific functions, including those with formulas or *LotusScript* programs.

## Navigator Pane ★NEW★

An optional component of the *Database Window* designed to display *Navigators*.

## Notes Client

A copy of Notes, Notes Desktop, Notes Express, or *Notes Mail* running on a computer.

## Notes Server

A copy of the Notes Server software running on a computer. Notes Server software is designed to allow *Notes Clients* to share *databases*, support *Notes Mail*, and facilitate *Workflow*. A *Notes Server* may also use the *InterNotes Web Retriever* to allow *Notes Clients* running the *InterNotes Web Browser* access to the Internet via Notes.

## Notes Mail

*Notes Mail* allows a *Notes Client* to communicate electronically with other Notes users. *Notes Mail* requires a *Notes Client* to have a connection to least one *Notes*

*Server*. If you are not connected to a *Notes Server* via a network, you can still use *Notes Mail* by connecting to a *Notes Server* via modem and telephone line.

A Notes mail message is the same as any Notes *Document*. For example, you can change fonts and colors, add file *attachments* and *OLE* objects, and include *tables*, graphics, *buttons*, and *Document, Database, or View Links*. Each Notes user has a database in which to store mail messages.

## Object Linking and Embedding (OLE)

A standard designed to allow applications to store and update data in its native format promoted by Microsoft.

## Panes

See *Database Window, Programmer's Pane, Preview Pane, View Pane,* and *Navigator Pane*.

## Personal Name and Address Book ★*NEW*★

See *Name and Address Book*.

## Preview Pane ★*NEW*★

An optional pane of the *Notes Client* that allows you to preview the currently selected *Document* in a *View*. Once a *Document* is opened, the *Preview Pane* can allow you to preview a Document's *Parent Document* or *Response*, or the contents of Documents linked using *Document Links*.

## Private Folders ★*NEW*★

See *Folders*.

## Programmer's Pane ★*NEW*★

A Pane that is opened in the Database Window whenever a user is editing a *button* or other Notes design element (*View, Form, Field,* etc.) Commonly used by *Database Designers*.

# Replica ID

A unique identifier that is a part of every Notes *database*. Databases that share the same *Replica ID* are called *replicas*. Only databases that are replicas can exchange information through *Replication*.

To view the *Replica ID* of a *database*, select the database on the *Workspace* and choose **File, Database, Properties...** from the *Notes Client* menu. In the Properties for Database dialog box, click on the Information page to see an entry containing the database's *Replica ID*.

# Replication

Notes lets you keep multiple copies of a single *database*, called replicas, on multiple *Notes Servers* and Notes Clients. Replication is the process of exchanging modifications between replicas. Through *replication*, Notes makes all of the replicas essentially identical over time.

A replica has the same *Replica ID* as the original database.

# Replicator

A page on the Notes Workspace that allows users to centralize replication tasks.

# Rich Text Fields

See *Fields*.

# Shared Folders

See *Folders*.

# Selective Replication

Notes lets you replicate a subset of documents to a replica so you can limit the size of replicas. Selective Replication can save disk space, reduce the amount of time a Mobile Notes Client spends connected to a *Notes Server* and allow you to only work with information in a database that is relevant.

## Server Connection Document

A Document in the *Name and Address Book* that tells a *Notes Client* or a *Notes Server* what telephone number to dial to connect to remote servers or what network protocol to use to reach a *Notes Server* on a Local Area Network (LAN) or Wide Area Network (WAN).

## SmartIcons

*SmartIcons* are buttons that perform an action (for example, italicizing selected text) in Notes when you click them. For many tasks, it's faster to click *SmartIcons* than it is to pull down menus or recall and type keyboard shortcuts.

## Status Bar

A group of clickable areas at the bottom of the *Notes Client* that allow you to quickly perform routine tasks in Notes. A portion of the status bar is dedicated to displaying messages from the *Notes Client* to the user.

## Table

A Notes element that can be inserted into a *rich text field* that allows you to present information in rows and columns. If you are familiar with the concept of tables from other database languages (such as SQL), it is important to Note that tables in Notes are more like the tables feature in a word processing package than in a database (that is, they contain static information, not dynamic subsets of data).

## Using Document

An optional *Document* in a Notes *Database* that is used by the *Database Designer* to provide users with help for using the database's features. It can be opened by selecting a database on the *Workspace* and choosing **Help, Using This Database...** from the *Notes Client* menu.

## Uniform Resource Locator (URL)

A string of characters designed to allow World Wide Web browsers to locate documents and files on the Internet.

## User ID

A *User ID* is a file that uniquely identifies a Notes user. Every Notes user—person or server—has a *User ID*. Your *User ID* determines access privileges between your *Notes Client* and *Notes Servers*.

## View

*Views* are lists of *Documents* in a Notes *database*. Views can select, sort, or categorize documents in different ways. Views use the *Fields* stored in each *Document* to display information, such as who created the *Document*, when it was created, what the subject is, etc.

A *View* may show all *Documents* in a database or only a selection of *Documents*.

## View Link  ★NEW★

*View Links* are special *buttons* that can be included in a *rich text field* by a user. They are created by selecting a *View* and choosing **Edit, Copy As Link, View Link** from the *Notes Client* menu. This moves the *View Link* to the clipboard, from which it can be pasted into one or more *rich text fields* by the user. When a user double-clicks a *View Link*, a *Database Window* with the *View* specified by the link is opened at the Notes Client.

---

NOTE

*View Links* do not override the *Access Control List* or other security settings (if you create a *View Link* and send it to a person via *Notes Mail* to a user who does not have access to the database that contains the *View*, he will not be able to use the link).

---

## View Pane  ★NEW★

An area of the *Database Window* dedicated to displaying the contents of the currently selected *View* or *Folder* in a Notes *database*.

## Workflow

Any combination of Notes' features that automates processes or tasks. *Workflows* can be simple, using a single *Action*, or complex, requiring hundreds of lines of code in Lotus *@Function* language or *LotusScript*.

## Workspace

The primary interface between the *Notes Client* and the user. The *Workspace* consists of a number of tabbed pages. Each tabbed page can contain icons for Notes *databases* located on the *Notes Client* or on one or more *Notes Servers*.

A special *Workspace Page* called the *Replicator* allows users to centralize replication tasks.

## @Commands

Pronounced "at - commands." A subset of *@Functions*.

## @Functions

Pronounced "at - functions." A programming language (also called *Function Language)* that allows *Database Designers* and users to create *Agents* to perform specific tasks. *@Functions* are more advanced than *Actions*, but not as robust as *LotusScript*. Prior to Notes Release 4, *@Functions* were the only development language. By supporting *@Functions* in Release 4, even though the more powerful LotusScript language is available to developers, Lotus helps maintain backwards compatibility with *databases* created using a previous version of Notes.

# Index

# W

# About the Disk

To help you get the most from the step-by-step exercises included in this book, a single 3.5" floppy diskette with a Notes Database is included. This database contains a number of Documents designed to illustrate many important concepts in Lotus Notes.

It is recommended that you copy the database TYLNDISC.NSF from the diskette to a subdirectory or folder beneath your Notes data directory.

For example: If you are using Windows 95/NT/3.1, it is likely that your Lotus Notes software is installed in a directory called NOTES. Beneath this directory is subdirectory called DATA. I suggest you create a subdirectory beneath DATA called TYLN, and copy the database on the included disk to it. The path for your database would then be NOTES\DATA\TYLN\TYLNDISC.NSF.

See Appendix B for further details.